The Way of Torah

The Religious Life in History Series
FREDERICK J. STRENG, *Series Editor*

The Way of Torah

An Introduction to Judaism

FIFTH EDITION/COMPLETELY REVISED

Jacob Neusner
University of South Florida

Wadsworth Publishing Company
Belmont, California
A Division of Wadsworth, Inc.

Religion Editor: Peggy Adams
Editorial Assistant: Amy Havel
Production Editor: Deborah Cogan
Managing Designer: Cloyce J. Wall
Print Buyer: Randy Hurst
Permissions Editor: Peggy Meehan
Copy Editor: Rebecca Smith
Composition: Scratchgravel Publishing Services
Cover Designer: Cloyce J. Wall
Cover Photograph: Bettmann Archives
Printer: Malloy Lithographing, Inc.

1 2 3 4 5 6 7 8 9 10—97 96 95 94 93

Library of Congress Cataloging-in-Publication Data

Neusner, Jacob, 1932–
    The way of Torah: an introduction to Judaism / Jacob Neusner. —
5th ed., completely rev.
        p.   cm. — (The Religious life in history series)
    Includes bibliographical references and index.
    ISBN 0-534-16938-4
    1. Judaism.   I. Title.   II. Series.
BM565.N487   1992
296—dc20   92-12408

For William Scott Green and Rebecca Fox,
Noah and Ethan

Contents

Foreword

THE RELIGIOUS LIFE IN HISTORY series is intended as an introduction to a large, complex field of inquiry: religious experience in particular cultural and historical contexts. It seeks to present the depth and richness of religious concepts, forms of worship, spiritual practices, and social institutions found in living traditions throughout the world.

As specialists in the languages and cultures in which each religion is found, the authors are able to illuminate the meanings of religious perspectives and practices as other human beings have experienced them. To communicate these meanings to readers who have had no special training in these cultures and religions, the authors have attempted to provide clear, nontechnical descriptions and interpretations of religious life.

Some of the religious traditions are defined primarily by a geographical context, others by root metaphors, religious practices, or social institutions that have developed over several cultures and continents. Likewise, different aspects of religious traditions provide diverse foci of interpretation. Sometimes symbols or cosmological doctrines, other times social institutions or spiritual practices are emphasized by spokespersons within the religious traditions.

The Religious Life in History series is concerned with historical contexts and developments as well as the meaning of religious experience and behavior found in various traditions. In the narrative description of a tradition the various cultural forms are interpreted in terms of their cultural context, demonstrating both the diverse expressions and the commonalities of religious life. Most of the basic narrative texts have a complementary anthology, which includes translations of some of the primary religious materials used by the participants of a tradition, descriptions of rituals or devotees' experiences, and brief interpretive studies of key cultural phenomena that function religiously for practitioners. Besides individual volumes on different religions, the series offers a core book on the study of religious meaning that describes several modes and structures of religious awareness and examines different study approaches. In addition, each basic book presents a list of readings in specific topics and a description of helpful teaching aids.

During more than two decades of use the series has experienced a wide readership. A continuing effort is made to update the scholarship, simplify the organization of material, and clarify concepts through the publication of revised editions. The authors have been gratified with the response to their efforts to introduce people to various forms of religious life. We hope readers will find these volumes "introductory" in the most significant sense: an introduction to a new perspective for understanding themselves and others.

FREDERICK J. STRENG
Series Editor

Preface to the Fifth Edition

MY MAIN INTERESTS in this revision of a now much studied book are to help you (1) see Judaism as a whole, as a system, and (2) understand the principal epochs in the history of that system. I want you to know more than isolated facts about this holiday or that custom, bits and pieces of a religious world glimpsed only partially and out of context. I want you to know that within Judaism holidays, beliefs, practices, and ways of living and of shaping the life cycle all express a single and whole conception of the world, of the human being, of the character of humanity, and of the supernatural meaning of the Jewish people. For Judaism, a Judaism, is not "this and that" but rather whole and encompassing—that is, it is a mode of creating and interpreting the world. It is a system of holiness in which each and every element relates to all other elements, and together they form a holy way of life and a holy world in time and beyond.

Moreover, this particular mode of the sacred is so shaped as to make sense of and to respond to the distinctive human situation of the Jewish people; hence, our attention focuses on the "ecology" of Judaism, a phrase I shall define in Chapter 3. I am certain that, when you are able to enter through your imagination into the human situation of the Jews, you will also grasp in some measure the human meaning of Judaism as a mode of interpreting and shaping that human situation. Beyond that point, as students of religion, we cannot go. For that is the frontier between the realm of interpretation and understanding, which belongs only to the Judaists, the believers and practitioners of Judaism. The distinction between the Judaists, people who live by and believe in a Judaism, and the Jewish people, who are all those born of a Jewish mother or converted to Judaism, is fundamental. This is a history of Judaism, not a history of the Jews. We cannot compose as a single, harmonious, and continuous history the diverse and often unrelated histories of various groups of Jews in diverse times and places. But as this book shows, we most certainly can provide a cogent account of the history of Judaism, seen whole and in its principal components.

What holds all Judaic religious systems together is a single ecology, made up of two components: (1) the permanent and ubiquitous appeal to the Torah, the Five Books of Moses (Genesis, Exodus, Leviticus, Numbers, and Deuteronomy), and (2) the inquiry into the Torah to make sense of the diverse circumstances of various groups, all of them identifying with the "Israel" of whom the Torah speaks—and all of them small, weak, scattered, and concerned with their status as a small minority, wherever they are (including, in our own time, the Jewish state of Israel in the Land of Israel, which in its time and place is small, weak, and uncertain in its own context). These two components, then—an ongoing reference to a single holy writing and a permanent social situation—define the ecosystem in which any Judaism must take shape.

Obviously, by using the word *ecology*, borrowed from the natural sciences, I want to introduce an unusual metaphor into the study of religions. Ecology is a branch of science concerned with the interrelationship of organisms and their environments. By "ecology of religions" I mean the study of the relationship between a religious way of viewing the world and living life and the historical and social situation of the people who view the world and live life in accord with the teachings of their religion. The Jewish people are a very small group, spread over many countries.

One fact of their natural environment is that they form a distinct group in diverse societies.

A second fact is that they constitute solely a faith-community with few, if any, shared social or cultural traits.

A third fact is that they look back on an exceptionally long, and in some ways painful, history.

A world view suitable for the Jews must make sense of their unimportance and explain their importance. It must deal with the issues of the long history of the group. Above all, it must make sense of the continuing life of the group, persuading its members that forming a distinct and distinctive community is important and worth carrying on. The interplay between the political, social, and historical life of the Jews and their conceptions of themselves in this world and under the aspect of God's will and Torah constitutes the focus for the inquiry—the "ecological" inquiry—that, I think, makes the study of Judaism accessible.

I may have made a mistake in introducing this metaphor—ecology of Judaism—into the intellectual framework of this book. But I think it is important to find language to focus on the curious interplay between the history of Judaism and the history of the Jewish people and to do so without reducing the history of Judaism to a minor detail in the history of the Jewish people. Judaism cannot be studied or even defined outside the historical experience of the Jewish people. But it also cannot be studied solely within that experience, as if there is no such thing as Judaism but merely the evanescent culture of the Jewish group. There *is* such a thing as (a) Judaism, which may stand definition and analysis in the same way that any other religion may be defined and analyzed. A Judaism is no less difficult to define and describe than any other religious system. It holds no mysteries accessible only to people who originate in a Jewish family, and nothing about Judaism is inaccessible to the accepted methods and procedures of the academic study of religions.

What is it, then, that makes Judaism especially interesting? In my judgment, it is that curious interplay between the social and historical environment of the Jews and the religious character of Judaism. The one defines the questions; the other answers them. In the interplay between question and answer is the work of ecology of religions—if, as I hope, I have not erred in converting to the present purpose a metaphor that may convey nothing but confusion. Time will tell.

This fifth edition, completely revised, suggests that my approach to the academic study of religion, exemplified by the case of Judaism, will enjoy a hearing into the twenty-first century. The first edition of this book was published in 1969. The third edition coincided with the celebration of the *bar mitzvah* of my firstborn, in 1978. The fourth edition went to press as he entered his senior year of college and went on to service as an ensign in the United States Navy, as his two brothers wended their way through college, and as his sister proceeded through high school. The fifth edition goes to press as my third son begins his marriage. As my children—Samuel, Eli, Noam, and Margalit—have grown and changed in the twenty-three years since this textbook began its life, so have my wife Suzanne and I grown and changed, she in her art, I in my labor of learning. The fact that this book takes up a fresh perspective on a subject I have worked on so long testifies to my goal: to remain still a beginner, still a learner, everything new and fresh every morning.

This fifth edition also reflects the wonderful new circumstance in which I do my work, at the University of South Florida. Here I find the students open to learning and responsive to the challenges of thought and criticism. Here I find encouragement for my work. So this book is a more ambitious statement to beginners in the field than any I had imagined possible. I pay tribute to my students, my colleagues, and our president and deans for their success in showing that a university can be truly professional, truly committed to excellence, truly devoted to the public interest.

The dedication of this book now shifts to celebrate trust: on the one side the happy marriage and family of my friend and co-worker, William Scott Green, and his wife, Rebecca Fox, and their children, Noah and Ethan, and on the other side friendship based on long-term collaboration in solving intellectual problems. Surely well-placed trust is to be celebrated in a book that has now endured for most of my professional life and now passes well into its third decade.

J. N.
St. Petersburg, Florida
July 28, 1991
My fifty-ninth birthday

Related Reading

YOU WILL FIND extensive readings from primary sources complementing this book in its companion anthology, *The Life of Torah: Readings in the Jewish Religious Experience*. Appropriate selections illustrative of the main points of *The Way of Torah* are in *The Life of Torah* as follows:

Acknowledgments

I DERIVED MUCH BENEFIT from the anonymous readers of the four prior editions of *The Way of Torah*, from both their specific corrections and also their more general comments on how to make this a still more useful textbook than it has been. Since learning proceeds apace and we gain a better grasp of things as time passes, there certainly will be a sixth edition. I earnestly solicit the critical comments of colleagues, teachers and students alike, who may be able to assist me in making this a still more perspicacious and informative textbook than I have succeeded in making it to date.

I gratefully acknowledge permission to reprint copyrighted material:

From Judah Goldin (trans.), *The Grace After Meals* (New York: Jewish Theological Seminary of America, 1955), pp. 9, 15*ff*.

From Maurice Samuel (trans.), *Haggadah of Passover* (New York: Hebrew Publishing, 1949), pp. 9, 13, 26, 27.

From Israel Abrahams, *Hebrew Ethical Wills* (Philadelphia: Jewish Publication Society, 1948), pp. 207–218.

From *Weekday Prayer Book*, ed. by Rabbinical Assembly of America Prayerbook Committee, Gershon Hadas, Chairman, and Jules Harlow, Secretary (New York: Rabbinical Assembly of America, 1962), pp. 42, 45–46, 50–54, 97–98.

From Jules Harlow (ed.), *A Rabbi's Manual* (New York: Rabbinical Assembly of America, 1965), pp. 45, 96.

From A. S. Halkin, "The Judeo-Islamic Age," in *Great Ages and Ideas of the Jewish People*, ed. by Leo Schwarz (New York: Random House, 1956).

From Isaak Heinemann, *Judah Halevi, Kuzari* (London: East & West Library, 1957).

From Franz Kobler, *Letters of Jews Through the Ages* (London: East & West Library, 1952), pp. 565–567. © Horovitz Publishing Co. Ltd., 1952.

From *Prayer in Judaism*, by Bernard Martin, pp. 84–85, © 1968 by Basic Books, Inc., Publishers, New York.

From Sholom Alchanan Singer (trans.), *Medieval Jewish Mysticism: The Book of the Pious* (Northbrook, Ill.: Whitehall, 1971), pp. 37–38.

Reprinted from *Profiles of Eleven*, by Melech Epstein, p. 17, by permission of Wayne State University Press. © 1965 Wayne State University Press.

From "The Mystical Elements of Judaism," by Abraham J. Heschel, in *The Jews: Their History, Culture, and Religion*, edited by Louis Finkelstein, vol. II, pp. 932–951. © 1949, 1955, 1960, 1971 by Louis Finkelstein. By permission of Harper & Row, Publishers, Inc.

Table of Dates

ca. 200	Judah the Patriarch, head of Palestinian Jewish community, promulgates Mishnah
ca. 220	Babylonian academy founded at Sura by Rab
ca. 250	Pact between Jews and Persian King, Shapur I: Jews to keep state law; Persians to permit Jews to govern selves, live by own religion
297	Founding of school at Pumbedita, in Babylonia, by Judah b. Ezekiel
ca. 330	Pumbedita school headed by Abbaye, then Rava, lays foundation of Babylonian Talmud
ca. 400	Talmud of Land of Israel completed Rab Ashi begins to shape Babylonian Talmud, which is completed by 600
ca. 450	Genesis Rabbah, commentary out of Genesis on meaning of Israel's history, and Leviticus Rabbah, historical laws of Israel's society developed out of book of Leviticus, are completed
ca. 475–500	*Pesiqta deRav Kahana,* set of essays on salvation of Israel in messianic time, expected fairly soon, worked out
630–640	Moslem conquest of Middle East
ca. 700	Saboraim complete final editing of Babylonian Talmud
ca. 750	*Problems* of Ahai Gaon, compilation of legal discourses
ca. 780	Death of Anan b. David, leader of Karaite revolt against rabbinic Judaism
882	Birth of Saadya, leading theologian, author of *Doctrines and Beliefs*
ca. 950	*Book of Creation*, mystical work, brief statement on how phenomena of world evolved from God
1040	Birth of Rashi, greatest medieval Bible and Talmud commentator
1096	First Crusade; Jews massacred in Rhineland by crusader armies
1138	Birth of Moses Maimonides
1141	Death of Judah Halevi
1179	Third Lateran Council issues anti-Semitic decrees
1180	Maimonides completes code of Jewish law
1187	Saladin recaptures Jerusalem from crusaders
1190	Riots at Lynn; massacre of Jews at York, England
1233	Inquisition at Aragon
1244	Ritual burning of Talmuds at Paris by church authorities
1247	Papal bull against ritual murder libel
1264	Charter of Boleslav the Pious
1283–1287	Riots against Jews in Rhineland
1290	Expulsion of Jews from England
1298–1299	Riots against Jews of Germany in Rhindfleisch; 1320–1321, Pastoureaux; 1336–1337, Armleder

1306, 1311, 1322, 1349, 1394	Expulsions of Jews from France
1328	Massacres in Navarre
1348–1350	Black death; Jews massacred; migration to Poland begins en masse
1385	Spanish Jews forbidden to live in Christian neighborhoods
1391	Massacres of Spanish Jewry, forced conversions to Christianity
1492	Jews expelled from Spain
1496	Jews expelled from Portugal; mass conversions to Christianity
1506	Secret Jews (*Maranos*) killed in Lisbon
1516	Ghetto introduced at Venice; Jews forced to live in separate neighborhood
1520	First printed edition of Babylonian Talmud
1521	Jewish migrations to Palestine
1542–1543, 1546	Luther preaches against Jews
1553	Talmud burned in Italy
1567	Publication of *Shulhan Arukh*, code of Jewish law, by Joseph Karo
1624	Ghetto law instituted at Ferrara, Italy
1648	Massacres of Polish and Ukrainian Jews
1654	Jewish community founded in New Amsterdam (New York)
1655	Jews readmitted to England by Oliver Cromwell
1658	Newport, Rhode Island, Jewish community founded
1665	Sabbatai Zevi proclaimed Messiah in Smyrna, Turkey
1670	Jews expelled from Vienna
1712	First public synagogue in Berlin
1760	Death of Baal Shem Tov, founder of Hasidism
1772	Rabbis of Vilna oppose Hasidism
1786	Death of Moses Mendelssohn, philosopher of Jewish Enlightenment
1789	U.S. Constitution guarantees freedom of religion
1791	Jews receive full citizenship in France
1796	Jews receive full citizenship in Batavia (Holland)
1807	Sanhedrin called by Napoleon
1812	Jews receive partial citizenship in Prussia
1815	Polish Constitution omits Jewish rights
1825	Jews granted full citizenship in state of Maryland
1832	Jews receive full rights in Canada
1847	Birth of Solomon Schechter, leader of Conservative Judaism in the United States
1866	Emancipation of Jews of Switzerland
1868	Emancipation of Jews of Austria-Hungary
1870	Unification of Italy; ghettos abolished
1873	Founding of Union of American Hebrew Congregations (Reform)

1982	Invasion of Lebanon; Christian Lebanese massacre of Palestinian women and children precipitates moral crisis in state of Israel; Kahan Commission report invokes Scripture and Talmud in condemning massacre on basis of collective responsibility
1984	First woman ordained as Conservative rabbi by Jewish Theological Seminary of America
1986	Orthodox rabbinical leader addresses Reform rabbis, and vice versa, amid talk of schism in Judaism because of changes in law to treat child of Jewish father and non-Jewish mother as born Jew; established law regards only child of Jewish mother as Jew by birth

PART ONE

Defining Judaism

CHAPTER 1

Defining a Religion

RELIGION AS AN ACCOUNT OF THE SOCIAL ORDER

Judaism is a religion, so we begin by asking what we mean when we define religion or a religion. In general, people define religions by saying what the people who follow that religion believe. But belief is too small a conception of what a religion is and accomplishes. First, religion is public—it is social, something people do together—and what people believe tells us only about what individuals think. Second, religion governs what we do, telling us who we are and how we should live, while what people believe tells us only about attitudes. Religion therefore encompasses not only beliefs or attitudes—matters of mind and intellect—but also actions and conduct.

So religion combines these two: belief, attitude, or world view, which we may call *ethos*, and also behavior, way of life, or right action, which we may call in a broad and loose sense *ethics*. But because religion forms the basis of life of not individuals or families but people otherwise unrelated to one another, it must be seen as an account of a social entity or a social group—for instance, a church or a holy people or a nation. In that sense, religion explains the social world made up by people who believe certain things in common and act in certain aspects of their lives in common. Thus religion accounts for the social entity, which we may call, for the sake of symmetry, *ethnos*. These three things together—ethos, ethics, and ethnos—define religion, which is the foundation of the life of many human social entities. Indeed, only when we understand that religion does its work in the social world can we begin to grasp why religion is the single most powerful social force in the life and politics of the world today, as in nearly the whole of recorded history.

How does religion work? A religious system—way of life, world view, theory of the social entity that lives by the one and believes in the other—

identifies an urgent and ongoing question facing a given social group and provides an answer that for the faithful is self-evidently valid. To study any vital religion is to address a striking example of how people explain to themselves, by appeal to God's will or word or works, who they are as a social entity. Religion, as a powerful force in human society and culture, is realized not only or mainly in theology; religion works through the social entity that embodies that religion. Religions form social entities— "churches" or "peoples" or "holy nations" or monasteries or communities—that, in the concrete, constitute the "us," as against "the nations" or merely "them." Religions carefully explain, in deeds and in words, who that "us" is—and they do it every day. To see religion in this way is to take religion seriously as a way of realizing, in classic documents, a large conception of the world.

RELIGION AS TRADITION OR AS SYSTEM

Religion may represent itself as a tradition, meaning, the increment of the ages. Or it may come forth as a cogent statement, a well-crafted set of compelling answers to urgent questions. A religious tradition covers whatever the received sedimentary process has handed on. A religious system addresses in an orderly way a world view, a way of life, and a defined social entity. And both processes of thought, the traditional and the systematic, obey their own rules. The life of intellect may commence morning by morning. Or it may flow from an ongoing process of thought, in which one day begins where yesterday left off and one generation takes up the task left by its predecessors.

A system of thought by definition starts fresh, defines first principles, augments and elaborates them in balance, proportion, and above all logical order. In a traditional process, by contrast, we never start fresh but only add to an ongoing increment of knowledge, doctrine, and mode of making judgment. And in the nature of such an ongoing process, we never start fresh but always pick and choose, in a received program, the spot we choose to augment. The former process, the systematic one, begins from the beginning and works in an orderly, measured, and proportioned way to produce a cogent and neatly composed statement—a philosophy, for instance. On the other hand, tradition by its nature is supposed to describe not a system, whole and complete, but a process of elaboration of a given, received truth: exegesis, not fresh composition. And in the nature of thought, what begins in the middle is unlikely to yield order and system and structure laid forth *ab initio*. In general terms, systematic thought is philosophical in its mode of analysis and explanation, and traditional thought is historical in its manner of drawing conclusions and providing explanations.

Insofar as *tradition* refers to the matter of process, it invokes specifically an incremental and linear process that step by step transmits out of the past statements and wordings that bear authority and are subject to study, refinement, preservation, and transmission. In such a traditional process, by definition, no one starts afresh to think things through. Each participant in the social life of intellect makes an episodic and ad hoc contribution to an agglutinative process, yielding over time (to continue the geological metaphor) a sedimentary deposit. The opposite process we may call systematic, in that, starting as if from the very beginning and working out the fundamental principles of things, the intellect constructs a freestanding and well-proportioned system, unbound by received perspectives and propositions. In architecture terms, the difference is like that between a city that just grows and one that is planned; in other terms, the difference is between a scrapbook and a fresh composition, a composite commentary and a work of philosophical exposition.

The one thing a traditional thinker in religion knows, as against a system builder in religion, is that he or she stands in a long process of thought, with the sole task of refining and defending received truth. But the systematic thinker affirms the task of starting fresh, seeing things all together, all at once, in the right order and proportion, as a composition not merely a composite, held together by an encompassing logic. A tradition requires exegesis, a system, exposition. A tradition demands the labor of harmonization and elaboration of the given. A system begins with its harmonies in order and requires not elaboration but merely a repetition, in one detail after another, of its main systemic message. A tradition does not repeat but only renews received truth; a system always repeats because it is by definition encompassing, everywhere saying one thing, which by definition is always new. A system in its own terms has no history; a tradition defines itself through the authenticity of its history. And that brings us to Judaism in particular.

CHAPTER 2

Defining Judaism

THE DIVERSITY OF JUDAISMS

The study of Judaism requires us to survey thousands of years of continuous human existence. The issue of this book is how to define and interpret the continuity of a religion-culture. For over the span of thirty-five hundred years of an ongoing life of a group, much changes and little, if anything, remains the same. If we define a religion as what people believe, then we turn the study of religion into opinion polling. And because minds change over time, we must cope with chaos. If we define religion in terms of the individual—for example, "religion is a matter of ultimate concern"—then we increase the imponderables, since we do not then know how to distinguish religion from other matters of ultimate concern. So defining a religion has itself to be defined: What do we do when we define a religion? To what do we refer?

When we speak of *Judaism*, therefore, we must ask ourselves what we mean. How may we define the whole despite the diversity of the parts? One solution to this problem is to take full account of diversity and change. We do so not to pretend that many things are really one but to find a way of describing, analyzing, and interpreting diversity within a realm of commonality. That is to say, there never has been a single encompassing Judaism, present beneath the accidents of difference. There have been only diverse Judaisms. But these Judaisms do form a whole; seen all together over time and all at once in comparison to other religion-cultures, these Judaisms do bear traits that distinguish all of them from all other religion-cultures and permit us to identify the Judaisms as a cogent set of systems.

For a homely example of the problem, consider how we define the college or university at which we study. Is it only us, here and now? Or is it everyone who has come and will come? Do we define only the buildings, not the people? The faculty, in flux and change? The alumni, who connect and depart and reconnect? *What* do we define when we say what we think our college or university really is? We have to specify the facts that we require to describe our entity, we have to analyze those facts so as to gain perspective on them, and that requires us to compare one set of facts to another set of facts of the same kind. We then have to interpret those facts in a broader context, to make sense of this thing, this college, this university, in its still greater social and historical setting. Knowing how to define the river as distinct from the water that rushes by will tell us, also, what we do when we study Judaism.

Social Entity, Way of Life, World View: Ethnos, Ethics, Ethos

How shall we know when we have a Judaism? The answer to that question draws us to the data—the facts—that we must locate and describe, analyze, and interpret. The first requirement is to find a group of Jews who see themselves as "Israel"—that is, the Jewish People who form the family and children of Abraham, Isaac, Jacob, Sarah, Rebecca, Leah, and Rachel, the founding fathers and mothers. That same group must tell us that it uniquely constitutes "Israel," not *an* Israel, the descriptive term we use.

The second requirement is to identify the forms through which that distinct group expresses its world view. Ordinarily we find that expression in writing, so we turn to the authoritative holy books that the group studies and deems God-given—that is, the group's Torah, or statement of God's revelation to Israel. Since we use the word *Torah* to mean biblical books, starting with the Five Books of Moses (Genesis, Exodus, Leviticus, Numbers, and Deuteronomy), we must remind ourselves that the contents of the Torah have varied from one Judaism to the next. Some groups regard as holy what other groups reject or ignore. A more suitable word than *Torah*, therefore, is *canon*, meaning the collection of authoritative writings. The canon contains much of the group's world view and describes its way of life.

We of course err if we treat as our sole source of facts only what is in writing. A group expresses its world view in many ways, through dance, drama, rite, and ritual; through art and symbol; through politics and ongoing institutions of society; through where it lives, what it eats, what it wears, what language it speaks, and the opposites of all these: what it will not eat, where it will not live. Synagogue architecture and art bear profound messages, powerful visible messages. The life cycle, from birth through death, the definition of time and the rhythm of the day, the week, the month, and the year—all of these testify to the world view and the way of life of the social group that, all together, all at once, constitute a Judaism.

In the long history of the Jews, groups of people who regarded themselves as "Israel"—that is, groups of Jews—have framed many Judaisms. What permits us to make sense of the history of these Judaisms is the fact that, over time, we are able to identify periods in which a number of Judaisms competed and other times in which a single Judaism predominated. The historical perspective therefore permits us to sort out the

Judaisms that have flourished, keeping each by itself for the purpose of description, analysis, and interpretation, and also to hold the Judaisms together in a single continuum over time and space, the whole of which, all together and all at once, makes sense. By recognizing that a given Judaism came into existence at a time in which Judaisms competed and by understanding that, at another point, a single Judaism defined the Jews' way of life, world view, and social existence as a distinct entity, we may understand how the diverse facts—writings, theologies, definitions of what matters in everyday life, doctrines of the end of time and the purpose of life—fit together or do not.

Diverse Histories of Jews: The History of Judaism

In studying the history of Judaism, we concentrate not on the Jews as an ethnic group but on the Judaic religious systems that various ethnic groups in diverse times and places, all of them regarding themselves as "Jewish" or as "Israel," have set forth as an account of the social world. The Jews as a people have not had a single, unitary, and continuous history. They have lived in many places—centuries here, centuries there—and what happened in one place rarely coincided with what happened in some other place. When Jews flourished on the Iberian peninsula, those in other parts of Western Europe—for example, England, France, and Germany—perished; when in 1492 and 1497 the Spanish and Portuguese governments expelled Muslims and Jews, Jews in Poland and in the Turkish empire flourished. Only rarely did the histories of many distinct and different communities of Jews coincide—for example, in the horror of the mass extermination of European Jews between 1933 and 1945 in Germany and German-occupied Europe.

But if the ethnic group proves too diverse and distinct to treat as whole and harmonious (except as a matter of theology in the conception of Israel, God's first love, or as a matter of ideology in the conception that the Jews form a people, one people), we can treat as a coherent whole, harmonious and unitary, the history of the Judaic religious system, or Judaism.

DEFINING A JUDAISM

The approach I work out here requires us to describe not Judaism as a whole but *a Judaism*—that is to say, a single religious system. It is composed of three elements: a world view, a way of life, and a social group that, in the here and now, embodies the whole. The world view explains the life of the group, ordinarily referring to God's creation, the revelation of the Torah, the goal and end of the group's life in the end of time. The way of life defines what is special about the life of the group. The social group, in a single place and time, then forms the living witness and testimony to the system as a whole and finds in the system ample explanation for its very being. That is *a Judaism*.

THE PERIODS IN THE HISTORY OF JUDAISMS AND THE PARAMOUNT STATUS OF ONE JUDAISM

Let me specify the periods of the history of Judaism. I see four: (1) an age of diversity, (2) an era of definition, (3) a time of essential cogency, and (4) a new age of diversity. Since the definition of Judaism rests on historical facts in the life of Israel, the Jewish people, I have to list the four facts of political history that mark off everything else:

586 B.C.E.*   Destruction of the First Temple in Jerusalem by the Babylonians

The ancient Israelites, living in what they called the Land of Israel, produced Scriptures that reached their present form in the aftermath of the destruction of their capital city and Temple. Whatever happened before that time was reworked in the light of that event and the meaning imputed to it by authors who lived afterward. All Judaisms, from 586 B.C.E. forward, appeal to the writings produced in the aftermath of the destruction of the First Temple. Therefore we must regard the destruction of that Temple as the date that marks the beginning of the formation of Judaism(s).

C.E. 70   Destruction of the Second Temple in Jerusalem by the Romans

After 586 B.C.E., the Jews' leaders—the political classes and priesthood—were taken to Babylonia, the homeland of their conquerors, where they settled down. A generation later, Babylonia fell under the rule of the Persians, who permitted Jews to return to their ancient homeland. A small number did so, where they rebuilt the Temple and produced the Hebrew Scriptures. The Second Temple of Jerusalem lasted from about 500 B.C.E. to C.E. 70, when the Romans—by that time ruling the entire Middle East, including the Land of Israel, mainly through their own friends and allies—put down a Jewish rebellion and destroyed Jerusalem again. The second destruction proved final and marked the beginning of the Jews' history as a political entity defined in social and religious terms but not in territorial ones. That is, the Jews formed a distinct religious-social group, but all of them did not live in any one place, and some lived nearly everywhere in the West, within the lands of Christendom and Islam alike.

C.E. 640   Conquest of the Near and Middle East and North Africa by the Muslims

The definition of the world in which the Jews would live was completed when the main outlines of Western civilization had been worked out. These encompassed Christendom in Western and Eastern Europe, including the world west of the Urals in Russia, and Islam, in command of North Africa and the Near and Middle East and, in later times, destined to conquer much of India and the Far East (Malaysia and Indonesia in particular), as well as sub-Saharan Africa.

---

*We use B.C.E., meaning Before Common Era, instead of B.C., and C.E., meaning Common Era, for A.D., preferring a neutral and not theological designation of eras.

*During this long period, the Jews in Christendom and Islam alike ordinarily en-
joyed the status of a tolerated but subordinated minority and were free to practice their religion and sustain their separate group existence. Of still greater
importance, both Christianity and Islam affirmed the divine origin of the Jews'
holy book, the Torah, and acknowledged the special status among the nations of
Israel, the Jewish people.*

1787 and 1789   Adoption of the American Constitution and the French
                 Revolution

*Adoption of the U.S. Constitution and the French Revolution marked the be-
ginning of an age of political change that reshaped the world in which the
West, including Western Jewries, lived. Politics became essentially secular, and
political institutions no longer acknowledged supernatural claims of special status accorded either to a church or to a religious community. The individual
person, rather than the social group, was the focus of politics. The change
meant that the Jews would be received as individuals and given rights equal to
those of all others, but at the same time "Israel" as a holy people and community no longer would enjoy special status and recognition.*

Now for the history of Judaism by its principal periods of formation,
let me offer the following scheme:

First age of diversity: ca. 500 B.C.E. to C.E. 70

Age of definition: ca. C.E. 70 to 640

Age of cogency: ca. C.E. 640 to 1800

Second age of diversity: ca. 1800 to the present

The *first age of diversity* begins with the writing down, in more or less
their present form, of the Scriptures of ancient Israel, beginning with the
Five Books of Moses. Drawing on writings and oral traditions of the period before the destruction of the First Temple of Jerusalem, in 586 B.C.E.,
the surviving leadership of that Temple and court, the priests, produced
most of the books we now know as the Hebrew Bible ("Old Testament,"
or "Tanakh"), specifically the Pentateuch, or Five Books of Moses; the
prophetic writings from Joshua and Judges through Samuel and Kings
and Isaiah; Jeremiah, Ezekiel, and the twelve smaller books of prophetic
writings; and some of the other Scriptures as well. During this same period, diverse groups of Jews, living in the Land of Israel as well as in
Babylonia to the east and in Alexandria, Egypt, to the west, took over
these writings and interpreted them in diverse ways. Hence, during the
period from the formation of the Torah-book to the destruction of the Second Temple, there were many Judaisms.

The *age of definition*, beginning with the destruction of the Second
Temple in C.E. 70, saw the diverse Judaisms of the preceding period give
way, over a long period, to a single Judaism. That was the system worked
out by the sages who, after C.E. 70, developed a system of Judaism linked
to Scripture but enriched by an autonomous corpus of holy writings. This
Judaism is marked by its doctrine of the dual media by which the Torah

was formulated and transmitted: in writing and by memory, hence orally. The doctrine of the dual Torah, written and oral, thus defined the canon of Judaism. The written Torah encompassed much the same books that the world at large knows as the Old Testament. The oral Torah added the writings of the sages: the Mishnah, a philosophical law code produced ca. C.E. 200; two massive commentaries on the Mishnah; and the two Talmuds, one produced in the Land of Israel and called the Yerushalmi, or Jerusalem Talmud, ca. C.E. 400, the other produced in Babylonia and called the Bavli, or Talmud of Babylonia, ca. C.E. 600. In that same age, alongside Mishnah-commentary, systematic work on Scripture yielded works organized around particular books of the written Torah, parallel to works organized around particular tractates of the Mishnah. These encompassed Sifra, parallel to the book of Leviticus; Sifré, parallel to Numbers; another Sifré, parallel to Deuteronomy; works containing statements attributed to the same authorities who stand behind the Mishnah, to be dated sometime between 200 and 400; Genesis Rabbah and Leviticus Rabbah, discursive works on themes in Genesis and Leviticus, edited between 400 and 450; Pesiqta deRav Kahana, a profoundly eschatological treatment of topics in pentateuchal writings, of about 450; and similar works. These writings all together, organized around first the Mishnah and then Scripture, composed the first works of the oral Torah. That is to say, the teachings of the sages, originally formulated and transmitted by memory, were the written-down contents of the oral Torah that God had revealed (so the system maintained) to Moses at Sinai. During the age of definition, that Judaism of the dual Torah reached its literary statement and authoritative expression.

The *age of cogency* is characterized by the predominance of the Judaism of the dual Torah, from the far west of Morocco to Iran and India and from Egypt to England. During this long period, the principal question facing Jews was how to explain the success of the successor religions, Christianity and Islam, which claimed to replace the Judaism of Sinai with a new testament, on the one side, or a final and perfect prophecy, on the other. Both religions affirmed but then claimed to succeed Judaism, and the Judaism of the dual Torah enjoyed success among Jews for making sense of the then-subordinated status of the enduring people and faith of Sinai. During this long period, heresies took shape, but the beliefs of the new systems responded to the structure of the established one, so that a principal doctrine—for example, the doctrine of the dual Torah, written and oral, or of the Messiah as a faithful sage—would take shape in opposition to the authoritative doctrines of the Judaism of the dual Torah.

The *second age of diversity* is marked not by the breaking apart of the received system but by the development of competing systems of Judaism. In this period new Judaisms came into being that entirely ignored the categories and doctrines of the received system, not responding to its concerns but to other issues altogether. The principal question addressed by the new systems concerned matters other than those found urgent by the received Judaism of the dual Torah, with its powerful explanation of the Jews' status in the divine economy. The particular points of stress, the

CHAPTER 3

The Ecology of Judaism

THE ECOLOGY OF RELIGION

Ecology is a branch of science concerned with the interrelationships of organisms and their environments. By "ecology of" I mean the study of the relationship between a particular religious system's way of viewing the world and living life and the historical, social, and especially political situation of the people who view the world and live life in accord with the teachings of their religion. The Jewish people form a very small group, spread over many countries. One fact of Jews' natural environment is that they form a distinct group in diverse societies. A second is that they constitute solely a community of fate and, for many, of faith—but that alone, in that they have few shared social or cultural traits. A third is that they do not form a single political entity. A fourth is that they look back on a very long and in some ways exceptionally painful history.

A world view suited to the Jews' social ecology must make sense of their unimportance and explain their importance. It must explain the continuing life of the group, which in important ways marks it as different from others, and persuade people that their distinct and distinctive community is important and worth carrying on. The interplay between the political, social, and historical life of the Jews and their conceptions of themselves in this world and the next—that is, their world view, contained in their canon and their way of life, explained by the teleology of the system and the symbolic structure that encompasses the two and stands for the whole all at once and all together—defines the focus for the inquiry into the ecology of Judaism.

One idea predominates in nearly all Judaic religious systems: the conception that the Jews are in exile but have the hope of coming home to their own land, which is the Land of Israel (also known as Palestine). The original reading of the Jews' existence as exile and return derives from the Pentateuch, the Five Books of Moses, which were composed as we now have them (out of earlier materials, to be sure) in the aftermath of the destruction of the Temple in 586 B.C.E. and in response to the exile to Babylonia. The experience addressed by the authorship of the document is that of exile and restoration. But that framing of events represents an act of powerful imagination and interpretation. That experience taught lessons that people claimed to learn out of the events they had chosen. The Pentateuch, which took shape in 450 B.C.E. when some Jews returned from Babylonia to Jerusalem, shows that people reached this conclusion: *The life of the group is uncertain, subject to conditions and stipulations. Nothing is set and given, all things are a gift: land and life itself. And what actually did happen in that uncertain world—exile but then restoration—marked the group as special, different, select.*

There were other ways of seeing things, and the pentateuchal picture was no more compelling than any other. Those Jews who did not go into exile, and those who did not "come home," had no reason to take the view of matters that characterized the authorship of Scripture. The life of the group need not have appeared more uncertain, more subject to contingency and stipulation, than the life of any other group. The land did not require the vision that imparted to it the enchantment, the personality, that in Scripture it received: "The land will vomit you out as it did those who were here before you." And the adventitious circumstance of Iranian imperial policy, a political happenstance, did not have to be recast into return. So nothing in the system of Scripture—exile for reason, return as redemption—followed necessarily and logically. Everything was invented, interpreted.

That experience of the uncertainty of the life of the group in the century or so from the destruction of the First Temple of Jerusalem by the Babylonians to the building of the Second Temple of Jerusalem by the Jews, with Persian permission and sponsorship returned from exile, formed the paradigm. With the promulgation ca. 450 B.C.E. of the "Torah of Moses" under the sponsorship of Ezra, the Persians' viceroy, all future Israels would then refer to that formative experience as it had been set down and preserved as the norm for Israel in the mythic terms of that "original" Israel—the Israel not of Genesis and Sinai and the end at the moment of entry into the promised land but the "Israel" of the families that recorded as the rule and the norm the story of both the exile and the return. In that minority genealogy, that story of exile and return, alienation and remission, imposed on the received stories of pre-exilic Israel and adumbrated time and again in the Five Books of Moses and addressed by the framers of that document in their work overall, we find that paradigmatic statement in which every Judaism, from then to now, found its structure and deep syntax of social existence, the grammar of its intelligible message.

No Judaism recapitulates any other, and none stands in a linear and incremental relationship with any prior one. But all Judaisms recapitulate that single paradigmatic experience of the "Torah of Moses," the authorship that reflected on the meaning of the events of 586–450 B.C.E. selected for the composition of history and therefore interpretation. That experience (in theological terms) rehearsed the conditional moral existence of sin and punishment, suffering and atonement and reconciliation and (in social terms) rehearsed the uncertain and always conditional national destiny of disintegration and renewal of the group. That moment is captured within the Five Books of Moses. People had had an extraordinary experience of exile and return. The conclusions drawn from that experience would inform the attitude and viewpoint of all the Israels beyond.

Let me now spell out this theory, accounting for the character and definition of all the diverse Judaisms that have taken shape since the destruction of the First Temple of Jerusalem in 586 and the return to Zion, the building of the Second Temple of Jerusalem, and the writing down of the Torah, a process complete in 450 B.C.E. Since the formative pattern imposed that perpetual, self-conscious uncertainty, treating the life of the group as conditional and discontinuous, Jews have asked themselves who they are and invented Judaisms to answer that question. Accordingly, because of the definitive paradigm affecting their group life in various contexts, no circumstances have permitted Jews to take for granted their existence as a group. Looking back on Scripture and its message, Jews have ordinarily treated as special, subject to conditions, and therefore uncertain what (in their view) other groups enjoyed as unconditional and simply given. Why the paradigm renewed itself is clear: This particular view of matters generated expectations that could not be met, hence created resentment—and then provided comfort and hope that made possible coping with that resentment. To state my thesis with appropriate emphasis: *Promising what could not be delivered, then providing solace for the consequent disappointment, the system at hand precipitated in age succeeding age the very conditions necessary for its own replication.*

There have been many Judaisms, each with its indicative symbol and generative paradigm, each pronouncing its world view, prescribing its way of life, and identifying the particular Israel that in its view is bearer of God's original promise. But each Judaism retells in its own way and with its distinctive emphases the tale of the Five Books of Moses, the story of a no-people that becomes a people, that has what it gets only on condition, and that can lose it all by virtue of its own sin. That is a terrifying, unsettling story for a social group to tell of itself, because it imposes acute self-consciousness and chronic insecurity upon what should be the level plane and firm foundation of society. That is to say, the collection of diverse materials joined into a single tale on the occasion of the original exile and restoration because of the repetition in age succeeding age also precipitates the recapitulation of the interior experience of exile and restoration—always because of sin and atonement. So it is the Pentateuch that shaped the imagination of Jews wherever they lived, it is their social condition as a small and scattered group that made the question raised by the pentateuchal narrative urgent, and it is the power of the Pentateuch both to ask and to answer the question that has preoccupied Jews (that is to say, "Israel") whenever and wherever they have lived.

CHAPTER 4

The Four Periods in the History of Judaism

THE FIRST AGE OF DIVERSITY (ca. 500 B.C.E. to C.E. 70)

The destruction of Jerusalem in 586 B.C.E. produced a crisis of faith,[1] be-cause ordinary folk supposed that the god of the conquerors had con-quered the God of Israel. Israelite prophets saw matters otherwise. Israel had been punished for her sins, and it was God who had carried out the punishment. God was not conquered but vindicated. The pagans were merely his instruments. Moreover, God could be served anywhere, not only in the holy and promised land of Israel. Israel in Babylonian exile continued the cult of the Lord through worship, psalms, and festivals; the synagogue, a place where God was worshipped without sacrifice, took shape. The Sabbath became Israel's sanctuary, the seventh day of rest and sanctification for God. When, for political reasons, the Persians chose to restore Jewry to Palestine and many returned (ca. 500 B.C.E.), the Jews were not surprised, for they had been led by prophecy to expect that, with the expiation of sin through suffering and atonement, God would once more show mercy and bring them homeward. The prophets' mes-sage was authenticated by historical events.

In the early years of the Second Temple (ca. 450 B.C.E.), Ezra, the priest-scribe, came from Babylonia to Palestine and brought with him the To-rah-book, the collection of ancient scrolls of law, prophecy, and narrative. Jews resolved to make the Torah the basis of national life. The Torah was publicly read on New Year's Day in 444 B.C.E., and those assembled pledged to keep it. Along with the canonical Scriptures, the Jews needed oral traditions, explanations, instructions on how to keep the law, and ex-egeses of Scripture to apply the law to changing conditions of everyday life. A period of creative interpretation of the written Torah began, one that has yet to conclude. From that time forward, the history of Judaism became the history of the interpretation of Torah and its message for each successive age.

The next great event in the history of the Jews was the destruction of the Second Temple in c.e. 70. A political and military event, its religious consequences were drawn by Yohanan ben Zakkai and other great rabbis of the age. These rabbis, heirs of the tradition of oral interpretation and instruction in Torah and the continuators of the prophets of old, taught that the God of Israel could still be served by the Jewish people, who had not been abandoned by God but once more chastised. The rabbis in the following talmudic story—told not after 70 but after a deep disappointment three hundred years later—taught that, by obedience to Torah, Israel would again be restored to its land:

> When a disciple of Yohanan ben Zakkai wept at seeing the Temple Mount in ruins, Yohanan asked him, "Why do you weep, my son?"
> "This place, where the sins of Israel were atoned, is in ruins, and should I not weep?" the disciple replied.
> "Let it not be grievous to your eyes, my son," Yohanan replied, "for we have another means of atonement, as effective as Temple sacrifice. It is deeds of loving-kindness, as it is said [Hosea 6:6], *For I desire mercy and not sacrifice.*"

In our own century, we have seen how historical events—the destruction of European Jewry, the creation of the state of Israel—defined the issues that Judaic religious systems would have to address. So we cannot find it surprising that once again a historical event produced a major religious revolution in the life of Judaism. That revolution is embodied in the pages of the Palestinian and Babylonian Talmuds, compendia of Judaic law, lore, and theology produced by the rabbis of Palestine and Babylonia on the basis of the ancient oral tradition and finally edited in the fifth and sixth centuries c.e. Once and for all, the rabbis defined "being Jewish" in terms of laws universally applicable, laws that might be kept by Jews living in every civilization. Wherever Jews might go, they could serve God through prayer, study of the Torah, practice of the commandments, and acts of loving kindness. All Jews were able to study. No clerical class was required, only learned men. So rabbis took the priests' place as teachers of the people. The Jews thus formed a commonwealth within an empire, a religious nation within other nations, living in conformity with the laws of alien governments but in addition carrying out their own Torah. It was a commonwealth founded on religious belief, a holy community whose membership was defined by obedience to laws believed given at Sinai and interpreted and applied by rabbinical sages to each circumstance of daily life.

We see, therefore, that in the biblical period, approximately fourteen centuries before the first century c.e., religious experiences and beliefs of various kinds took shape among diverse groups of Jewish people, the people of ancient (and modern) Israel. One principal development in that long period was the Hebrew Scriptures, called by Christians the Old Testament and by Jews *Tanakh* (for the letters beginning the Hebrew words for the three parts of the document: *Torah,* or Pentateuch; *Nebi'im,* or Prophets; and *Ketubim,* or Writings—hence *T-N-K*). As we must realize, the Hebrew Scriptures are a mosaic of different kinds of books—about different sorts of religious experiences and teachings—all addressed to a single group of people, ancient Israel, and all united solely by their common audience.

The formative generations of rabbinic Judaism, the next period before us, drew upon more than the ancient Hebrew Scriptures. The formative generations flowed out of particular groups in the world of Judaism, which read these Scriptures in a particular way and which had a distinctive approach to the religious life of the community of Israel. We must pay attention to three main components of the religious life of the Jews in the last two centuries B.C.E. and the first century C.E. These components, not mutually exclusive, were the priests, with their commitment to the Temple of Jerusalem and its sacred offerings and to governance of the people of Israel in accord with the orderly world created by and flowing out of the Temple; the scribes, with their commitment to the ancient Scriptures and their capacity to interpret and apply these Scriptures to the diverse conditions of the life of the people (later on, the heirs of the scribes would gain the honorific title of "rabbi," which was not distinctive to their group of Jews or even to the Jews); and the messianic Zealots, who believed that God would rule the Jews when foreign rulers had been driven out of the Holy Land. Obviously, these three components were talking about different things to different people.

Of these three groups, one predominated in the shaping of events in the first century C.E., and the other two fused thereafter. The messianic Zealots, until the destruction of the Temple of Jerusalem in C.E. 70, were the most powerful force in the history of the Jews. For they precipitated the single most important event of the time, the war fought against Rome from C.E. 66 to 73, climaxed by the fall of Jerusalem in C.E. 70. And the messianic Zealots must have remained paramount for another three generations, since the next major event in the history of the Jews was yet a second and still more disastrous holy and messianic war against Rome, fought under the leadership of Ben Kosiba (also called *Bar Kokhba,* the Star's Son) from C.E. 132 to 135. That war surely was a mass uprising, which tells us that a large part of the population was attracted to the Zealot way of thinking.

The other two groups—the priests and the scribes—with their interest in continuity, order, and regularity, lost out both times. The priests of the Temple saw the destruction of their sanctuary in C.E. 70 and realized after C.E. 135 that it would not be rebuilt for a long time. The scribes who taught Scriptures and administered their law witnessed the upheavals of society and the destruction of the social order that war inevitably brings in its aftermath. While both groups doubtless shared in the messianic hopes, they most certainly could not have sympathized with the policies and disastrous programs of the messianic Zealots.

THE AGE OF COGENCY (ca. C.E. 640 to 1800)

The age of cogency ran on into the nineteenth century. That does not mean there were no other Judaic systems. It means that the Judaism of the dual Torah set the standard. A heresy selected its "false doctrine" by defining something in a way different from the Judaism of the dual Torah. There were shifts and changes of all sorts. But the Judaism of the dual Torah absorbed into itself and its structure powerful movements, such as philosophy and mysticism (called *kabbalah*), and found strength in both of them. The philosopher defended the way of life and world view of the Judaism of the dual Torah. The mystic observed the faith defined by the Judaism of the dual Torah as the vehicle for gaining his or her mystical experience. So although the Judaism of the dual Torah was cogent for nineteen centuries, it is not because the system remained intact and unchanged but because it was forever able to take within itself, treat as part of its system of values and beliefs, a wide variety of new concepts and customs. This is an amazingly long time for something so volatile as a religion to have remained essentially stable and to have endured without profound shifts in symbolic structure, ritual life, or modes of social organization for the religious community. The Judaism that predominated during this long period and that has continued to flourish in the nineteenth and twentieth centuries bears a number of names: *rabbinic* because of the nature of its principal authorities, who are rabbis; *talmudic* because of the name of its chief authoritative document after the Hebrew Scriptures, which is the Talmud; *classical* because of its basic quality of endurance and prominence; or simply *Judaism* because no other important alternative was explored by Jews.

What provided the stability and essential cogency of rabbinic Judaism during the long period of its predominance was its capacity—in its modes of thought, its definitions of faith, worship, and the right way to live—to take into itself and to turn into a support and a buttress for its own system a wide variety of separate and distinct modes of belief and thought. Of importance were, first, the philosophical movement and, second, the mystical one. Both put forward modes of thought quite distinct from those of rabbinic Judaism.

Philosophers of Judaism raised a range of questions and dealt with those questions in ways essentially separate from the established and accepted rabbinic ways of thinking about religious issues. But all the philosophers of Judaism not only lived in accord with the rabbinic way of life; all of them were entirely literate in the Talmud and related literature, and many of the greatest philosophers were also great Talmudists. The same is to be said of the mystics. Their ideas about the inner character of God, their quest for a fully realized experience of union with the presence of God in the world, their particular doctrines, with no basis in the talmudic literature produced by the early rabbis, and their intense spirituality—all were thoroughly "rabbinized," or brought into conformity with the lessons and way of life taught by the Talmud. In the end, rabbinic Judaism received extraordinary reinforcement from the spiritual resources generated by the mystic quest. Both philosophy and mysticism found their way into the center of rabbinic Judaism. Both of them were shaped by minds that, to begin with, were infused with the content and spirit of rabbinic Judaism.

THE SECOND AGE OF DIVERSITY
(ca. 1800 to the present)

It is only in modern times that other than religious consequences have been drawn from cataclysmic historical events. Because Judaism had developed prophecy and rabbinic leadership, it was able to overcome the disasters of 586 B.C.E. and C.E. 70. The challenge of modern times comes not only from the outside but also from within: the nurture of new religious leadership for Jews facing a world of new values and ideals. Religion provides a particularly subtle problem for students of the process of modernization. In such areas as politics and economics, that which is "modern" may meaningfully be set apart from that which is "traditional," but in religion the complexities of the process of social change become most evident, the certainties less sure. Even the very definition of the problem to be studied poses difficulty. We refer to "the impact of cultural modernization upon traditional religion" as though religion is a *given*, "a compact entity inherited from the past in a particular form," and as though modernization is also a *given*, a process with a fixed direction.[2] According to the "impact theory," it is *modern* culture that acts on *traditional* religion, just as economic and political patterns are "modernized."

As Wilfred Cantwell Smith points out, the impact theory "is altogether too externalist," for it minimizes the "*interiorization* of modernity in the religious life of all communities," a process that takes place from within as much as from without. It underestimates the dynamism of the so-called tradition, ignoring its own evolution, as in the development of Hasidism and the Jewish Enlightenment (which we will soon study). We speak of "the impact" of one thing upon another only at the risk of vast oversimplification. The dynamic is *within* as well as *upon* tradition.

Smith further asks whether we can speak of the "traditional religion *and* modern culture" and finds difficulty in so doing. He points out that the supposed dichotomy between religion and culture emerges uniquely in the West, which "not only conceptualizes, but institutionalizes, the two separately." "Traditional religion and modern culture" is not only a Western concept but a Western *phenomenon*, Smith says. If Judaism is a Western religion, then the dichotomy fails even here. Smith raises the issue: Is it meaningful to speak of "religion" at all in non-Western contexts? "Hinduism is a modern Western concept, which formulates in Western cultural terms that which can more accurately . . . be characterized as Hindu culture," Smith says, and the same may be said of Judaism. He concludes: "In non-Western societies there is no such thing as religion, there is only culture." Many of the specifically Jewish problems we shall consider derive from that fact.

Smith thus emphasizes that the very concept of a "religious phenom-enon" existing apart from culture is one of the very *significations* of "mod-ernization." Hence the isolation of something called "traditional religion" is similarly a by-product of modernization. The very recognition of the category of *tradition* represents the first step toward the disintegration of that tradition. As a Muslim theologian said, "There is no hope in return-ing to a traditional faith after it has once been abandoned, since the es-sential condition in the holder of a traditional faith is that he should not know he is a traditionalist." Smith seems to offer a paraphrase: "The emergence of Hinduism and Islam as 'traditional religions' is itself a symptom of modern culture." So, too, he states, "Curiously, this modern-cultural phenomenon of something called 'traditional religions' turns out to be not only not traditional, but also not religious." By "religious," Smith refers to two qualities—first, timelessness and, second, a sense of daily presence: "If religion is anything at all, it is something that links the present moment to eternity." As long as religion is a "living reality," im-mediately present in the lives of the communicants, as long as the law is practiced, not merely obeyed, as long as society represents the corporate stage for living out the divinely ordained duty—then "the religious tradi-tion" is fully *traditional*.

The issue is, therefore, more adequately stated by Smith as follows: "*to discern and to delineate what is happening to man's religiousness in the flux and turmoil of the modern world.*" A corollary, peculiarly modern issue, which will be of special concern here, is what is happening to the "religious-ness" of people who, in Smith's words, "either do not express their reli-giousness formally at all, or, if they do, express it in new, untraditional ways." The question is a broad one. Religious phenomena in the past ex-pressed an inner orientation in the lives of people. If so, what is happen-ing today to the human person and to the qualities of life that those tradi-tions used to represent and to foster? This investigation is here subsumed under the narrow and yet exemplary rubric of "Judaism": What has hap-pened to Jewish human beings?

JEWS AS AN ETHNIC GROUP AND JUDAISM
AS A RELIGION IN MODERN TIMES

Two points come clear: First, Jews persisted in an extraordinary belief rooted not in reality but in their own fantasies, that someday things would be better, that somehow problems would find solutions, and that people were not fated to repeat their old mistakes forever and ever. They retained the faith that times would change for the better and that faith called forth from them extraordinary changes in their normal patterns of behavior. In 1665–66—the time of the (false) Messiah, Sabbatai Zevi—that faith led them to sell all their possessions and await the great day. In the years after 1897—the time of the beginning of modern Zionism, the po-litical movement that created the state of Israel—that faith demanded that they leave their homelands for a Mediterranean country previously

known only in prayer, dream, and Scripture. So the very substance of the
"tradition" continued unchanged. The psychic realities embodied in it
seem, in retrospect, to have endured amid all kinds of changes.

On the other hand, Jews so fundamentally changed that they could no
longer talk about reality in the arcane metaphysics of the tradition but
rather had to adapt for their own use the equally metaphysical language
of democratic socialism and nineteenth-century romantic nationalism.
Sabbatai Zevi and Theodor Herzl could not have been more different;
and yet, had their followers met, they might have seen in the sparkle of
one another's eyes, in the radical willingness to act, in the hopeful, fren-
zied optimism, something not wholly unfamiliar.

From such a perspective one may readily perceive the unreality of the
"impact theory" and of formulating the issue in terms of "modernization
and religion." What we want to know is not how matters *progressed* to
their present state, but rather: What changed? And what remained the
same? What is constant in the human experience, and what has been altered in the passage of time, in the movement of people from one place to
another, and in the alteration of inherited patterns of economic, social,
and political behavior? And of greatest interest in the Jewish paradigm:
How has the inherited tradition shaped, as much as it has been shaped
by, the processes of change we call, for convenience, modernization?
These questions will occupy us in Part Five.

What made the modern period *modern?* The break with those long centuries in which Judaism was defined by the rabbis of the Talmud was
marked by the fact that classical Judaism became implausible in the face
of the contemporary context. Many Jews, emerging from the perspectives
of rabbinic world views, found that the promise of modernity was closed
off by those world views. The long-time reticence about Messiah and the
messianic age did not credibly explain that wonderful age people thought
had dawned: an age of liberalism in acceptance of difference in general
and an age in which Jews in particular might find themselves citizens like
all others, subject to a common law and enjoying common rights. One
important component in the shift of Judaism in the modern period, therefore, is the demise of long-established skepticism in the face of claims of
messiahs and new dawns and new ages. Through much of the nineteenth
century, and even down to World War II, that skepticism proved to be
incredible and implausible.

The second reason that classical Judaism was found to be unlikely
contradicts the first. From the last third of the nineteenth century onward, many Jews began to understand that the promises of Enlightenment and of Emancipation would never be kept—indeed, were false to
begin with. There was no place in Western civilization for the Jews, who
had to build their own state as a refuge from the storms that were coming upon them. These Jews rejected that fundamental teleological optimism, rationalism, yielding patience, and quietism with which classical
Judaism had viewed the world. They did not believe that the world was
so orderly and reliable as Judaism had supposed. They regarded Judaism as a misleading and politically unwise view of the Jewish people
and their worldly context. What was needed was not prayer, study of

Torah, and a life of compassion and good deeds. What the hour demanded was renewed action, a reentry into politics, and the
repoliticization of the Jewish people. Zionism was the movement that redefined the Jewish people into a nation and revived the ancient political
status of the Jews. Insofar as Zionism saw the world as essentially irra-
tional and unreliable, unable to proceed in the orderly, calm, reasonable
fashion in which Judaism assumed the world would always do its business, Zionism marked an end to Judaism as it had been known. The fact
that in time to come Zionism would, as we shall see, take up the old
messianic language and symbolism of Judaism and make over these ancient vessels into utensils bearing new meaning is not to be ignored. But
at its beginning, Zionism marked a break from Judaism, not because of
Zionism's messianic fervor but because of its rejection of the quiet confidence, rationalism, and optimism of rabbinic Judaism.

Thus, these two things—the promise of emancipation and the advent
of racist and political anti-Semitism—fell so far outside the world view of
rabbinic Judaism that they could not be satisfactorily interpreted and explained within the established system. The result, as we shall observe
later on, is the breakdown of the Judaic system for many, many Jews. The
system of Judaism was not overturned; for these people, it simply had
become implausible. It had lost the trait of self-evidence. To state matters
very simply: Rabbinic Judaism was and is a system of balance between
cosmic, teleological optimism and short-term skepticism, a system of
moderation and restraint, of rationalism and moderated feeling. Just as it
came into being in response to the collapse of unrestrained messianism,
feelings unleashed and hopes unbounded by doubt, so it came to an end,
where and when it did come to an end, in a renewed clash with those
very emotions and aspirations that in the beginning it had overcome: pas-
sionate hope and unrestrained, total despair. A system of optimistic skepticism and skeptical optimism, a world grasped with open arms and
loved with a breaking heart, could never survive those reaches toward
the extremes, those violations of the rules and frontiers of moderate and
balanced being, that characterize modern times.

CHAPTER 5

The Holy Scriptures of Ancient Israel and the History of Judaism

THE TORAH OF JUDAISM COMPRISES NOT ONLY THE WRITTEN TORAH

Judaism begins in the Hebrew Scriptures, called by Christianity "the Old Testament," but Judaism is not the religion of the Old Testament, any more than Christianity is. Judaism, as we shall see, is the religion of the dual Torah, written and oral, of Sinai: that other, oral Torah teaches the meaning of the written one. To see how this duality works, let us begin with the picture of creation found in a document that forms part of the oral Torah and compare it to the creation-narrative of Scripture:

> In the beginning, two thousand years before the heaven and the earth, seven things were created: the Torah, written with black fire on white fire and lying in the lap of God; the Divine throne, erected in the heavens . . .; Paradise on the right side of God; Hell on the left side; the Celestial Sanctuary directed in front of God, having a jewel on its altar graven with the name of the Messiah, and a Voice that cries aloud, Return, Oh you children of men.[1]

This creation account from classical talmudic Judaism may come as a surprise to readers more familiar with a different creation-legend of Scripture:

> In the beginning God created the heavens and the earth. The earth was without form and void, and darkness was upon the face of the deep. The spirit of God was moving over the face of the waters. And God said, Let there be light, and there was light.
> —**Genesis 1:1–4**

Genesis says nothing about what happened before creation. God alone is responsible for the works of creation, and what he made was heaven and earth. The talmudic creation-legend, by contrast, begins with the creation of the Torah and concludes with the powerful "Voice that cries. . . ."

Clearly, Judaism conceives of creation not solely within the biblical account, known to Christianity as well, but also within the rabbinic account cited here. What that means is simple: Judaism is not the religion of the Old Testament; rather, it is a development out of the ancient Hebrew Scriptures as much as Christianity is. But few people who are not Jewish, and not too many more who are Jewish, know that fact. Let us dwell on this observation: Judaism as it has flourished for many centuries has become, in modern times, an unknown religion even among its own community. If we say to a Jew today, "Tell me the Jewish story of creation," we may hear, "In the beginning God created. . . ." If, having the advantage of advanced education in the study of religions, we persist, "But what about the seven things created before creation?" an ordinary Jew will probably have no idea what we mean. The difficulty in studying Judaism is that in modern, Western society, the classic forms coexist, or compete, with strikingly different but no less interesting views, experiences, and definitions of Judaism.

So, while everybody knows that "Judaism" is the religion of the Old Testament, that is only partly true. Every Judaism appeals to the "Old Testament"—that is, the written Torah. But just as Christianity reads the Old Testament through the New Testament, so any Judaism will read the written Torah in light of a further tradition, or a broader concept of what the Torah encompasses. That explains why, although it is true that the history of Judaism begins with the Hebrew Bible, the history of the Hebrew Bible does not begin with the events depicted in it. It starts long afterward. We revert to the Hebrew Scriptures (or, as we shall learn to call those writings, "the written Torah") because all Judaisms retell, in one way or another, the Old Testament story, each with its own points of interest and emphasis. For every Judaism, Israel's history begins, in the biblical narrative, with the creation of the world and ends with the redemption of mankind and the conclusion of history.

IDENTIFYING ONESELF AS "ISRAEL"

Every group of Jews—that is, every "Israel"—is going to trace its origin to Abraham, who migrated from Mesopotamia and became a sojourner in the land of Canaan (the present-day land of Israel). That migration was given religious significance: Abraham left the gods of this world—idols called "no-gods"—to serve the Lord, Creator of heaven and earth. His descendants, Isaac and Jacob, were bearers of the promise God had made to Abraham that, through him, the families of man would bless themselves and that Abraham would be the father of a great people. Jacob, who was also called Israel, went down to Egypt in the time of famine, when his son Joseph served Pharaoh, and there his children multiplied. A pharaoh arose who did not know Joseph; he oppressed the children of Israel until they cried out to the God of their fathers. God sent Moses to redeem Israel from the bondage of Egypt, to bring them through the wilderness to the Promised Land. So goes the biblical legend. It has been adopted by many peoples. When Jews call themselves "Israel," meaning "the people" (not the state of Israel, which is a separate matter), they adopt the written Torah as their own story. They see it not merely as a spiritual paradigm but as a personal, concrete history, the family history of Israel after the flesh.

In retrospect, we see that, as the biblical record has it, the great event of the Exodus from Egypt culminated in the Mosaic revelation; the monarchy of King David, several centuries afterward, so shaped the Israelite imagination as to produce histories, psalms, and above all the messianic hope attached to the Davidic line. The destruction of the northern part of the kingdom, the ten tribes of Israel, in 722 B.C.E. provoked magnificent prophecy. The end of the southern kingdom, Judah—that is, the destruction of its city and the Temple of Jerusalem in 586 B.C.E. and the exile of Judeans (Jews or *Yehudim*) to Babylonia—resulted in the formation of much of the Hebrew Bible as we know it.

The conquest of Jerusalem by the Romans in C.E. 70 led to the foundation of classical, rabbinic Judaism under the leadership of Yohanan ben Zakkai and other great rabbis. The Moslem conquest of the Middle East in C.E. 640 renewed the philosophical and mystical inquiry. The advent of modern times—marked by the political emancipation of Western European Jewry, the destruction of European Jewry, and the creation of the state of Israel—has also had important religious consequences.

The fate of the Jewish people and the faith of Judaism were forever bound up with one another. One became a Jew—that is, part of the Jewish people—not through ethnic or territorial assimilation, but through profession of faith in one God and adoption of the laws of the Torah. Professing that faith and practicing those laws make a person into a Jew.

The beginning of Israel-the-people marked the appearance not only of a new group but also of an entirely new religious ideal, monotheism. To understand what was new in the biblical legacy, one must know what was old. Biblical writers invariably misrepresented paganism, calling it the worship of wood and stone, of dumb idols—that is, fetishism. What was actually central to paganism was the deification of worldly phenomena (not the simple carving of idols), the view that all manifestations of nature are aspects of a "mysterious supernatural vitality."[2] Israel began with the affirmation that God is transcendent over creation. God created the world and is wholly different from it. He has no myth, no birth. He is not subject to nature, to anything above himself, to any primordial reality. He is sovereign, and there is no realm beyond him.

Moses transformed the liberation of slaves into the birth of a nation[3] and made the birth of a nation into the creation of a new faith. He did so by pronouncing the redemption to be the work of the supreme God, who revealed his will through the liberation from Egyptian slavery. The Lord further made a covenant at Sinai, a contract, that Israel should be his people and he should be their God, that Israel should do his will and he should protect and defend them. That will was both universal and specific. Some of the commandments concerned only Israel; others, including respect for the sanctity of life, marriage, property, and justice, pertained to everyone. Ethics applied to the entire nation. A new moral category, the people, was created, which bore ethical and legal responsibilities beyond those that earlier pertained to individuals.

The creation of the monarchy, ca. 1000 B.C.E., a political event, called forth prophecy of religious significance. The king was not to be deified; he, too, was not God but subject to the law of God. When political and military disasters produced social disintegration, prophets came forward as apostles of God, emphasizing the primacy of morality. What was new was the conviction that the cult, while cherished as the link between heaven and earth, had no intrinsic, but only contingent, value. God demanded justice, mercy, and loving kindness. God accepts the sacrifices of upright people; sacrifice by itself does not make a difference. The cult is profoundly appreciated and central to the life of the faith, but morality takes a premier place over the cult. History was decided not by force but by the moral condition of the people. Idolatry, a religious matter, and social corruption, a moral one—these were the predominating facts in the shaping of the people's political destiny. The prophets looked forward to the end of days, when God would make himself known to the nations as he was now known to Israel. Thus history was seen as a succession of events that were not meaningless but rather pointed toward a goal, the fulfillment of the divine, moral law. Through prophecy, Israelite religion created the notion of a single, all-encompassing, universal history of mankind. All of these powerful writings would flow into every Judaic system. But each would define its terms and then discover in the written Torah what its religious system required.

PART TWO

The Holy Books
of Judaism

CHAPTER 6

The Mishnah

From what time may they recite the Shema in the evening? From the hour that the priests enter [their homes] to eat their heave offering, "until the end of the first watch," the words of R. Eliezer. But sages say, "Until midnight." Rabban Gamaliel says, "Until the rise of dawn." There was the case in which his [Gamaliel's] sons returned from a banquet hall [after midnight]. They said to him, "We did not [yet] recite the Shema." He said to them, "If the dawn has not yet risen, you are obligated to recite [the Shema]. And [this applies] not only [in] this [case]. Rather, [as regards] all [commandments] which sages said [may be performed] 'Until midnight,' the obligation [to perform them persists] until the rise of dawn." [For example,] the offering of the fats and entrails—their obligation [persists] until the rise of dawn [see Leviticus 1:9, 3:3-5]. And all [sacrifices] which must be eaten within one day, the obligation [to eat them persists] until the rise of dawn. If so why did sages say [that these actions may be performed only] until midnight? In order to protect man from sin.

—**Mishnah-tractate Berakhot chapter 1, paragraph 1, the opening lines of the Mishnah**

So begins the Mishnah. Not a very promising start! Falling into the hands of someone who has never seen the writing before, the Mishnah must cause puzzlement. From the first line to the last, discourse takes up questions internal to a system that is never introduced. The Mishnah provides information without establishing context. It presents disputes about facts hardly urgent outside of a circle of faceless disputants. Consequently, we start with the impression that we join a conversation already long under way about topics we can never grasp anyhow. Even though the language is our own, the substance is not. We feel as if we are in a transit lounge at a distant airport. We understand the words people say but are baffled by their meanings and concerns, above all by the urgency in their voices: What are you telling me? Why must I know it? Who cares if I do not? No one can take for granted that what is before us makes sense in any context but the Mishnah's own inaccessible world. Each step in the inquiry into the meaning and importance of the document must be laid forth with ample preparation, taken with adequate care. For before us is a remarkable statement of concerns for matters not only wholly remote from our own world but, in the main, alien to the world of the people who made the Mishnah itself. It is as if people sat down to write letters about things they had never seen to people they did not know—letters from an unknown city to an undefined and unimagined world. The Mishnah is from no one special in utopia, to whom it may concern. And yet, by the end of these pages, I hope you will agree with me that the Mishnah presents a magnificent example of how religious sages formulate a theory and account of the social order: everything all together, all at once, that we need to know to live a good and holy life in a community.

DEFINING THE MISHNAH: THE FIRST HOLY BOOK IN JUDAISM AFTER THE HEBREW SCRIPTURES

Defining the Mishnah presents difficulties, because the Mishnah does not identify its authors. It permits only slight variations, if any, in its authorities' patterns of language and speech, so there is no place for individual characteristics of expression. It nowhere tells us when it speaks. It does not address a particular place or time and rarely speaks of events in its own day. It never identifies its prospective audience. There is scarcely a *you* in the entire mass of sayings and rules. The Mishnah begins nowhere. It ends abruptly. There is no predicting where it will commence and no explaining why it is done. Where, when, why the document is laid out and set forth are questions not deemed urgent and not answered.

Indeed, the Mishnah contains not a hint about what its authors conceive their work to be. Is it a law-code? Is it a schoolbook? Since it makes statements describing what people should and should not do, or rather do and do not do, we might suppose it is a law-code. Since, as we shall see in a moment, it covers topics of both practical and theoretical interest, we might suppose it is a schoolbook. But the Mishnah never expresses a hint about its authors' intent. The reason is that the authors do what they must to efface all traces not only of individuality but even of their own participation in the formation of the document. So it is not only a letter from utopia to whom it may concern. It also is a letter written by no one person but not by a committee either. Nor should we fail to notice, even at the outset, that while the Mishnah clearly addresses Israel, the Jewish people, it is remarkably indifferent to the Hebrew Scriptures. The Mishnah makes no effort at imitating the Hebrew of the Hebrew Bible, as do the writers of the Dead Sea Scrolls. The Mishnah does not attribute its sayings to biblical heroes, prophets, or holy men, as do the writings of the pseudoepigraphs of the Hebrew Scriptures. The Mishnah does not claim to emerge from a fresh encounter with God through revelation, as is not uncommon in Israelite writings of the preceding four hundred years; the Holy Spirit is not alleged to speak here. So all the devices by which other Israelite writers gain credence for their messages are ignored. Perhaps the authority of the Mishnah was self-evident to its authors. But self-evident authorities or not, they in no way take the trouble to explain to their document's audience why people should conform to the descriptive statements contained in their holy book.

If, then, we turn to the contents of the document, we are helped not at all in determining the place of the Mishnah's origination, the purpose of its formation, the reasons for its anonymous and collective plane of discourse and monotonous tone of voice. For the Mishnah covers a carefully defined program of topics. But the Mishnah never tells us why one topic is introduced and another is omitted or what the agglutination of these particular topics is meant to accomplish in the formation of a system or imaginative construction. Nor is there any predicting how a given topic will be treated, why a given set of issues will be explored in close detail and another set of possible issues ignored. Discourse on a theme begins and ends as if all things are self-evident, including the reason for beginning at one point and ending at some other. In all one might readily imagine, upon first glance at this strange and curious book, that what we have is a rule book. It appears on the surface to be a book lacking all traces of eloquence and style, revealing no evidence of system and reflection, serving no important purpose. At first glance it is yet another sherd from remote antiquity, no different from the king-lists inscribed on the ancient sherds, the random catalogue of (to us) useless, meaningless facts: a cookbook, a placard of posted tariffs, detritus of random information, accidentally thrown upon the currents of historical time. Who would want to have made such a thing? Who would now want to refer to it?

The answer to that question is deceptively straightforward: The Mishnah is important because it is a principal component of the canon of Judaism. Indeed, that answer begs the question: Why should some of the ancient Jews of the Holy Land have brought together these particular facts and rules into a book and set them forth for the Israelite people? Why should the Mishnah have been received, as much later it certainly was received, as a half of the "whole Torah of Moses at Sinai"? The Mishnah was represented, after it was compiled, as the part of the "whole Torah of Moses our rabbi" that had been formulated and transmitted orally, so it bore the status of divine revelation right alongside the Pentateuch. Yet it is already entirely obvious that little in the actual contents of the document evoked the character or the moral authority of the written Torah of Moses. Indeed, since most of the authorities named in the Mishnah lived in the century and a half prior to the promulgation of the document, the claim that things said by men known to the very framers of the document in fact derived from Moses at Sinai through a long chain of oral tradition contradicted the well-known facts of the matter. So this claim presents a paradox even on the surface: How can the Mishnah be deemed a book of religion, a program for consecration, a mode of sanctification? Why should Jews from the end of the second century to our own day have deemed the study of the Mishnah to be a holy act, a deed of service to God through the study of an important constituent of God's Torah, God's will for Israel, the Jewish people?

In fact, the Mishnah is precisely that, a principal holy book of Judaism. The Mishnah has been and now is memorized in the circle of all those who participate in the religion, Judaism. Of still greater weight, the two great documents formed around the Mishnah and so shaped as to serve, in part, as commentaries to the Mishnah—namely, the Babylonian Talmud and the Palestinian Talmud—form the center of the curriculum of Judaism as a living religion. Consequently, the Mishnah is necessary to the understanding of Judaism. It hardly needs saying that people interested in the study of religions surely will have to reflect upon the same questions I have formulated within the context of Judaism—namely, how such a curious compilation of materials may be deemed a holy book. And self-evidently, scholars of the formative centuries of Christianity, down to the recognition of Christianity as a legal religion in the fourth century, will be glad to have access to a central document of the kind of Judaism taking shape at precisely the same time as the Christianity they study was coming into being. In all, we need not apologize for our interest in this sizable monument to the search for a holy way of life, for Israel is represented, full and whole, in this massive thing, the Mishnah.

DESCRIBING THE MISHNAH: ITS CONTENTS AND CONTEXT

Let me now briefly describe the Mishnah. It is a six-part code of descriptive rules formed toward the end of the second century C.E. by a small number of Jewish sages and put forth as the constitution of Judaism under the sponsorship of Judah the Patriarch, the head of the Jewish community of the Land of Israel at the end of that century. The reason the document is important is that the Mishnah forms the foundation for the Babylonian and Palestinian Talmuds. It therefore stands alongside the Hebrew Bible as the holy book upon which the Judaism of the past nineteen hundred years is constructed. The six divisions are (1) agricultural rules; (2) laws governing appointed seasons, such as Sabbaths and festivals; (3) laws on the transfer of women and property, including the transfer of women from one man (father) to another (husband); (4) the system of civil and criminal law (corresponding to what we today should regard as "the legal system"); (5) laws for the conduct of the cult and the Temple; and (6) laws on the preservation of cultic purity both in the Temple and under certain domestic circumstances, with special reference to the table and bed. These divisions define the range and realm of reality.

The world addressed by the Mishnah is hardly congruent with the world view presented within the Mishnah. Let us now consider the time and context in which the document took shape. The Mishnah is made up of sayings bearing the names of authorities who lived, as I just said, in the later first and second centuries. (The book contains very few names

of people who lived before the destruction of the Temple of Jerusalem, in
C.E. 70.) These authorities generally fall into two groups, two distinct sets of names, each set of names randomly appearing together but rarely, if ever, with names of the other set. One set of names is generally supposed to represent authorities who lived between the destruction of the Temple in 70 and the advent of the second war against Rome, led by Simeon bar Kokhba, in 132. The other set of names belongs to authorities who flourished between the end of that war, ca. 135, and the end of the second century. The Mishnah itself is generally supposed to have come to closure at the end of the second century, and its date, for conventional purposes only, is ca. C.E. 200. Now, of these two groups—sages from 70–130 and from 135–200—the latter is represented far more abundantly than the former. Approximately two-thirds of the named sayings belong to mid-second-century authorities. This is not surprising, since these are the named authorities whose students (mainly unnamed) collected, organized, and laid out the document as we now have it. In all, the Mishnah represents the thinking of Jewish sages who flourished in the middle of the second century. That group took over whatever they had in hand from the preceding century, and from the whole legacy of Israelite literature even before that time, and revised and reshaped the whole into the Mishnah. Let us briefly consider their world.

In the aftermath of the war against Rome in 132–135, the Temple was declared permanently prohibited to Jews, and Jerusalem was closed off to them as well. So there was no cult, no Temple, no holy city to which, at this time, the description of the Mishnaic laws applied. We observe at the very outset, therefore, that a sizable proportion of the Mishnah deals with matters to which the sages had no material access or practical knowledge at the time of their work. For we have seen that the Mishnah contains a division, namely the fifth, on the conduct of the cult, as well as one on the conduct of matters so as to preserve the cultic purity of the sacrificial system along the lines laid out in the book of Leviticus, the sixth division. In fact, a fair part of the second division, on appointed times, takes up the conduct of the cult on special days—for example, the sacrifices offered on the Day of Atonement, Passover, and the like. Indeed, what the Mishnah wants to know about appointed seasons concerns the cult far more than it concerns the synagogue. For its part, the fourth division, on civil law, presents an elaborate account of a political structure and system of Israelite self-government—in tractates Sanhedrin and Makkot, not to mention Shebuot and Horayot. This system speaks of king, priest, Temple, and court. But it was not the Jews, their kings, priests, or judges, but the Romans who governed in the Land of Israel in the second century. Nevertheless, it would appear that well over half the document before us speaks of cult, Temple, government, priesthood. As we shall see, moreover, the Mishnah takes up a profoundly priestly and Levitical conception of sanctification. When we consider that, in the very time in which the authorities before us did their work, the Temple lay in ruins, the city of Jerusalem was prohibited to all Israelites, and the Jewish government and administration that had centered on the Temple and based its authority on the holy life lived there were in ruins, the fantastic character of the Mishnah's address to its own catastrophic day becomes clear. Much of the Mishnah speaks of matters not in being in the time in which the Mishnah was created, because the Mishnah wishes to make its statement on what really matters.

In the age beyond catastrophe, the problem is to reorder a world off course and adrift, to gain reorientation for an age in which the sun has come out after the night and the fog. The Mishnah is a document of imagination and fantasy, describing how things "are" out of the sherds and remnants of reality but, in larger measure, building social being out of beams of hope. The Mishnah tells us something about how things were but everything about how a small group of men wanted things to be. The document is orderly, repetitious, careful in both language and message. It is small-minded, picayune, obvious, dull, routine—everything its age was not. The Mishnah stands in contrast to the world to which it speaks. Its message is one of small achievements and modest hope. It means to defy a world of large disorders and immodest demands. The heirs of heroes build an unheroic folk in the new and ordinary age. The Mishnah's message is that what a person wants matters in important ways. It states that message to an Israelite world that can shape affairs in no important ways and speaks to people who by no means will the way things now are. The Mishnah therefore lays down a practical judgment on, and in favor of, the imagination and will to reshape reality, regain a system, reestablish that order upon which trustworthy existence is to be built.

The Judaism shaped by the Mishnah consists of a coherent world view and a comprehensive way of living. It is a world view that speaks of transcendent things, a way of life in response to the supernatural meaning of what is done, a heightened and deepened perception of the sanctification of Israel in deed and in deliberation. Sanctification means two things: first, distinguishing Israel in all its dimensions from the world in all its ways; second, establishing the stability, order, regularity, predictability, and reliability of Israel at moments and in contexts of danger. Danger means instability, disorder, irregularity, uncertainty, and betrayal. Each topic of the system as a whole takes up a critical and indispensable moment or context of social being. Each orders what is disorderly and dangerous. Through what is said in regard to each of the Mishnah's principal topics, what the system as a whole wishes to declare is fully expressed. Yet if the parts severally and jointly give the message of the whole, the whole cannot exist without all of the parts, so well joined and carefully crafted are they all.

THE MISHNAH'S JUDAISM

Let me now describe and briefly interpret the six components of the Mishnah's system. The critical issue in the economic life, which means in farming, is in two parts, revealed in the first division, Agriculture. First, Israel, as tenant on God's holy land, maintains the property in the ways God requires, keeping the rules that mark the land and its crops as holy.

Next, the hour at which the sanctification of the land comes to form a critical mass, namely in the ripened crops, is the moment ponderous with danger and heightened holiness. Israel's will so affects the crops as to mark a part of them as holy, the rest of them as available for common use. The human will is determinative in the process of sanctification.

In the second division, what happens on the land at certain times, at Appointed Times, marks off spaces of the land as holy in yet another way. The center of the land and the focus of its sanctification is the Temple. There the produce of the land is received and given back to God, the one who created and sanctified the land. At these unusual moments of sanctification, the inhabitants of the land in their social being in villages enter a state of spatial sanctification. That is to say, the village boundaries mark off holy space, within which one must remain during the holy time. This division is expressed in two ways. First, the Temple itself observes and expresses the special, recurring holy time. Second, the villages of the land are brought into alignment with the Temple, forming a complement and completion to the Temple's sacred being. The advent of the appointed times precipitates a spatial reordering of the land, so that the boundaries of the sacred are matched and mirrored in village and in Temple. At the heightened holiness marked by these moments of Appointed Times, therefore, the occasion for an affective sanctification is worked out. Like the harvest, the advent of an appointed time, a pilgrim festival, also a sacred season, is made to express that regular, orderly, and predictable sort of sanctification for Israel that the system as a whole seeks.

If for a moment we now leap over the next two divisions, the third and fourth, we come to the counterpart of the divisions of Agriculture and Appointed Times. These are the fifth and sixth divisions, namely Holy Things and Purities, which deal with the everyday and the ordinary as against the special moments of harvest, on the one side, and the special time or season, on the other.

The fifth division is about the Temple on ordinary days. The Temple, the locus of sanctification, is conducted in a wholly routine and trustworthy, punctilious manner. The one thing that may unsettle matters is the intention and will of the human actor. This element is therefore subjected to carefully prescribed limitations and remedies. The division of Holy Things generates its companion, the sixth division, the one on cultic cleanness, Purities. The relationship between the two is like that between Agriculture and Appointed Times—the former locative, the latter utopian, the former dealing with the fields, the latter with the interplay between fields and altar.

Here, too, in the sixth division, once we speak of the one place of the Temple, we also address the cleanness that pertains to every place. A system of cleanness—taking into account what imparts uncleanness and how it does so, what is subject to uncleanness and how that state is overcome—is fully expressed once more in response to the participation of the human will. Without the wish and act of a human being, the system does not function. It is inert. Sources of uncleanness, which come naturally and not by volition, and modes of purification, which work naturally and not by human intervention, remain inert until human will has imparted susceptibility to uncleanness—that is, introduced into the system food and drink, bed, pot, chair, and pan, which to begin with form the focus of the system. The movement from sanctification to uncleanness takes place when human will and work precipitate it.

Now let us return to the middle divisions, the third and fourth, on Women and Damages. They take their place in the structure of the whole by showing the congruence, within the larger framework of regularity and order, of human concerns of family and farm, politics and workaday transactions among ordinary people. For without attending to these matters, the Mishnah's system does not encompass what it is meant to comprehend and order. So what is at issue is fully cogent with the rest.

In the case of Women, the third division, attention focuses on the point of disorder marked by the transfer of that disordering anomaly, woman, from the regular status provided by one man to the equally trustworthy status provided by another. That is the point at which the Mishnah's interests are aroused: once more, predictably, the moment of disorder.

In the case of Damages, the fourth division, there are two important concerns. First, there is the paramount interest in preventing, so far as possible, the disorderly rise of one person and fall of another and in sustaining the status quo of the economy, the house and household, of Israel, the holy society in eternal stasis. Second, there is the necessary concomitant in the provision of a system of political institutions to carry out the laws preserving the balance and steady state of persons.

The two divisions that take up topics of concrete and material concern, the formation and dissolution of families and the transfer of property in that connection, the transactions that through torts and through commerce lead to exchanges of property and the potential dislocation of the state of families in society, are both locative and utopian. They deal with the concrete locations in which people make their lives, household and street and field, the sexual and commercial exchanges of a given village. But they pertain to the life of all Israel, both in the land and otherwise. These two divisions, together with the household ones of Appointed Times, constitute the sole opening outward toward the life of utopian Israel, that diaspora in the far reaches of the ancient world, in the endless span of time. From the Mishnah's perspective, this community is not only in exile but unaccounted for outside the system, for the Mishnah declines to recognize and take it into account. Israelites who dwell in the land of (unclean) death instead of in the Holy Land simply fall outside of the range of (holy) life. Priests, who must remain cultically clean, may not leave the land, and neither may most of the Mishnah.

CHAPTER 7

Women in Judaism:
The Evidence of the Mishnah

WOMEN AS THE INDICATOR OF THE CHARACTER OF A RELIGIOUS SYSTEM

The social vision of the Judaism of the Mishnah says the same thing about everything. Accordingly, knowing the urgent question and the self-evidently valid answer of the system, we can predict what the system has to say about any topic it chooses to treat. The social vision of the Mishnah's Judaism encompasses issues of gender, social structure and construction, wealth and transactions in property, and the organization of the castes of society. In all these matters the system seeks the principles of order and proper classification, identifying as problems the occasions for disorder and improper disposition of persons or resources. The fact that we can find our document saying one thing about many things tells us that the document stands for a well-considered view of the whole. When we come to the theological and philosophical program of the same writing, that consistent viewpoint will guide us to what matters and what is to be said about what matters.

The principal focus of a social vision framed by men, such as that of the Mishnah, not only encompasses but also focuses upon woman, who is perceived as the indicative abnormality in a world in which man is normal. But to place into perspective the Mishnah's vision of woman, we have to locate woman within the larger structure defined by the household. That is for two reasons. First of all, as a matter of definition, woman forms the other half of the whole that is the householder. Second, since, as we have already seen, the household forms the building block of the social construction envisioned by the Mishnah's framers, it is in that setting that every other component of the social world of the system must situate itself.

In the conception at hand, which sees Israel as made up, on earth, of households and villages, the economic unit also framed the social one, and the two together composed, in conglomerates, the political one. Hence a political economy (*polis, oekos*) was initiated within an economic definition formed out of the elements of production. That development explains why woman cannot be addressed outside the framework of the economic unit of production defined by the household. Throughout, the Mishnah makes a single cogent statement that the organizing unit of society and politics finds its definition in the irreducible unit of economic production. The Mishnah conceives no other economic unit of production than the household, although it recognizes that such existed; its authorship perceived no other social unit of organization than the household and the conglomeration of households, although that limited vision omitted all reference to substantial parts of the population perceived to be present, such as craftsmen, the unemployed, the landless, and the like. But what about woman in particular?

The framers of the Mishnah, for example, do not imagine a household headed by a woman; a divorced woman is assumed to return to her father's household. The framers make no provision for the economic activity of isolated individuals, out of synchronic relationship with a household or a village made up of householders. Accordingly, craftsmen and day laborers or other workers, skilled and otherwise, enter the world of social and economic transactions only in relationship to the householder. The upshot, therefore, is that the social world is made up of households, and since households may be made up of many families—husbands, wives, children, all of them dependent upon the householder—households in no way are to be confused with the family. The indicator of the family is kinship, that of the household propinquity or residence. Yet, even residence is not always a criterion for membership in the household unit, since the craftsmen and day laborers are not assumed to live in the household compound at all. The household forms an economic unit, with secondary criteria deriving from that primary fact.

The Mishnaic law of women defines the position of women in the social economy of Israel's supernatural and natural reality. That position acquires definition in relationship to men, who give form to the Israelite social economy. It is effected through both supernatural and natural, this-worldly action. What man and woman do on earth provokes a response in heaven, and the correspondences are perfect. So the position of women is defined and secured in heaven and here on earth, and that position, always and invariably relative to men, is what comes into consideration. The principal point of interest on the Mishnah's part is the time at which a woman changes hands. That is, she becomes, and ceases to be, holy to a particular man when she enters and leaves the marital union. These are the dangerous and disorderly points in the relationship of woman to man—therefore, as I said, to society.

Five of the seven tractates that pertain to women and family are devoted to the transfer of women, the formation and dissolution of the marital bond. Of them, three treat what is done here on earth by man— that is, formation of a marital bond through betrothal and marriage contract and dissolution through divorce and its consequences: Qiddushin, Ketubot, and Gittin. One of them is devoted to what is done here on earth by woman: Sotah. Yebamot, greatest of the seven in size and informal and substantive brilliance, deals with the corresponding heavenly intervention into the formation and dissolution of marriage: the effect of death on the marital bond and the dissolution, through death, of that bond. The other two tractates, Nedarim and Nazir, draw into one the two realms of reality, heaven and earth, as they work out the effects of vows—generally taken by married women and subject to the confirmation or abrogation of the husband—to heaven. These vows make a deep impact on the marital relationship of the woman who has taken such vows. So, in all, we consider the natural and supernatural character of the woman's relationship to the social economy framed by man: the beginning, end, and middle of that relationship.

PROPER CONDUCT WITH WOMEN

One of the many important issues worked out in the Mishnah concerns proper conduct with women. Here we see how the Mishnah sets forth its ideas on avoiding improper sexual relations:

MISHNAH-TRACTATE QIDDUSHIN
4:12

    A. A man should not remain alone with two women, but a woman may remain alone with two men.

    B. R. Simeon says, "Also: One may stay alone with two women, when his wife is with him.

    C. "And he sleeps with them in the same inn,

    D. "Because his wife keeps watch over him."

    E. A man may stay alone with his mother or with his daughter.

    F. And he sleeps with them with flesh touching.

    G. But if they [the son who is with the mother, the daughter with the father] grew up, this one sleeps in her garment, and that one sleeps in his garment.

    —M. Qiddushin 4:12

4:13–14

    A. An unmarried man may not teach scribes.

    B. Nor may a woman teach scribes.

    C. R. Eliezer says, "Also: He who has no wife may not teach scribes."

    —M. Qiddushin 4:13

    A. R. Judah says, "An unmarried man may not herd cattle.

    B. "And two unmarried men may not sleep in the same cloak."

    C. And sages permit it.

    D. Whoever has business with women should not be alone with women.

    E. And a man should not teach his son a trade which he has to practice among women.

    F. R. Meir says, "A man should always teach his son a clean and easy trade. And let him pray to him to whom belong riches and possessions.

G. "For there is no trade which does not involve poverty or wealth.

H. "For poverty does not come from one's trade, nor does wealth come from one's trade.

I. "But all is in accord with a man's merit."

J. R. Simeon b. Eleazar says, "Have you ever seen a wild beast or a bird who has a trade? Yet they get along without difficulty. And were they not created only to serve me? And I was created to serve my Master. So is it not logical that I should get along without difficulty? But I have done evil and ruined my living."

L. Abba Gurion of Saidon says in the name of Abba Gurya, "A man should not teach his son to be an ass-driver, a camel-driver, a barber, a sailor, a herdsman, or a shopkeeper. For their trade is the trade of thieves."

M. R. Judah says in his name, "Most ass-drivers are evil, most camel-drivers are decent, most sailors are saintly, the best among physicians is going to Gehenna, and the best of butchers is a partner of Amalek."

N. R. Nehorai says, "I should lay aside every trade in the world and teach my son only Torah.

O. "For a man eats its fruits in this world, and the principal remains for the world to come.

P. "But other trades are not that way.

Q. "When a man gets sick or old or has pains and cannot do his job, lo, he dies of starvation.

R. "But with Torah it is not that way.

S. "But it keeps him from all evil when he is young, and it gives him a future and a hope when he is old.

T. "Concerning his youth, what does it say? *They who wait upon the Lord shall renew their strength* (Isaiah 40:31). And concerning his old age what does it say? *They shall still bring forth fruit in old age* (Psalms 92:14).

U. "And so it was with regard to the patriarch Abraham, may he rest in peace, *And Abraham was old and well along in years, and the Lord blessed Abraham in all things* (Genesis 24:1)

V. "We find that the patriarch Abraham kept the entire Torah even before it was revealed, since it says, *Since Abraham obeyed my voice and kept my charge, my commandments, my statutes, and my laws* (Genesis 26:5)."

—M. Qiddushin 4:14

Mishnah-tractate 4:13 refers to teachers of young children. The teachers should not be brought into close association with the mothers (A) or fathers (B) of the children. The formal and substantive traits of what follows require no comment.

To appreciate these rules, we have to remember that what the Mishnah's authors say about one thing they say about all things. Hence, if we want to understand how the Mishnah's Judaism treats women, we have to ask how the Mishnah's Judaism deals with any important subject. We see that the Mishnah wants men and women to preserve relationships that are chaste and dignified. The authors of the document know full well

that each sex desires the other—that is the foundation of the social order:
family, home, household. But a well-ordered society is a predictable one, which keeps in check the natural desires of women and men.

A STEADY-STATE WORLD OF
PERMANENCE AND ORDER

What the Mishnah really wants is for nothing to happen. The Mishnah presents a tableau, a wax museum, a diorama. It portrays a world fully perfected and so fully at rest. The one thing the Mishnah does not want to tell us is about change, how things come to be what they are. That is why there can be no sustained attention to the priesthood and its rules, the scribal profession and its constitution, the class of householders and its interests. The Mishnah's pretense is that all of these have come to rest. They compose a world in stasis, perfect and complete, made holy because it is complete and perfect. It is an economy—again, in the classic sense of the word—awaiting the divine act of sanctification that, as at the creation of the world, would set the seal of holy rest upon an again-complete creation, just as in the beginning. There is no place for the actors when what is besought is no action whatsoever but only unchanging perfection. There is room only for a description of how things are: the present tense, the sequence of completed statements and static problems. All the action lies within, in how these statements are made.

Essentially, the Mishnah's authorship aimed at the fair adjudication of conflict, worked out in such a way that no party gained, none lost, in any transaction. The task of Israelite society, as they saw it, is to maintain perfect stasis, to preserve the prevailing situation, to secure the stability of not only relationships but also status and standing. To this end, in the interchanges of buying and selling, giving and taking, borrowing and lending, transactions of the market and exchanges with artisans and craftsmen and laborers, it is important to preserve the essential equality, not merely equity, of exchange. Fairness alone does not suffice. *Status quo ante* forms the criterion of the true market, reflecting as it does the exchange of value for value, in perfect balance. That is the way that, in reference to the market, the systemic point of urgency, the steady state of the polity, therefore also of the economy, is stated. The upshot of their economics is simple. No party in the end may have more than what he or she had at the outset, and none may emerge as the victim of a sizable shift in fortune and circumstance. All parties' rights in the stable and unchanging political economy are preserved. When, therefore, the condition of a person is violated, the law will secure the restoration of the antecedent status.

Critical to the social system of the Mishnah is its principal social entity, the village, comprising households, imagined as a society that never changes in any important way. The model, from household to village to "all Israel," comprehensively describes whatever of "Israel" the authorship at hand has chosen to describe. We have therefore to identify as systemically indicative the centrality of political economy—"community, self-sufficiency, and justice"—within the system of the Mishnah. It is no surprise, either, that the point of originality of the political economy of the Mishnah's system is its focus upon the society organized in relationship to the control of the means of production—namely, the farm, for the household is always the agricultural unit.

In the context of a world of pervasive diversity, the Mishnah's authorship set forth a fantastic conception of a simple world of little blocks formed into big ones: households into villages, no empty spaces but also no vast cities. In the conception of the authorship of the Mishnah, community or village (*polis*) is made up of households, and the household (*bayit/oikos*) constituted the building block of both society or community and also economy. It follows that the household forms the fundamental, irreducible, and of course representative unit of the economy, the means of production, the locus and the unit of production. We should not confuse the household with class status—for example, thinking of the householder as identical with the wealthy. The opposite is suggested on every page of the Mishnah, in which householders vie with craftsmen for ownership of the leavings of the loom and the chips left behind by the adze. Rather, the household forms an economic and a social classification defined by function, specifically economic function. A poor household was a household, and (in theory, because the Mishnah's authorship knows none such in practice) a rich landholding that did not function as a center for a social and economic unit—that is, as a rural industrial farm—was not a household. The household constituted the center of the productive economic activities we now handle through the market. Within the household all local—as distinct from cultic, economic, therefore social—activities and functions were held together. For the unit of production composed also the unit of social organization and, of greater import still, the building block of all larger social and political units, with special reference to the village.

In its identification of the householder as the building block of society, to the neglect of the vast panoply of "others" or "nonhouseholders," including after all that half of the whole of the Israelite society comprising women, the Mishnah's authorship reduced the dimensions of society to only a single component in it: the male landowner engaged in agriculture. But that is the sole option open to a system that, for reasons of its own, wished to identify productivity with agriculture, individuality in God's image with ownership of land, and social standing and status consequently with ownership and control of the land, which constituted the sole systemically consequential means of production. If we were to list all of the persons and professions who enjoy no role in the system, or who are treated as ancillary to the system, we would have to encompass not only workers—the entire landless working class!—but also craftsmen and artisans, teachers and physicians, clerks and officials, traders and merchants, the whole of the commercial establishment, not to mention women as a caste.

Fair and just to all parties, the authorship of the Mishnah nonetheless speaks in particular for the landholding, proprietary Israelite. The

Mishnah's problems are the problems of the householder, its perspectives are his. Its sense of what is just and fair expresses the landholder's sense of the givenness and cosmic rightness of the present condition of society. These are men of substance and of means, however modest, aching for a stable and predictable world in which to tend their crops and herds, feed their families and dependents, keep to the natural rhythms of the seasons and lunar cycles, and in all live out their lives within strong and secure boundaries on earth and in heaven. This is why the sense of landed place and its limits, the sharp lines drawn between village and world on the one side, Israelite and Gentile on the second, and temple and world on the third evoke metaphysical correspondences. Householder, which is Israel, in the village and temple beyond, form a correspondence. Only when we understand the systemic principle concerning God in relationship to Israel in its land shall we come to the fundamental and generative conception of the householder as the centerpiece of society.

In this regard, therefore, the Mishnah's social vision finds within its encompassing conception of who forms the *polis* and who merely occupies space within the polis its definition of the realm to which "economics" applies. In the Mishnah's social vision, the householder is the active force, and women, among all other components of the actual economy (as distinct from the economics), prove systemically inert. Of course, the Mishnah's social vision thus ignores most of the actuality of the Jewish people in the Land of Israel in the first and second centuries. But then what of the economically active members of the polis, the ones who had capital and knew how to use it? If they wished to enter that elevated "Israel" that formed the social center and substance of the Mishnah's Israel, they had to purchase land. The Mishnah's social vision thus describes a steady-state society.

THE HOUSEHOLD, THE FAMILY, AND WOMEN

So, for the Mishnah the center and focus of interest lie in the village, the household and family and home, a patriarchal conception. The village is made up of households, each a unit of production in farming. The households are constructed by and around the householder, father of an extended family, including his sons and their wives and children, his servants, his slaves (bondsmen), and the craftsmen to whom he entrusts the tasks he does not choose to do. The concerns of householders are transactions in land. Their measurement of value is expressed in acreage of top, middle, and bottom grade. Through real estate, critical transactions are worked out. The marriage settlement depends on real property. Civil penalties are exacted through payment of real property. The principal transactions to be taken up are those of the householder who owns beasts that do damage or suffer it; who harvests his crops and sets some aside and so by his own word and deed sanctifies them for use by the castes scheduled from on high; who uses or sells his crops and feeds his family; and who, if he is fortunate, will acquire still more land. It is to householders—the pivot of society and its bulwark, the units of which the village is composed, the corporate component of the society of Israel in the limits of the village and the land—that the Mishnah is addressed. The householder, as I said, is the building block of the house of Israel, of its economy in the classic sense of the word in Greek, *oikos,* meaning household, which yields our word *economics.* To that conception of the household, the woman is essential. But it would be many centuries, as we shall see in a later chapter, before women would take a central role in Judaism. Only in the twentieth century were women ordained as rabbis and then not in the Judaism that claimed to be authentic to the Mishnah and the Talmud, Orthodox Judaism, but in the Judaism that proclaimed itself a reforming movement, Reform Judaism, and in its path Reconstructionist and Conservative Judaisms too.

Through its six divisions, the Mishnah sets forth a coherent world view and comprehensive way of living for holy Israel. It is a world view that speaks of transcendent things, a way of life in response to the supernatural meaning of what is done, a heightened and deepened perception of the sanctification of Israel in deed and in deliberation. Sanctification means two things: first, distinguishing Israel in all its dimensions from the world in all its ways, and second, establishing the stability, order, regularity, predictability, and reliability of Israel at moments and in contexts of danger. Danger means instability, disorder, irregularity, uncertainty, and betrayal. Each topic of the system as a whole takes up a critical and indispensable moment or context of social being. Each orders what is disorderly and dangerous. Through what is said in regard to each of the Mishnah's principal topics, what the system as a whole wishes to declare is fully expressed. These writers are obsessed with order and compelled by a vision of a world in which all things are in their right place, each bearing its own name, awaiting the benediction that comes when, everything in order, God pronounces the benediction and brings about sanctification of the whole. So much for the Mishnah. What about the Talmud?

CHAPTER 8

The Mishnah and the Talmud

A TALMUD AS A COMMENTARY TO THE MISHNAH

The Talmud is a commentary on the Mishnah. In fact, there are two talmuds, one produced in the Land of Israel and completed about C.E. 400, called the Talmud of the Land of Israel, the other produced in Babylonia, in the Iranian Empire (present-day Iraq) and completed about 600, called the Talmud of Babylonia, or in Hebrew the Bavli. Each of these extensive documents selected tractates of the Mishnah for comment. But the two Talmuds are quite distinct; they differ in their choices of tractates that require analysis, and their treatment of the tractates they do choose is quite distinct. The Talmud of the Land of Israel deals with thirty-nine tractates of the Mishnah's sixty-two, and the Talmud of Babylonia deals with thirty-seven.

To sample the kind of religious writing we find in the Talmud's reading of the Mishnah, we consider the single most important statement of the Mishnah. It is the rule that defines who is and who is not a Jew— that is, "Israel, the holy people." It does so by explaining who belongs and who does not: "All Israel" will not die but will rise from the dead at the end of days; then those who do not "have a portion in the world to come" will not be part of Israel in the resurrection. Excluded are those who deny the resurrection of the dead or deny that the Torah teaches that the dead will live and that the Torah was given by God ("does not come from Heaven") and those who deny the principles of the faith ("an Epicurean"):

MISHNAH-TRACTATE SANHEDRIN 11:1–2

    A. All Israelites have a share in the world to come,

    B. as it is said, "your people also shall be all righteous, they shall inherit the land forever; the branch of my planting, the work of my hands, that I may be glorified" (Isaiah 60:21).

C. And these are the ones who have no portion in the world to come:

D. He who says, the resurrection of the dead is a teaching which does not derive from the Torah, and the Torah does not come from Heaven; and an Epicurean.

The Babylonian Talmud to this passage begins with two questions in mind. First, is the rule of the Mishnah fair? Second, how on the basis of the written Torah do we know the fact taken for granted by the oral Torah—namely, that the resurrection of the dead will take place and that the Torah itself says so? First comes the justification of God's way:

BABYLONIAN TALMUD TRACTATE SANHEDRIN FOLIO PAGES 90A–B

I. A. [With reference to the Mishnah's statement, *And these are the ones who have no portion in the world to come*]: Why all this [that is, why deny the world to come to those listed]?

B. On Tannaite authority [it was stated], "Such a one denied the resurrection of the dead, therefore he will not have a portion in the resurrection of the dead.

C. "For all the measures [meted out by] the Holy One, blessed be he, are in accord with the principle of measure for measure."

What someone denies shall be denied to that person; hence, it is only fair that someone who does not believe in the resurrection will not live when the dead are raised up. But where in Scripture do we find that fact? The Talmud proceeds to many pages of proofs, among which the following provide a taste of the discussion:

IV. A. It has been taught on Tannaite authority:

B. R. Simai says, "How on the basis of the Torah do we know about the resurrection of the dead?

C. "As it is said, 'And I also have established my covenant with [the patriarchs] to give them the land of Canaan' (Exodus 6:4).

D. "'With you' is not stated, but rather, 'with *them*,' indicating on the basis of the Torah that there is the resurrection of the dead."

V. A. *Minim* [believers, sectarians, sometimes identified as Jews who believed in Jesus as the Messiah, hence Christian Jews] asked Rabban Gamaliel, "How do we know that the Holy One, blessed be he, will resurrect the dead?"

B. He said to them, "It is proved from the Torah, from the Prophets, and from the Writings." But they did not accept his proofs.

C. He said to them, "From the Torah: for it is written, 'And the Lord said to Moses, Behold, you shall sleep with your fathers and rise up' (Deuteronomy 31:16)."

D. They said to him, "But perhaps the sense of the passage is, 'And *the people* will rise up' (Deuteronomy 31:16)?"

E. He said to them, "From the Prophets: as it is written, 'Thy dead men shall live, together with my dead body they shall arise. Awake and sing, you that live in the dust, for your dew is as the dew of herbs, and the earth shall cast out its dead' (Isaiah 26:19)."

F. They said to him, "But perhaps that refers to the dead whom Ezekiel raised up."

He said to them, "From the Writings, as it is written, 'And the roof of your mouth, like the best wine of my beloved, that goes down sweetly, causing the lips of those who are asleep to speak' (Song of Songs 7:9)." . . .

L. [The *minim* would not concur in Gamaliel's view] until he cited for them the following verse: "'Which the Lord swore to your fathers to give to them' (Deuteronomy 11:21)—to *them* and not to you, so proving from the Torah that the dead will live."

We see how the Talmud of Babylonia has faithfully expounded the Mishnah's teaching, so forming an expansion and explanation of the oral Torah's claim.

THE TALMUD AND THE MISHNAH AS PART OF THE ORAL TORAH

Now let us step back and examine the importance of the Talmuds in the history of Judaism, beginning with their reading of the Mishnah. The most important statement concerning the Mishnah made by the two Talmuds is not set forth in so many words but is contained in every page of the two writings. It is that the Mishnah is part of the Torah and that, in commenting on the Mishnah, the authors of the two Talmuds were explaining the meaning of the Torah. This was expressed in a simple way. The framers of the two Talmuds tried to show how most of the rules of the Mishnah derive from statements in the Scriptures. So the Mishnah was shown to depend upon the written Torah.

Not only so, but in the first important piece of writing after the Mishnah was closed, a collection of sayings attributed to sages of the Mishnah, called the Sayings of the Fathers (in Hebrew: *Pirqé Abot*), the Mishnah is shown to form part of the chain of tradition that began at Sinai. This proposition is contained in a rather subtle exposition. First of all, it is alleged that when God gave the Torah to Moses at Sinai, he handed on a tradition that was to be memorized and repeated, master to disciple, for all time. This other medium by which the Torah was revealed was oral; hence "the oral Torah" referred to the part of the Torah formulated and handed on in memory. The story of this other part of the Torah, the oral part, is contained in a few words of a document called the Sayings of the Founders (in Hebrew: *Pirqé Avot*), a writing of about C.E. 250 read in the synagogue, chapter by chapter, as a principal part of Torah-study.

> Moses received Torah at Sinai and handed it on to Joshua, Joshua to elders, and elders to prophets. And prophets handed it on to the men of the great assembly. They said three things: "Be prudent in judgment. Raise up many disciples. Make a fence for the Torah." Simeon the Righteous was one of the last survivors of the great assembly. He would say: "On three things does the world stand: On the Torah, and on the Temple service, and on deeds of loving kindness."
>
> —**Avot 1:1–2**

What is striking in this statement is three allegations. First we find the claim that a tradition from God's revelation to Moses at Sinai continues beyond the figures we know in the holy Scriptures of ancient Israel (the Old Testament), specifically Joshua and the prophets. The "men of the great assembly" and Simeon the Righteous stand in the chain of tradition from Sinai, but they are not figures out of the Old Testament. It follows that there is that other Torah, one not in writing, namely the orally formulated and orally transmitted part of the Torah. The second claim is that this other Torah comes down through the relationship of master to disciple, who becomes a master later on. The third striking fact is that what is stated is not a citation of Scripture but a saying that stands on its own. Simeon's saying is part of that Torah from Sinai, for example, but it does not refer to or quote Scripture. This same chapter then goes on to include sayings by various other sages, onward to figures who are cited many times in the pages of the Mishnah itself, Hillel and Shammai. By citing these figures within the chain of tradition from Sinai, the framer of the passage was able to show that the Mishnah contains part of the Torah of Sinai, the oral part.

Certainly the single most important figure in the chain of tradition from Sinai onward to the sages who created the Mishnah itself is Hillel, a sage who flourished about the same time as Jesus and to whom is attributed a statement strikingly like the Golden Rule: "What is hateful to yourself, do not do to anybody else. That is the whole of the Torah. All the rest is commentary. Now go learn." Both the teaching of Hillel and that of Jesus on the Golden Rule—"Do unto others as you would have them do unto you"—state in other language the commandment of the Torah at Leviticus 19:18: "You shall love your neighbor as yourself." Many great sages of Judaism have maintained that that statement summarizes the whole of Judaism. A further statement in Hillel's name forms the foundation of the morality of Judaism:

> "If I am not for myself, who is for me? And when I am for myself, what am I? And if not now, when?"
> —**Avot 1:13**

The collection of sayings gathered in the Sayings of the Founders appears now as part of the most important holy book of Judaism after the written Torah, and that is the Mishnah, a philosophical law code written down ca. C.E. 200.

Scripture, the written Torah, and the Mishnah, the oral Torah, received extensive commentaries. Books of the written Torah, such as Genesis, Exodus, Leviticus, Numbers, and Deuteronomy, were given extensive commentaries, called in Hebrew *midrash* (plural *midrashim*). And right alongside, the Mishnah too was given its extensive commentary. This is called in Hebrew a *talmud* (plural *talmudim*), and there are two of them, the Talmud of the Land of Israel, ca. C.E. 400, and the Talmud of Babylonia, ca. C.E. 600. The fact that the written Torah and the Mishnah are treated in precisely the same way—that is to say, they are read in a close and careful manner so as to discover their meaning for the world today—

proves that the Mishnah enjoyed a unique position as part of the Torah. The two Talmuds then provided an authoritative explanation of what the oral part of the Torah meant and how it was to be observed.

TORAH IN TWO MEDIA, WRITTEN AND ORAL

The conception of another form of the Torah, an oral, memorized form, is expressed in the following passage of the Talmud of the Land of Israel, where we find the theory that there is a tradition separate from, and in addition to, the written Torah. This tradition it knows as "the teachings of scribes." The Mishnah is not identified as the collection of those teachings.

III. A. Associates in the name of R. Yohanan: "The words of scribes are more beloved than the words of Torah and more cherished than words of Torah: 'Your palate is like the best wine' (Song of Songs 7:9)."

B. Simeon bar Ba in the name of R. Yohanan: "The words of scribes are more beloved than the words of Torah and more cherished than words of Torah: 'For your love is better than wine' (Song of Songs 1:2)." . . .

D. R. Ishmael repeated the following: "The words of Torah are subject to prohibition, and they are subject to remission; they are subject to lenient rulings, and they are subject to strict rulings. But words of scribes all are subject only to strict interpretation, for we have learned there: He who rules, 'There is no requirement to wear phylacteries,' in order to transgress the teachings of the Torah, is exempt. But if he said, 'There are five partitions in the phylactery, instead of four,' in order to add to what the scribes have taught, he is liable [Mishnah-tractate Sanhedrin 11:3]."

E. R. Haninah in the name of R. Idi in the name of R. Tanhum b. R. Hiyya: "More stringent are the words of the elders than the words of the prophets. For it is written, 'Do not preach'—thus they preach—one should not preach of such things (Micah 2:6). And it is written, '[If a man should go about and utter wind and lies, saying,] "I will preach to you of wine and strong drink," he would be the preacher for this people!' (Micah 2:11).

F. "A prophet and an elder—to what are they comparable? To a king who sent two senators of his to a certain province. Concerning one of them he wrote, 'If he does not show you my seal and signet, do not believe him.' But concerning the other one he wrote, 'Even though he does not show you my seal and signet, believe him.' So in the case of the prophet, he has had to write, 'If a prophet arises among you . . . and gives you a sign or a wonder. . . .' (Deuteronomy 13:1). But here [with regard to an elder:] '. . . according to the instructions which they give you . . .' (Deuteronomy 17:11) [without a sign or a wonder]."

—**Talmud of the Land of Israel tractate Abodah Zarah 2:7**

What is important in the foregoing anthology is the distinction between teachings contained in the Torah and teachings in the name or authority of "scribes." These latter teachings are associated with quite specific details of the law and are indicated in the Mishnah's rule itself. Furthermore, at *E* we have "elders" (that is, sages) as against prophets. What happens to the Mishnah in the two Talmuds shows us how the later sages viewed the Mishnah.

That view may be stated very simply. The Mishnah rarely cites verses of Scripture in support of its propositions. The two Talmuds routinely adduce scriptural bases for the Mishnah's laws. The Mishnah seldom undertakes the exegesis of verses of Scripture for any purpose. The two Talmuds consistently investigate the meaning of verses of Scripture and do so for a variety of purposes. Accordingly, the two Talmuds, subordinate as they are to the Mishnah, regard the Mishnah as subordinate to and contingent upon Scripture. That is why, in the two Talmuds' view, the Mishnah requires the support of proof-texts of Scripture.

A broad shift was taking place in the generations that received the Mishnah—that is, over the third and fourth centuries. If the sages of the second century, who made the Mishnah as we know it, spoke in their own name and in the name of the logic of their own minds, those who followed, certainly the ones who flourished in the later fourth century and onward to the sixth, who produced the two Talmuds, took a quite different view. Reverting to ancient authority like others of the age, they turned back to Scripture, deeming it the source of certainty about truth.

The result for the history of Judaism may be stated very briefly. The history of Judaism proceeded in three stages: the written Torah, defining the basic issues of Israel's life; then the Mishnah, contributing to the dual Torah the revision of the theory of Israel's sanctification, in response to the destruction of the Second Temple; and third the two Talmuds and related writings, adding to the complete account of Israel's supernatural life the reaffirmation of salvation in response to the advent of triumphant Christianity. In the formation of the one whole Torah, the Mishnah is a version of the Judaism of the dual Torah that reached writing before Christianity made an impact on the Judaic sages, whereas the two Talmuds and their associates show us the changes that were made in the encounter with Christianity as the triumphant religion of the Roman state. The Judaism that took shape in the Land of Israel in the fourth century, attested by documents brought to closure in the fifth, responded to that Christianity and in particular to its challenge to the Israel of that place and time. That Judaism flourished in Israel, the Jewish people, as long as the West was Christian. That, sum and substance, is the story of the most important Judaic system of all times.

THE ORAL TORAH AND THE
CHALLENGE OF CHRISTIANITY

What shifted in the two Talmuds' transformation of the received system was their theologians' redefinition of salvation from the here and now to the end of time. And that change, of course, was not only plausible; it also was necessary in light of the catastrophe at hand. The reason for transferring the hope for salvation from now to the end of time derives from a political event in some ways bearing greater weight than the destruction of the Temple in 70. It is the success of the competing and rival version of the written Torah, Christianity, with its fully articulated Bible made up of the Old Testament and the New Testament, with its claim to succeed and replace the old Israel, with its proof for the kingship of Jesus as Christ in the Christian empire, and with its dismissal of Israel after the flesh as now rejected and set aside by God.

With the triumph of Christianity through Constantine and his successors in the West, from the legalization of Christianity in 312 to its establishment as religion of the state by the end of the fourth century, Christianity's explicit claims, now validated in world-shaking events of the age, demanded a reply. The sages of the two Talmuds provided it. At those very specific points at which the Christian challenge met head on old Israel's world view, sages' doctrines responded. What did Israel's sages have to present as the Torah's answer to the cross? It was the Torah. This took three forms. First, the Torah was defined in the doctrine of the Mishnah's status as oral and memorized revelation and, by implication, of the status of other rabbinical writings. Moreover, the Torah was presented as the encompassing symbol of Israel's salvation. Finally, the Torah was embodied in the person of the Messiah, who of course would be a rabbi. The Torah in all three modes confronted the cross, with its doctrine of the triumphant Christ, Messiah and king, ruler now of earth as of heaven. That is why the dual Torah formed the generative symbol for the Judaism that triumphed. It dealt with the urgent and critical question that had to be confronted, and it provided an answer that to believers was self-evidently valid: both necessary and sufficient.

CHAPTER 9

The Midrash

WHAT IS MIDRASH?

The Judaism of the dual Torah produced a commentary on the oral Torah in the form of the two Talmuds. It also produced a commentary on the written Torah in the form of collections of scriptural explanation that are called Midrashim. *Midrash* in Hebrew means investigation, and when applied to Scripture, *Midrash* means investigation of the meaning of Scripture, hence interpretation. There are three types of interpretation of Scripture characteristic of Midrash-compilations. In the first, the focus of interest is individual verses of Scripture, and interpreting those verses in the sequence in which they appear forms the organizing principle of sustained discourse. In the second, the center of interest attends to the testing and validating of large-scale propositions, which, through the reading of individual verses, an authorship wishes to test and validate. In that rather philosophical trend in rabbinic Bible interpretation, the interpretation of individual verses takes a subordinated position, the appeal to facts of Scripture in the service of the syllogism at hand. The third approach directs attention not to concrete statements of Scripture, whether in sequences of verses or merely individual verses or even words or phrases, but to entire compositions of Scripture: biblical themes, stories. This investigation of Scripture's meaning generates Midrash as narrative: the imaginative recasting of Scripture's stories in such a way as to make new and urgent points through the retelling.

Rabbinic Bible interpretation read the Hebrew Scriptures as the written half of the whole Torah—that is, the dual Torah revealed in two media, writing and memory, by God to Moses at Sinai. The other half of that same Torah, the oral part, derives from oral formulation and oral transmission of God's word, finally preserved in the teachings of the Judaic sages themselves. Midrash so works as to lead us into the world of the Hebrew Bible as that holy Scripture entered into Judaism. For the Holy

Scriptures were transformed by the Judaic sages or rabbis of the formative centuries of Western civilization, from the first century to the seventh. *Through the workings of Midrash, the Hebrew Bible became the written half of the one whole Torah, oral and written, revealed by God to Moses our Rabbi at Mount Sinai.* Midrash works in three dimensions: first, as an explanation of meaning imputed to particular verses of Scripture; second, as a mode of stating important propositions, syllogisms of thought, in conversation with verses or sustained passages of Scripture; and third, as a way of retelling scriptural stories in such a way as to impart to those stories new immediacy.

By the word *Midrash*, people commonly mean one of three things. First comes the sense of Midrash as the explanation, by Judaic interpreters, of the meaning of individual verses of Scripture. The result of the interpretation of a verse of Scripture is called a Midrash-exegesis. Second, the result of the interpretation of Scripture is collected in Midrash-compilations, or what I call a Midrash-document. Third, the process of interpretation—for instance, the principles guiding the interpreter—is called Midrash-method.

Let us now proceed to a simple definition for the word *Midrash*, with close attention to the literary and social context in which the writings of Midrash are produced and to the techniques of Midrash-exegesis. The best definition derives from Gary G. Porton,[1] who states:

> Midrash is "a type of literature, oral or written, which has its starting point in a fixed, canonical text, considered the revealed word of God by the Midrashist and his audience, and in which this original verse is explicitly cited or clearly alluded to." . . . For something to be considered Midrash it must have a clear relationship to the accepted canonical text of Revelation. Midrash is a term given to a Jewish activity which finds its locus in the religious life of the Jewish community.* While others exegete their revelatory canons and while Jews exegete other texts, only Jews who explicitly tie their comments to the Bible engage in Midrash.[2]

What is important in Porton's definition are three elements: (1) exegesis (2) starting with Scripture and (3) ending in community.

Porton identifies five types of Midrashic activity: the rabbinic; the Midrash found in the Hebrew Scriptures themselves, such as Deuteronomy's rewriting of Exodus, Numbers, and Leviticus; translations (called in Hebrew and Aramaic *Targumim*); the rewriting of the biblical narrative; and the *Pesher*-Midrash of an apocalyptic order. Porton writes as follows:

> A further form of non-rabbinic Midrash from the turn of the eras is the rewriting of the biblical narrative. Such works as the *Liber Antiquitatum Biblicarum* of Pseudo-Philo, the *Genesis Apocryphon*, and *Jubilees* fall into this category. If we could establish that the early sections of Josephus'

---

*I distinguish between Midrash and exegesis only by assigning the former word to activity within the Israelite community. However, it should be clear that there may be extensive parallels between Midrash, which occurs within an Israelite context, and exegesis, which occurs in other religious and cultural systems.

Antiquities and Philo's many allegories and his *Life of Moses* were written for communities which accepted the authority of the biblical texts upon which these writers built, these too could be fit into this category.

The *pesharim* found among the writings from Qumran represent yet another type of ancient Jewish Midrash, for its apocalyptic tone and its exclusive concern with the history of the Dead Sea Community set it apart from the other examples of ancient Jewish exegetical activity.

Rabbinic Midrash represents an independent phenomenon, for the rabbis are a distinct class within the Jewish community of Late Antiquity. The definitive characteristic of the ancient rabbi was his knowledge and how he attained it. What a rabbi knew distinguished him from the rest of the Jewish community, and the fact that he had gained his information by studying with another rabbi who participated in a chain of tradition which stretched back to God and Moses on Mount Sinai also set him apart in his larger environment. A rabbi's knowledge began with the Written Torah, the five books of Moses, the public record of the perfect revelation from the perfect God, and from there it moved into the Oral Torah, that part of revelation which had been handed down from God to Moses our Rabbi and from Moses our Rabbi, through an unbroken chain, to the rabbis of Late Antiquity. The Oral Torah is the record of rabbinic attempts to solve problems encountered in the Written Torah, for among other things it filled in the details, explained unclear matters and expanded upon enigmatic passages found in the Written Torah. The Oral Torah also offered the rules and methods according to which the Written Torah was to be interpreted and upon which an understanding of it should be based. In short, the Oral Torah provided the guidelines that made possible the understanding of and the application of Scripture's lessons in contemporary life. The Oral Torah was the key to unlocking the mysteries of the Written Torah, and the rabbis were the only ones who possessed this key. Rabbinic Midrash is the type of Midrash produced by this small segment of the Jewish population of Palestine and Babylonia during the first seven centuries of the common era.

Rabbinic Midrash is based on several presuppositions. The rabbis believed that the Written Torah was the accurate and complete public record of a direct revelation from the One, Unique, and Perfect God to His people; therefore, nothing in the Bible was unimportant or frivolous.

Every letter, every verse, and every phrase contained in the Bible was important and written as it was for a specific reason. The Bible contained no needless expressions, no "mere" repetitions, and no superfluous words or phrases. The assumption that every element of the biblical text was written in a specific way in order to teach something underlies the Midrashic activity of the rabbis.

Furthermore, the rabbis believed that everything contained in Scriptures was interrelated. Often, one verse is explained by reference to another verse. A section of the Prophets may be used to explain a verse from the Torah, or a portion of the Torah may explain a passage from the Writings.

In addition, the rabbis believed that any given biblical verse was open to more than one possible interpretation. Taken as a whole, the rabbinic Midrashic collections offer a wide variety of explanations of the same verses, the Hebrew Bible. Even within a single collection we often find contradictory Midrashic statements standing side by side. Moreover, especially in the earlier collections of rabbinic Midrash, we find attempts to prove that reason unaided by revelation is fallible.

A common Midrashic activity is to refute a reasonable or logical conclusion merely by citing a verse from Scripture. The Midrashic activity
was important, for without it, people might not act in proper ways and
might misunderstand the realities of the world, man and God. Therefore,
the Midrashic activity represents the other side of the coin from the
mishnaic activity of the rabbinic class.

These are some of the principal technical aspects of how sages read a
verse of Scripture. We move now to the theological side of matters.

HOW THE SAGES OF JUDAISM READ THE BOOK OF GENESIS AS A PARABLE FOR THEIR OWN TIME

From this definition, let us turn to a concrete example of how the sages of
the Midrash read Scripture. Our case in point is the book of Genesis,
which is examined in the Midrash-compilation Genesis Rabbah, a document that took shape in the century beyond Constantine, ca. 400–450. The
sages who composed Genesis Rabbah read Scripture's account of creation
and the beginnings of Israel, in which God set forth to Moses the entire
scope and meaning of Israel's history among the nations and salvation at
the end of days. Genesis drew their attention more than any other book
of the Pentateuch (the five books of Moses). Sages read Genesis not as a
set of individual verses, one by one, but as a single and coherent statement, whole and complete. So in a few words let me restate the conviction of the framers of Genesis Rabbah about the message and meaning of
the book of Genesis:

> "We now know what will be in the future. Just as Jacob had told his sons
> what would happen in time to come, just as Moses told the tribes their
> future, so we may understand the laws of history if we study the Torah.
> And in the Torah, we turn to beginnings: the rules as they were laid out
> at the very start of human history. These we find in the book of Genesis,
> the story of the origins of the world and of Israel.
> "The Torah tells us not only what happened but why. The Torah per-
> mits us to discover the laws of history. Once we know those laws, we
> may also peer into the future and come to an assessment of what is go-
> ing to happen to us—and, especially, of how we shall be saved from our
> present existence. Because everything exists under the aspect of a time-
> less will, God's will, and all things express one thing, God's program and
> plan, in the Torah we uncover the workings of God's will. Our task as
> Israel is to accept, endure, submit, and celebrate." So our sages found les-
> sons not only for the future but also for today: hope, not despair, cour-
> age, not cowardice, belief and faith and trust in God in difficult times.

This is a fine example of how sages read Scripture so that things were not
what they seemed to be but meant something else altogether. In general,
people read the book of Genesis as the story of how Israel saw the past,
not the future: the beginning of the world and of Israel, humanity from
Adam to Noah, then from Noah to Abraham, and the story of the three
patriarchs and four matriarchs of Israel—Abraham, Isaac, Jacob, Sarah,

Rebecca, Leah, and Rachel—and finally of Joseph and his brothers—from creation to the descent into Egypt. But to the rabbis who created Genesis Rabbah, the book of Genesis tells the story of Israel, the Jewish people, in the here and now. The principle was that what happened to the patriarchs and matriarchs signals what will happen to their descendants; the model of the ancestors sends a message for the children. So the importance of Genesis, as the sages of Genesis Rabbah read the book, derives not from its lessons about the past but its message for Israel's present and, especially, its future.

In the way in which the sages of Genesis Rabbah dealt with this crisis, we follow in concrete terms what it means to see things as other than what they seem. Specifically, the sages conceded that Christian Rome required attention in a way pagan Rome had not. Furthermore, they appealed to their established theory of who Israel is in order to find a place for Rome. They saw Israel as one big family, the children of Abraham, Isaac, Jacob. To fit Rome into the system, they had to locate for Rome a place in the family. Scripture, we now recognize, speaks of deeper truths. Hence when Scripture told the story of certain members of the family, "we" who understand Scripture know that what is meant is a member whom only we recognize. Specifically, Rome now is represented by Esau: Jacob's brother, Jacob's enemy. Or Rome may be Ishmael or Moab. "And we? We are Israel." Scripture therefore tells the story of Esau and Jacob, who are in today's world Rome and Israel. And Jacob supplants, Jacob wins the blessing and the patrimony and the birthright—and Jacob will again. Things are not what they seem, Scripture speaks of things other than those on the surface, and Midrash-exegesis, working out this mode of Midrash-process, collected in Midrash-documents, tells that story.

That is an example of reading one thing in light of something else and everything as though it meant something other than what it said. Identifying Rome as Esau is a fresh idea. In the Mishnah, two hundred years earlier, Rome appears as a place, not as a symbol. But in Genesis Rabbah, Rome is symbolized by Esau. Why Esau in particular? Because Esau is sibling: relation, competitor, enemy, brother. In choosing Rome as the counterpart to Israel, the sages simply opened Genesis and found there Israel—that is, Jacob and his brother, his enemy, Esau. Why not understand the obvious? Esau stands for Rome, Jacob for Israel, and their relationship represents then what Israel and Rome would work out in the fourth century, the first century of Christian rule. Esau rules but Jacob possesses the birthright. Esau/Rome is the last of the four great empires (Persia, Media, Greece, Rome). On the other side of Rome? Israel's age of glory. And why is Rome now brother? Because, after all, the Christians do claim a common patrimony in the Hebrew Scriptures and do claim to form part of Israel. That claim was not ignored, it was answered: Yes, you are part of Israel, the rejected part. Jacob bears the blessing and transmits the blessing to humanity, Esau does not.

That concession—Rome is a sibling, a close relative of Israel—represents an implicit recognition of Christianity's claim to share the patrimony of Judaism, to be descended from Abraham and Isaac. So how are we to deal with the glory and the power of our brother, Esau? And what are we to say about the claim of Esau to enthrone Christ? And how are we to assess today the future history of Israel, the salvation of God's first, best love? It is not by denying Rome's claim but by evaluating it, not by turning a back to the critical events of the hour but by confronting those events forcefully and authoritatively. In this instance we see how rabbinic Midrash resorted to an allegorical or parabolic reading of Scripture to bring to Scripture the issues of the age and to discover God's judgment of those issues. We now turn to a detailed examination of how the sages spelled out what Scripture really means. To the sages, Genesis reported what really happened. But as we see throughout, Genesis also spelled out the meanings and truth of what happened. In the following passage we have Esau in place of Rome:

GENESIS RABBAH LXI:VII

2. A. *"[But to the sons of his concubines, Abraham gave gifts, and while he was still living,] he sent them away from his son Isaac, eastward to the east country]"* (Genesis 25:6):
   B. He said to them, "Go as far to the east as you can, so as not to be burned by the flaming coal of Isaac."
   C. But because Esau came to make war with Jacob, he took his appropriate share on his account: *"Is this your joyous city, whose feet in antiquity, in ancient days, carried her afar off to sojourn? Who has devised this against Tyre, the crowning city?"* (Isaiah 23:7).
   D. Said R. Eleazar, "Whenever the name of Tyre is written in Scripture, if it is written out [with all of the letters], then it refers to the province of Tyre. Where it is written without all of its letters [and so appears identical to the word for enemy], the reference of Scripture is to Rome. [So the sense of the verse is that Rome will receive its appropriate reward.]"

Section 2 carries forward the eschatological reading of the incident. Israel's later history is prefigured in the gift to Isaac and the rejection of the other sons. The self-evidence that Esau's reward will be recompense for his evil indicates that the passage draws upon sarcasm to make its point. Sages essentially looked to the facts of history for the laws of history. We may compare them to social scientists or social philosophers, trying to turn anecdotes into insight and to demonstrate how we may know the difference between impressions and truths. Genesis provided facts. Careful sifting of those facts will yield the laws that dictated why things happened one way rather than some other. The language of the narrative, as much as the substance, provided facts demanding careful study. We understand why sages thought so if we call to mind their basic understanding of the Torah. To them (as to many today, myself included), the Torah came from God and in every detail contained revelation of God's truth. Accordingly, just as we study nature and derive facts demanding explanation and yielding law, so we study Scripture and find facts susceptible of explanation and yielding truth.

Let us consider an exemplary case of how sages discovered social laws of history in the facts of Scripture. What Abraham did corresponds to what Balaam did, and the same law of social history derives proof from each of the two contrasting figures.

GENESIS RABBAH LV:VIII

1. A. *"And Abraham rose early in the morning, [saddled his ass, and took two of his young men with him, and his son Isaac, and he cut the wood for the burnt offering and arose and went to the place which God had told him]"* (Genesis 22:3):

   B. Said R. Simeon b. Yohai, "Love disrupts the natural order of things, and hatred disrupts the natural order of things.

   C. "Love disrupts the natural order of things we learn from the case of Abraham: *'. . . he saddled his ass.'* But did he not have any number of servants? But that proves love disrupts the natural order of things.

   D. "Hatred disrupts the natural order of things we learn from the case of Balaam: *'And Balaam rose up early in the morning and saddled his ass'* (Numbers 22:21). But did he not have any number of servants? But that proves hatred disrupts the natural order of things.

   E. "Love disrupts the natural order of things we learn from the case of Joseph: *'And Joseph made his chariot ready'* (Genesis 46:29). But did he not have any number of servants? But that proves love disrupts the natural order of things.

   F. "Hatred disrupts the natural order of things we learn from the case of Pharoah: *'And he made his chariot ready'* (Exodus 14:6). But did he not have any number of servants? But that proves hatred disrupts the natural order of things."

The social law about the overriding effect of love and hatred is proven by diverse cases, as we see.

Now we move from the laws of social history to the rules that govern Israel's history in particular:

2. A. Said R. Simeon b. Yohai, "Let one act of saddling an ass come and counteract another act of saddling the ass. May the act of saddling the ass done by our father Abraham, so as to go and carry out the will of him who speak and brought the world into being, counteract the act of saddling that was carried out by Balaam when he went to curse Israel.

   B. "Let one act of preparing counteract another act of preparing. Let Joseph's act of preparing his chariot so as to meet his father serve to counteract Pharaoh's act of preparing to go and pursue Israel."

   C. R. Ishmael taught on Tannaite authority, "Let the sword held in the hand serve to counteract the sword held in the hand.

   D. "Let the sword held in the hand of Abraham, as it is said, *'Then Abraham put forth his hand and took the knife to slay his son'* (Genesis 22:10) serve to counteract the sword taken by Pharoah in hand: *'I will draw my sword, my hand shall destroy them'* (Exodus 15:9)."

We see that the narrative is carefully culled for probative facts, yielding laws. One fact is that there are laws of history. The other is that laws may be set aside, by either love or hatred. Yet another law of history applies in particular to Israel, as distinct from the foregoing, deriving from the life of both Israel and the nations, Abraham and Balaam.

Here is an exercise in the recurrent proof of a single proposition that Abraham foresaw the future history of Israel, with special reference to the rule of the four monarchies—Babylonia, Media, Greece, then Rome—prior to the rule of Israel:

Genesis Rabbah XLIV:XVII

4. A. *"[And it came to pass, as the sun was going down,] lo, a deep sleep fell on Abram, and lo, a dread and great darkness fell upon him"* (Genesis 15:12):

   B. *". . . lo, a dread"* refers to Babylonia, as it is written, *"Then was Nebuchadnezzar filled with fury"* (Genesis 3:19).

   C. *". . . and darkness"* refers to Media, which darkened the eyes of Israel by making it necessary for the Israelites to fast and conduct public mourning.

   D. *". . . great . . ."* refers to Greece. . . .

   G. *". . . fell upon him"* refers to Edom [Rome], as it is written, *"The earth quakes at the noise of their fall"* (Jeremiah 49:21).

I find this a particularly moving tableau, with darkness descending and dread falling on Jacob. That tone also accounts for the power of the ideas at hand. Section 4 successfully links the cited passage once more to the history of Israel. Israel's history falls under God's dominion. Whatever will happen carries out God's plan. The fourth kingdom is part of that plan, which we can discover by carefully studying Abraham's life and God's word to him.

In the following selection, we see an explicit effort to calculate the time at which the end will come and Israel will be saved:

Genesis Rabbah XLIV:XVIII

1. A. *"Then the Lord said to Abram, 'Know of a surety [that your descendants will be sojourners in a land that is not theirs, and they will be slaves there, and they will be oppressed for four hundred years; but I will bring judgment on the nation which they serve, and afterward they shall come out with great possessions']"* (Genesis 15:13–14):

   B. *"Know"* that I shall scatter them.

   C. *"Of a certainty"* that I shall bring them back together again.

   D. *"Know"* that I shall put them out as a pledge [in expiation of their sins].

   E. *"Of a certainty"* that I shall redeem them.

   F. *"Know"* that I shall make them slaves.

   G. *"Of a certainty"* that I shall free them.

2. A. *". . . that your descendants will be sojourners in a land that is not theirs and they will be slaves there, and they will be oppressed for four hundred years:"*

   B. It is four hundred years from the point at which you will produce a descendant. [The Israelites will not serve as slaves for four hundred years, but that figure refers to the passage of time from Isaac's birth.]

C. Said R. Yudan, "The condition of being outsiders, the servitude,
the oppression in a land that was not theirs all together would
last for four hundred years, that was the requisite term."

Section 1 parses the cited verse and joins within its simple formula the
entire history of Israel, punishment and forgiveness alike. Section 2
parses the verse to follow, trying to bring it into line with the chronology
of Israel's later history.

The single most important paradigm for history emerged from the
deed at Moriah, the binding of Isaac on the altar as a sacrifice to God. The
binding of Isaac forms a critical motif in synagogue art as well, as the phi-
losopher-artists of synagogue decoration created their Midrash. Here is
how sages derive enduring rules of history and salvation from the story
of the willingness of Abraham to sacrifice even his son to God:

GENESIS RABBAH LVI:I

1. A. *"On the third day Abraham lifted up his eyes and saw the place afar off"*
(Genesis 22:4):
   B. *"After two days he will revive us, on the third day he will raise us up,
that we may live in his presence"* (Hosea 16:2).
   C. On the third day of the tribes: *"And Joseph said to them on the third
day, 'This do and live'"* (Genesis 42:18).
   D. On the third day of the giving of the Torah: *"And it came to pass on
the third day when it was morning"* (Exodus 19:16).
   E. On the third day of the spies: *"And hide yourselves there for three
days"* (Joshua 2:16).
   F. On the third day of Jonah: *"And Jonah was in the belly of the fish
three days and three nights"* (Jonah 2:1).
   G. On the third day of the return from the Exile: *"And we abode there
three days"* (Ezra 8:32).
   H. On the third day of the resurrection of the dead: *"After two days he
will revive us, on the third day he will raise us up, that we may live in
his presence"* (Hosea 16:2).
   I. On the third day of Esther: *"Now it came to pass on the third day
that Esther put on her royal apparel"* (Esther 5:1).
   J. She put on the monarchy of the house of her fathers.
   K. On account of what sort of merit?
   L. Rabbis say, "On account of the third day of the giving of the
Torah."
   M. R. Levi said, "It is on account of the merit of the third day of
Abraham: *'On the third day Abraham lifted up his eyes and saw the
place afar off'* (Genesis 22:4)."

The third day marks the fulfillment of the promise, at the end of time of
the resurrection of the dead, of Israel's redemption. The reference to the
third day at Genesis 22:2 then invokes the entire panoply of Israel's history. The relevance of the composition emerges at the end. Prior to the
concluding segment, the passage forms a kind of litany and falls into the
category of a liturgy. Still, the recurrent hermeneutic, which teaches that
the stories of the patriarchs prefigure the history of Israel, certainly makes
its appearance.

GENESIS RABBAH LVI:II

4. A. *". . . and we will worship [through an act of prostration] and come again to you"* (Genesis 22:5):
    B. He thereby told him that he would come back from Mount Moriah whole and in peace [for he said that *we* shall come back].
5. A. Said R. Isaac, "And all was on account of the merit attained by the act of prostration.
    B. "Abraham returned in peace from Mount Moriah only on account of the merit owing to the act of prostration: *'. . . and we will worship [through an act of prostration] and come [then, on that account,] again to you'* (Genesis 22:5).
    C. "The Israelites were redeemed only on account of the merit owing to the act of prostration: *'And the people believed . . . then they bowed their heads and prostrated themselves'* (Exodus 4:31).
    D. "The Torah was given only on account of the merit owing to the act of prostration: *'And prostrate yourselves afar off'* (Exodus 24:1).
    E. "Hannah was remembered only on account of the merit owing to the act of prostration: *'And they worshipped before the Lord'* (1 Samuel 1:19).
    F. "The exiles will be brought back only on account of the merit owing to the act of prostration: *'And it shall come to pass in that day that a great horn shall be blown and they shall come that were lost . . . and that were dispersed . . . and they shall worship the Lord in the holy mountain at Jerusalem'* (Isaiah 27:13).
    G. "The Temple was built only on account of the merit owing to the act of prostration: *'Exalt you the Lord our God and worship at his holy hill'* (Psalms 99:9).
    H. "The dead will live only on account of the merit owing to the act of prostration: *'Come let us worship and bend the knee, let us kneel before the Lord our maker'* (Psalms 95:6)."

Section 3 draws a lesson from the use of *thus* in the cited verses. The sizable construction at section 4 makes a simple point, to which our base verse provides its modest contribution. But its polemic is hardly simple. The entire history of Israel flows from its acts of worship ("prostration") and is unified by a single law. Every sort of advantage Israel has ever gained came about through worship. Hence what is besought, in the elegant survey, is the law of history. The Scripture then supplies those facts from which the governing law is derived. The lesson that Israel commands its own destiny through obedience to God emerges in every line of Genesis as sages' Midrash interprets the book. In the hands of the sages of Genesis Rabbah, the book of the beginnings tells the tale of the end-time.

CHAPTER 10

What About Judaism and Christianity: "Why Don't the Jews Believe in Jesus as Christ?"

WHY OR WHY NOT?

One final question demands attention before we proceed to our description of the way of Torah. It concerns the student of Judaism, of whatever origin, because of the *setting* in which the study of Judaism takes place. That is in a world made up of Christians of good will, interested in Judaism not only on its own account but also on account of its relationship to the origins and life of their religion, Christianity. The circumstance that Christianity reveres the sacred writings that Judaism knows as the written Torah and Christianity as the Old Testament is only part of the reason. The other part is that, as everyone knows, the earliest Christians were Jews and saw their religion as normative and authoritative: (a) Judaism. A natural question that troubles believing Christians, therefore, is why Judaism as a whole remains a religion that believes other things. Or, as Christians commonly ask, "Why did the Jews not 'accept Christ'?" Or "Why, after the resurrection of Jesus Christ, is there Judaism at all?" Often asked negatively, the question turns on why the Jews do not believe, rather than on what they do believe. Yet it is a constructive question even in the context of description and analysis, not religious polemic. For the question leads us deeper into an understanding not only of the differences between one religion and the other but also of the traits of the religion under study. In other words, it is a question of comparison—even though the question is not properly framed.

The asking of the question "Why not?" rather than "Why so?" reflects the long-term difficulty that the one group has had in making sense of the other. And my explanation of the difference between Christianity and Judaism rests on that simple fact. I maintain, as is clear, that each group has talked to its adherents about its points of urgent concern—that is, different people have talked about different things to different people. Incomprehension marks relations between Judaism and Christianity in the first century, yet the groups were two sectors of the same people. Each addressed its own agenda, spoke to its own issues, and employed language distinctive to its adherents. Neither exhibited understanding of what was important to the other. Recognizing that fundamental inner-directedness may enable us to interpret the issues and the language used in framing them. For if each party perceived the other through a thick veil of incomprehension, the heat and abuse that characterized much of their writing about each other testify to a truth different from that yielded by conventional interpretations. If the enemy is within, if I see only the mote in the other's eye, it matters little whether there is a beam in my own.

A FAMILY QUARREL, AN ISRAELITE CIVIL WAR

The key is this: the incapacity of either group to make sense of the other. We have ample evidence for characterizing as a family quarrel the relationship between the two great religious traditions of the West. Only brothers can hate so deeply yet accept and tolerate so impassively, as Judaic and Christian brethren have both hated yet taken for granted the other's presence. Christianity wiped out unbelievers, but under ordinary circumstances Christians adhered to the doctrine that the Jews were not to be exterminated. Nevertheless, from the first century onward, the echoes of Matthew's Pharisees as hypocrites and John's Jews as murderers poisoned the Christian conscience. Jews grudgingly recognized that Christianity was not merely another paganism. But in their awareness festered Tarfon's allegation that Christians knew God but denied him, knew the Torah but did violence against its meaning. Today we recognize in these implacably negative projections signs of frustration, anger at those who should know better than to act as they do, a very deep anger indeed.

The authors of the Gospels choose a broad range of enemies for Jesus and hence for the church. One group, the Pharisees, assumes importance in our eyes out of proportion to its place in the Gospels because the kind of Judaism that emerges from the first century draws heavily on the methods and values imputed to the Pharisees in the later rabbinic literature. So let us narrow our discussion from "Judaism," a word that can stand for just about anything, to that group among first-century Judaisms that in the event contributed substantially to the Judaism that later became normative. And when we speak of Christianity, following the same principle, let us specify a particular aspect of the rich and various belief of the church represented in the writings of the evangelists. That aspect, the common denominator of the Gospels, finds full expression in the simple claim that Jesus Christ came to save humanity. Hence we shall center on the salvific aspect of the Christianity represented by the Gospels (although not by them alone).

The Judaism defined by the system and method of the Pharisees, whom we met in connection with the destruction of the Second Temple by the Romans in 70, addressed the issue of the sanctification of Israel, whereas Christianity as defined by the evangelists took up the question of the salvation of Israel. Both were expressions of Israel's religion; one spoke of one thing, the other of something else. In retrospect, although they bear some traits in common, the two groups appear in no way comparable. Why not? The Gospels portray the first Christians as the family and followers of Jesus. So, as a social group, Christianity represented at its outset in a quite physical, familial, and genealogical way "the body of Christ." The Pharisees, by contrast, hardly formed a special group at all. It is easier to say what they were not than what they were. How so? Although the Pharisees appear as a political group by the first century in Josephus's writings about Maccabean politics, the Gospels and the rabbinic traditions concur that what made an Israelite a Pharisee was not exclusively or even mainly politics. The Pharisees were characterized by their adherence to certain cultic rules. They were not members of a family in any natural or supernatural sense. Their social affiliations in no way proved homologous.

Pharisees, some may object, surely appear as a "they"—that is, as a discernible type of Israelite. But if they formed some sort of distinct social group, and if that group took shape in various places around the country, we nevertheless cannot point to much evidence about its character. We have no documentation of any kind concerning the social traits of the Pharisees as a group. What we do have is considerable information on certain practices held to characterize and define people who were called Pharisees. If we eat our meals in one way rather than in some other, however, that common practice does not of itself make us a political party or, for that matter, a church; it makes us people who are willing to eat lunch together.

So, as a hypothesis permitting the argument to unfold, let me say that the Christians carried forward one aspect of Scripture's doctrine of Israel and the Pharisees another. The Hebrew Scriptures represent Israel as one very large family, descended from a single set of ancestors. The Christians adopted that theory of Israel by linking themselves, first of all, to the family of Jesus and his adopted sons, the disciples, and secondly, through him and them to his ancestry, to David and on backward to Abraham, Isaac, and Jacob (hence the enormous power of the genealogies of Christ). The next step, the spiritualization of that familiar tie into the conception of the church as the body of Christ, need not detain us. But Scripture did not restrict itself to the idea of Israel as family; it also defined Israel as a kingdom of priests and a holy people. That is the way taken by the Pharisees. Their Israel found commonality in a shared, holy way of life, required of all Israelites—so Scripture held. The Mosaic Torah defined that way of life in both cultic and moral terms, and the prophets laid great stress on the latter. What made Israel holy—its way of life, its moral character—depended primarily on how people lived, not on their shared genealogy.

Both Christians and Pharisees belonged to Israel but chose different definitions of the term. The Christians saw Israel as a family; the Pharisees saw it as a way of life. The Christians stressed their genealogy; the Pharisees their ethos and ethics. The Christian family held things in common; the holy people held in common a way of life that sanctified them. At issue in the argument between them are positions that scarcely intersect, held by groups whose social self-definitions are incongruent.

Christians were a group comprising the family of Israel, talking about salvation; Pharisees were a group shaped by the holy way of life of Israel, talking about sanctification. The two neither converse nor argue. Groups unlike each other in what, to begin with, defines and bonds them, groups devoid of a common program of debate, have no argument. They are different people talking about different things to different people. Yet, as is clear, neither group could avoid recognizing the other. What ensued was not a discussion, let alone a debate, but only a confrontation of people with nothing in common pursuing programs of discourse that do not in any way intersect. It is not much of an argument.

Why were the two groups fundamentally different? Why did each find the other just that—totally other? Certainly we can identify groups within the larger Israelite society through whom the Christian familists and the Pharisaic commensals could have come to compare themselves. Since the Essenes of Qumran laid great stress on observing cultic rules governing meals, Pharisees could have debated with them about which rules must be kept, how to do so, and what larger meaning inhered in them. Since the Essenes also emphasized the coming eschatological war and the messianic salvation of Israel, Christians could have conducted an argument with them about who the Messiah would be and when he would come. Christians and Pharisees, we can see, bear comparison in an essentially morphological dimension with the Essenes of Qumran. But in the terms I have defined, they cannot be so compared with each other.

DIFFERENT PEOPLE TALKING ABOUT
DIFFERENT THINGS TO DIFFERENT PEOPLE

Let me answer the question of the fundamental difference between the two religious traditions by pointing out what really does make parallel the formulation of the Judaism of each. I mean to make a very simple point. Christianity and Judaism each took over the inherited symbolic structure of Israel's religion. Each in fact did work with the same categories as the other. But in the hands of each, the available and encompassing classification system found wholly new meaning. The upshot was two religions out of one, each speaking within precisely the same categories but so radically redefining the substance of these categories that conversation with the other became impossible.

The similarity? Christ embodies God, just as the talmudic sage, or rabbi, in later times would be seen to stand for the Torah incarnate.

The difference? Christ brought salvation, and for the ages to come, the talmudic sage promised salvation.

Salvation, in the nature of things, concerned the whole of humanity; sanctification, equally characteristic of its category, spoke of a single nation, Israel. To save, the Messiah saves Israel amid all nations, because salvation categorically entails the eschatological dimension and so encompasses all of history. No salvation, after all, can last only for a little while or leave space for time beyond itself. To sanctify, by contrast, the sage sanctifies Israel in particular. Sanctification categorically requires the designation of what is holy against what is not holy. To sanctify is to set apart. No sanctification can encompass everyone or leave no room for someone in particular to be holy. One need not be "holier than thou," but the *holy* requires the contrary category, the *not-holy*. So, once more, how can two religious communities understand each other when one raises the issue of the sanctification of Israel and the other the salvation of the world? Again, different people are talking about different things to different people.

Mutual comprehension becomes still more difficult when the familiar proves strange, when categories we think we understand we turn out not to grasp at all. Using the familiar in strange ways was, I maintain, the most formidable obstacle to resolving the Jewish-Christian argument in the first century. Both Christians and Pharisees radically revised existing categories. To understand this total transvaluation, let us examine the principal categories of the inherited Israelite religion and culture. Once their picture is clear, we can readily grasp how, in both Christianity and Judaism, each category undergoes revision in definition and in content.

Recall the major trends in Judaism that earlier emerged: priests, scribes, and Zealots. To these we now return, remembering, of course, that there were other trends of importance as well. The principal Israelite categories are discernible both in the distinct types of holy men, whom we know as priests, scribes, and messiahs, and in the definitive activities of cult, school, government offices, and (ordinarily) the battlefield. Ancient Israel's heritage yielded the cult with its priests, the Torah with its scribes and teachers, and the prophetic and apocalyptic hope for meaning in history and an eschaton mediated by messiahs and generals. From these derive Temple, school, and (in the apocalyptic expectation) battlefield on earth and in heaven.

To seek a typology of the modes of Israelite piety, we must look for the generative symbol of each mode: an altar for the priestly ideal, a scroll of Scripture for the scribal ideal of wisdom, a coin marked "Israel's freedom: year one" for the messianic modality. In each of these visual symbols we perceive things we cannot touch, hearts and minds we can only hope to evoke. We seek to enter into the imagination of people distant in space and time. We must strive to understand the way in which they framed the world and encapsulated their world view in some one thing: the sheep for the priestly sacrifice, the memorized aphorism for the disciple, the stout heart for the soldier of light. Priest, sage, soldier—each stands for the whole of Israel. When all would meld into one, there would emerge a fresh and unprecedented Judaism, whether among the heirs of scribes and Pharisees or among the disciples of Christ.

The symbols under discussion—Temple-altar, sacred scroll, victory wreath for the head of the King-Messiah—largely covered Jewish society. We need not reduce them to their merely social dimensions to recognize that on them was founded the organization of Israelite society and the interpretation of its history. Let us rapidly review the social groups envisaged and addressed by the framers of these symbols.

The priest viewed society as organized along structural lines emanating from the Temple. His caste stood at the top of a social scale in which all things were properly organized, each with its correct name and proper place. The inherent sanctity of the people of Israel, through the priests' genealogy, came to its richest embodiment in the high priest. Food set apart for the priests' rations, at God's command, possessed the same sanctity; so, too, did the table at which priests ate. To the priest, for the sacred society of Israel, history was an account of what happened in, and (alas) on occasions to, the Temple.

To the sage, the life of society demanded wise regulations. Relationships among people required guidance by the laws enshrined in the Torah and best interpreted by scribes; the task of Israel was to construct a way of life in accordance with the revealed rules of the Torah. The sage, master of the rules, stood at the head.

Prophecy insisted that the fate of the nation depended on the faith and moral condition of society, a fact to which Israel's internal and external history testified. Both sage and priest saw Israel from the viewpoint of externality, but the nation had to live out its life in this world, among other peoples coveting the very same land, and within the context of Roman imperial policies and politics. The Messiah's kingship would resolve the issue of Israel's subordinate relationship to other nations and empires, establishing once and for all the desirable, correct context for priest and sage alike.

Implicit in the messianic framework was a perspective on the world beyond Israel for which priest and sage cared not at all. The priest perceived the Temple as the center of the world; beyond it he saw in widening circles the less holy, then the unholy, and further still the unclean. All lands outside the Land of Israel were unclean with corpse uncleanness; all other peoples were unclean just as corpses were unclean. Accordingly, in the world, life abided within Israel; and in Israel, within the Temple. Outside, in the far distance, were vacant lands and dead peoples, constituting an undifferentiated wilderness of death, a world of uncleanness. From such a perspective, no teaching about Israel among the nations, no interest in the history of Israel and its meaning, was likely to emerge.

The wisdom of the sage pertained in general to the streets, marketplaces, and domestic establishments (the household units) of Israel. What the sage said was wisdom as much for Gentiles as for Israel. The universal wisdom proved international, moving easily across the boundaries of culture and language, from eastern to southern to western Asia. It focused, by definition, on human experience common to all and undifferentiated by nation, essentially unaffected by the large movements of history. Wisdom spoke about fathers and sons, masters and disciples, families and villages, not about nations, armies, and destiny.

Because of their very diversity, these three principal modes of Israelite existence might easily cohere. Each focused on a particular aspect of the national life, and none essentially contradicted any other. One could worship at the Temple, study the Torah, and fight in the army of the Messiah—and some did all three. Yet we must see these modes of being, and their consequent forms of piety, as separate. Each contained its own potentiality to achieve full realization without reference to the others.

The symbolic system of cult, Torah and Messiah demanded choices. If one thing was most important, others must have been less important. Either history matters or it happens without significance, "out there." Either the proper conduct of the cult determines the course of the seasons and the prosperity of the Land, or it is "merely ritual," an unimportant external and not the critical heart. (We hear this judgment in, for example, the prophetic polemic against the cult.) Either the Messiah will save Israel, or he will ruin everything. Accordingly, although we take for granted that people could have lived within the multiple visions of priest, sage, and Messiah, we must also recognize that such a life was vertiginous. Narratives of the war of 66–73 emphasize that priests warned messianists not to endanger their Temple. Later sages, talmudic rabbis, paid slight regard to the messianic struggle led by Bar Kokhba, and after 70 sages claimed the right to tell priests what to do.

The way in which symbols were arranged and rearranged was crucial. Symbol change is social change. A mere amalgam of all three symbols hardly serves by itself as a mirror for the mind of Israel. The particular way the three were bonded in a given system reflects an underlying human and social reality. That is how it should be, since, as we saw, the three symbols—with their associated myths, the world views they projected, and the way of life they defined—stood for different views of what really matters. In investigating the existential foundations of the several symbolic systems available to Jews in antiquity, we penetrate to the bedrock of Israel's reality, to the basis of the life of the nation and of each Israelite, to the ground of being—even to the existential core that we the living share with them.

Let us unpack the two foci of existence: public history and private establishment. We may call the first "time." Its interest is in one-time, unique *events* that happen day by day in the here and now of continuing history. The other focus we may call "eternity." Its interest is in the recurrent and continuing *patterns* of life—birth and death, planting and harvest, the regular movement of the sun, moon, and stars in heaven, night and day, Sabbaths, festivals and regular seasons on earth. The two share one existential issue: How do we respond to the ups and downs of life?

The events of individual life—birth, maturing, marriage, death—do not make history, except for individuals. But the events of group life—the formation of groups, the development of social norms and patterns, depression and prosperity, war and peace—these do make history. When a small people coalesces and begins its course through history in the face of adversity, one of two things can happen. Either the group disintegrates in the face of disaster and loses its hold on its individual members, or the group may fuse, being strengthened by trial, and so turn adversity into renewal.

The modes around which Israelite human and national existence coalesced—those of priests, sages, and messianists (including prophets and apocalyptists)—emerge, we must remember, from national and social consciousness. The heritage of the written Torah (the Hebrew Scriptures or "Old Testament") was carried forward in all three approaches to Judaism. The Jewish people knew the mystery of how to endure through history. In ancient Israel, adversity elicited self-conscious response. Things did not merely *happen* to Israelites. God made them happen to teach lessons to Israel. The prophetic and apocalyptic thinkers in Israel shaped, reformulated, and interpreted events, treating them as raw material for renewing the life of the group.

History was not merely "one damn thing after another." It was important, teaching significant lessons. It had a purpose and was moving somewhere. The writers of Leviticus and Deuteronomy, of the historical books from Joshua through Kings, and of the prophetic literature agreed that, when Israel did God's will, it enjoyed peace, security, and prosperity; when it did not, it was punished at the hands of mighty kingdoms raised up as instruments of God's wrath. This conception of the meaning of Israel's life produced another question: How long? When would the great events of time come to their climax and conclusion? As one answer to that question, there arose the hope for the Messiah, the anointed of God, who would redeem the people and set them on the right path forever, thus ending the vicissitudes of history.

When we reach the first century C.E., we come to a turning point in the messianic hope. No one who knows the Gospels will be surprised to learn of the intense, vivid, prevailing expectation among some groups that the Messiah was coming soon. Their anticipation is hardly astonishing. People who fix their attention on contemporary events of world-shaking dimensions naturally look to a better future. That expectation is one context for the messianic myth.

More surprising is the development among the people of Israel of a second, quite different response to history. It is the response of those prepared once and for all to transcend historical events and to take their leave of wars and rumors of wars, of politics and public life. These persons, after 70, undertook to construct a new reality beyond history, one that focused on the meaning of humdrum, everyday life. We witness among the sages, ultimately represented in the Mishnah, neither craven nor exhausted passivity in the face of world-shaking events but the beginnings of an active construction of a new mode of being. They chose to exercise freedom uncontrolled by history, to reconstruct the meaning and ultimate significance of events, to seek a world within ordinary history, a different and better world. They undertook a quest for eternity in the here and now; they strove to form a society capable of abiding amid change and stress. Indeed, it was a fresh reading of the meaning of history. The nations of the world suppose that they make "history" and think that their actions matter. But these sages knew that it is God who makes history and that it is the reality formed in response to God's will that counts as history: God is the King of kings.

This conception of time and change had, in fact, formed the focus of the earlier priestly tradition, which was continued later in the Judaism called rabbinic or talmudic. This Judaism offered an essentially metahistorical approach to life. It lived above history and its problems. It expressed an intense inwardness. The Judaism attested in the rabbis' canon of writings emphasized the ultimate meaning contained within small and humble affairs. Rabbinic Judaism came in time to set itself up as the alternative to all forms of messianic Judaism—whether in the form of Christianity or militaristic zealotry and nationalism—which claimed to know the secret of history, the time of salvation, and the way to redemption. But paradoxically, the canonical writings of rabbis also disclosed answers to these questions. The Messiah myth was absorbed into the rabbis' system and made to strengthen it. The rabbinical canon defined in a new way the uses and purposes of all else that had gone before.

This approach to the life of Israel, stressing continuity and pattern and promising change only at the very end, when all would be in order, represents the union of two trends. The one was symbolized by the altar, the other by the Torah scroll—the priest and the sage. In actual fact, the union was effected by a kind of priest manqué and by a special kind of sage. The former was the Pharisee, the latter the scribe.

The scribes constituted a profession. They knew and taught Torah. They took their interpretation of Torah very seriously, and for them the act of study had special importance. The Pharisees were a sect and had developed a peculiar perception of how to live and interpret life: They acted in their homes as if they were priests in the Temple. Theirs was an "as if" way. They lived "as if" they were priests, "as if" they had to obey at home the laws that applied to the Temple. When the Temple was destroyed in 70, the Pharisees were prepared. They continued to live "as if" there were a new Temple composed of the Jewish people.

These, then, represent the different ways in which great events were experienced and understood. One was the historical-messianic way, stressing the intrinsic importance of events and concentrating on their weight and meaning. The other was the metahistorical, scribal-priestly-rabbinic way, which emphasized Israel's power of transcendence and the construction of an eternal, changeless mode of being in this world, capable of riding out the waves of history.

We may now return to our starting point, where Judaic and Christian religious life led in different directions. Judaic consciousness in the period under discussion had two competing but not yet "contradictory" symbol systems: the altar/scroll of the Pharisees and scribes; the wreath of the King-Messiah. What made one focus more compelling than the other? The answer emerges when we realize that each kind of piety addressed a distinctive concern; each spoke about different things to different people. We may sort out the types of piety by returning to our earlier observations. Priests and sages turned inward, toward the concrete, everyday life of the community. They addressed the sanctification of Israel.

Messianists and their prophetic and apocalyptic teachers turned outward, toward the affairs of states and nations. They spoke of the salvation of Israel. Priests saw the world of life in Israel and death beyond. They knew what happened to Israel without concerning themselves with a theory about the place of Israel among the nations. For priests, the nations formed an undifferentiated realm of death. Sages, all the more, spoke of home and hearth, fathers and sons, husbands and wives, the village and enduring patterns of life. What place was there in this domestic scheme for the realities of history, wars and threats of wars, the rise and fall of empires? The sages expressed the consciousness of a singular society amidst other societies. At issue for the priest/sage was being; for the prophet/messianist the issue was becoming.

The radical claims of such holiness sects as the Pharisees and Essenes, of professions such as the scribes, and of followers of messiahs—all expressed aspects of Israel's common piety. Priest, scribe, Messiah—all stood together with the Jewish people along the same continuum of faith and culture. Each expressed in a particular and intense way one mode of the piety that the people as a whole understood and shared. That is why we can move from the particular to the general in our description of the common faith in first-century Israel. That common faith, we hardly need argue, distinguished Israel from all other peoples of the age, whatever the measure of "hellenization" in the country's life; as far as Israel was concerned, there was no "common theology of the ancient Near East."

No wonder that the two new modes of defining Judaic piety that issued from the period before 70 and thrived long after that date—the Judaism framed by sages from before the first century to the seventh century and Christianity with its paradoxical King-Messiah—redefined that piety while remaining true to emphases of the inherited categories. Each took over the established classifications—priest, scribe, and Messiah—but infused them with new meaning. Although in categories nothing changed, in substance nothing remained what it had been. That is why both Christian and Judaic thinkers reread the received Scriptures—"the Old Testament" to the one, "the written Torah" to the other—and produced, respectively, "the New Testament" and the "oral Torah." The common piety of the people Israel in their land defined the program of religious life for both the Judaism and the Christianity that emerged after the caesura of the destruction of the Temple. The bridge to Sinai—worship, revelation, national and social eschatology—was open in both directions.

Thus Christ—as perfect sacrifice, teacher, prophet, and King-Messiah—in the mind of the Church brought together but radically recast the three foci of what had been the common piety of Israel in Temple times. Still later, the figure of the talmudic sage would encompass but redefine all three categories as well.

How so? After 70, study of Torah and obedience to it became a temporary substitute for the Temple and its sacrifice. The government of the sages, in accord with "the one whole Torah of Moses our rabbi," revealed by God at Sinai, carried forward the scribes' conception of Israel's proper government. The Messiah would come when all Israel, through mastery of the Torah and obedience to it, had formed the holy community that the Torah prescribed in the model of heaven revealed to Moses at Sinai. Jesus as perfect priest, rabbi, and Messiah was a protean figure. So was the talmudic rabbi as Torah incarnate, priest for the present age and, in the model of (Rabbi) David, progenitor and paradigm of the Messiah. In both cases we find an unprecedented rereading of established symbols.

The history of the piety of Judaism is the story of successive rearrangements and revisions of symbols. From ancient Israelite times onward, there would be no system of classification beyond the three established taxa. But no category would long be left intact in its content. When Jesus asked people who they thought he was, the enigmatic answer proved less interesting than the question posed. For the task he set himself was to reframe everything people knew through encounter with what they did not know: a taxonomic enterprise. When the rabbis of late antiquity rewrote in their own image and likeness the entire Scripture and history of Israel, dropping whole eras as though they had never been, ignoring vast bodies of old Jewish writing, inventing whole new books for the canon of Judaism, they did the same thing. They reworked what they had received in light of what they proposed to give. No mode of piety could be left untouched, for all proved promising. In Judaism from the first century to the seventh, every mode of piety would be refashioned in light of the vast public events represented by the religious revolutionaries—rabbi-clerk, rabbi-priest, rabbi-Messiah. Accordingly, the piety of Israel in the first century ultimately defined the structure of the two great religions of Western civilization: Christianity through its Messiah, for the Gentile; Judaism through its definition in the two Torahs of Sinai and in its embodiment in the figure of the sage, for Israel.

But believing Jews do not maintain so relativistic a picture of the types of Judaism that flourished in the early centuries of the Common Era. That is why it remains to be said that, judged by the criteria of the Torah, that is, of the Five Books of Moses, much that Jesus said in the Sermon on the Mount was precisely as new and alien as Jesus said it was, stressing, "You have heard it said . . . , but I say to you . . . ." Then as now, Jews believe in the Torah of Moses and form on earth and in their own flesh God's kingdom of priests and the holy people. And that belief requires faithful Jews to enter a dissent at the teachings of Jesus, on the grounds that those teachings at important points contradict the Torah. Where Jesus diverges from the revelation by God to Moses at Mount Sinai that is the Torah, all those who believe in Judaism—that is, the Torah—maintain that he is wrong and Moses is right. The reason is that Jesus claimed to reform and to improve. But Judaism then held and now maintains that Torah was and is perfect and beyond improvement, and the Judaism built upon the Torah and the prophets and writings—the originally oral parts of the Torah written down in the Mishnah, Talmuds, and Midrash—was and remains God's will for humanity. The enduring position of Judaism is this: Jesus cannot be said by the criteria of the Torah as understood by Judaism to have fulfilled the Torah or sustained the Torah or conformed to the Torah.

PART THREE

The Torah's World View

CHAPTER 11

The Evidence

In a history of nearly forty centuries, the Jews have produced rich and complex religious phenomena. Indeed, Judaic religious and historical data, like those of other religions, may seem at the outset to defy adequate description. The varieties of historical settings, rituals, intellectual and religious expressions, exegetical and theological literature can scarcely be satisfactorily apprehended in the modest framework of a lifetime of study. In working toward a definition of any religion, we must confront the same formidable complexities.

Our operative criteria of selection ought to be what phenomena are most widely present and meaningful. What, furthermore, is important as a representation of the reality both viewed and shaped by Judaism? The answers surely cannot be found only in philosophical, legal, mystical, or theological literature produced by and for a religious elite. We cannot suppose sophisticated conceptions of extraordinary people were fully grasped by common folk. Theological writings, although important, testify to the conceptions of reality held by only a tiny minority. The legal ideals and values of Judaism were first shaped by the rabbis, a class of religious virtuosi, and then imposed upon the life of ordinary people. Excluding learned theological and legal writings, the religious materials best conforming to our criteria are liturgical. The myths conveyed by prayer and associated rituals are universal, everywhere present, and meaningful in the history of Judaism. Of greatest importance, they provide the clearest picture of how Jews in archaic times envisioned the meaning of life and of themselves.

Before proceeding, we had best clarify the meaning of *mythic structure.* By myth, historians of religion do *not* mean something that is not true. They mean, in Streng's words, "that the essential structure of reality manifests itself in particular moments that are remembered and repeated from generation to generation."[1] These moments are preserved in myths.

This meaning is wholly congruent with the Judaic data we shall now consider. If, in general, myth has the power to transform life because "it reveals the truth of life," as Streng says,[2] then what is the nature of Judaic myth?

If a myth is present, it must infuse all details of the faith, for it carries the world view that comes to expression in the way of life, the pattern of deeds, the faith somehow hidden in every ceremony and rite, every liturgy, every sacred gesture and taboo. We must be able to locate it in commonplace, not merely extraordinary, events of piety. Liturgy provides the clearest and, at the same time, the most reliable evidence of the structure of Judaic myth. The reason is that the prayers were everywhere said with much the same structure and substance; they constituted the centerpiece of the religious life of expression. They carried the message of the faith, its view of the world, of history and of Israel, of the individual and of the holy community, and that message came to expression in emotionally powerful language and song, gesture and dance, procession and proclamation. The way of Torah carries us to the synagogue, to stand before the ark, as the doors open wide and reveal, inside, the Torah-scroll that stands for, symbolizes, the Torah: "This is the Torah that Moses set forth before the People, Israel, at the instruction of the Lord." Here is the proclamation of the faith, stated, sung, and acted out as the Torah is raised and shown, word for word, to the believing congregation.

The overall mythic structure of the Judaism of the dual Torah, which we now begin to describe, has three principal components: a story of creation, one of revelation, and one of redemption. God created the world, revealed the Torah, and will redeem the people of Israel—to whom God revealed the Torah—at the end of time through the sending of the Messiah. Sometimes the same elements will be given the shape of a story about God, Israel (the Jewish people), and the covenant effected through the keeping of the Torah—that is, through doing God's will for Israel. (This set of mythic statements is called by the New Testament scholar E. P. Sanders "covenantal nomism," meaning the keeping of the religious requirements of the Torah as an expression of loyalty to the covenant between God and Israel.)[3] In many of the religious statements we shall see, the main themes again and again are God's creation of the world, revelation of the Torah, and redemption of Israel. Naturally, it is possible to express these same themes in diverse ways, so that creation takes the form of the Garden of Eden story, redemption is symbolized by the going forth from Egypt, and revelation is reflected throughout in the use of Torah-symbols.

We shall consider several sorts of liturgies, for the Judaic Prayerbook—the *Siddur*—constitutes the corpus of Judaic dogma, rite, and myth for the Judaism of the dual Torah and its continuators and successors in contemporary Orthodoxy, Reform, Conservatism, and Reconstructionism. First comes the *Shema*, containing the fundamental principles of faith. Then we shall turn to the marriage liturgy to see how the vital myth reshapes a private experience into a moment of public and communal meaning. Third, we shall consider two disparate liturgies of self-consciousness, the family together at the Passover *seder* and the community

on the threshold of going forth from worship. Each prayer tells us about
how Jews see and define themselves in and apart from the world. We
shall see, in the Grace After Meals, how the land and Jerusalem enter the
Judaic imagination. We shall read a folk song, a message of prophecy, a
stanza of a modern nationalist anthem, and a messianic prayer in the
daily service, all addressed to the question *How long O Lord?*

As we proceed in our study, we draw on materials from the Hebrew
Scriptures—for instance, Psalms—as much as from documents generally
credited to talmudic rabbis, just as the rabbis themselves drew on the
Scriptures for a definition of Judaism. What we see in the profoundly biblical orientation of Judaism is that the talmudic rabbis did not start something essentially new but reshaped something that had been in existence
for a very long time. That means that the ecological framework to be interpreted by Judaism—that is, the context framed and shaped in the life
of the Jewish people—remained fairly stable, so that old ideas continued
to be found plausible and self-evident. In this respect, the claim of the
rabbinic version of Judaism to continue the Torah of Moses "our rabbi" is
by no means incredible, except as plain history. And (it goes without saying) the fact that a great many sources we shall adduce in evidence of the
inner life of Judaism are not distinctive to rabbinic perspectives of Judaism changes nothing. These are materials that talmudic rabbis found congenial to their conceptions. And they found them so because they could
and did read them as statements of ideas particular to the talmudic rabbis themselves.

Why should this expression of Judaism—that is, the world view expressed through the symbols of creation, revelation, and redemption—
have made sense and proved plausible for the Jews over a long period of
time? The reason is that the critical issues of Jews' historical life—Why do
we matter? Why should we go forward? How long will this situation
last?—are dealt with in a profound and transcendent way. Keep in mind
that the Jews have had to suffer for their faith and accept the condition of
a despised minority, a pariah people, everywhere they have lived. Even
in America today, many people look down on the Jews and think ill of
them. The Jews, for their part, have always had the choice of accepting
the dominant religion of their place of residence—Christianity in the
West, Islam in the Middle East—and so of leaving their condition as a pariah people. And some did. But most did not, just as the Jews of the modern period chose and continue to choose to be Jews, no matter what. Why
should they do this? Why do they do this? And what does it mean? This
barrage of questions deserves a simple answer.

In the classical myth, the meaning is found in the correspondence of
heaven and earth. The world was created for the sake of the Torah; the
Torah was revealed for the sake of Israel; and Israel, keeping the covenant through the Torah, will be redeemed in the end of time. To the
world, the Jews may seem to be pariahs, but Judaism knows they are
God's children, princes and princesses. The life of Torah is a sweet and
serene life. The rhythms of creation and Sabbath, revelation and Torah-
study, and redemption and the festivals (Passover, Tabernacles, Pentecost) join the lives of individual men and women to the patterns of the

transcendent and the holy. From the perspective of Judaism lived by the Jewish people, suffering has been the proof and vindication of the faith of Torah. The very regularity of creation—the waves on the ocean, the majesty and permanence of the mountains and the valleys—stands as witness to the truth of the faith of Torah. These are the lines of thought to be explored: the relationship between the Jews' historical and social realities and their self-understanding as shaped and expressed through their religion, Judaism.

We begin with the *Shema,* the proclamation of God's unity recited morning and evening in Judaic worship. This highly theological statement—that God is one and singular—is set into a context of prayers that convey much insight into the classical Judaic view of reality.

CHAPTER 12

Hear, O Israel

Evening and morning, the pious Jew proclaims the unity and uniqueness of God. The proclamation is preceded and followed by blessings. The whole constitutes the credo of the Judaic tradition. It is "what the Jews believe." Components recur everywhere. Let us first examine the prayer called *Shema* (Hear).

The recital of the *Shema* is introduced by a celebration of God as Creator of the world. In the morning, one says,

> Praised are You, O Lord our God, King of the universe.
> You fix the cycles of light and darkness;
> You ordain the order of all creation
> You cause light to shine over the earth;
> Your radiant mercy is upon its inhabitants.
> In Your goodness the work of creation
> Is continually renewed day by day. . . .
> O cause a new light to shine on Zion;
> May we all soon be worthy to behold its radiance.
> Praised are You, O Lord, Creator of the heavenly bodies.[1]

The corresponding prayer in the evening refers to the setting of the sun:

> Praised are You. . . .
> Your command brings on the dusk of evening.
> Your wisdom opens the gates of heaven to a new day.
> With understanding You order the cycles of time;
> Your will determines the succession of seasons;
> You order the stars in their heavenly courses.
> You create day, and You create night,
> Rolling away light before darkness. . . .
> Praised are You, O Lord, for the evening dusk.[2]

Morning and evening, the Jew responds to the natural order of the world with thanks and praise to God who created the world and who actively guides the daily events of nature. Whatever happens in nature gives testimony to the sovereignty of the Creator. And that testimony is not in unnatural disasters but in the most ordinary events: sunrise and sunset. These, especially, evoke the religious response to set the stage for what follows.

For the Jew, God is not merely Creator but purposeful Creator. The works of creation serve to justify and to testify to Torah, the revelation of Sinai. Torah is the mark not merely of divine sovereignty but of divine grace and love, source of life here and now and in eternity. So goes the second blessing:

> Deep is Your love for us, O Lord our God;
> Bounteous is Your compassion and tenderness.
> You taught our fathers the laws of life,
> And they trusted in You, Father and king.
> For their sake be gracious to us, and teach us,
> That we may learn Your laws and trust in You.
> Father, merciful Father, have compassion upon us:
> Endow us with discernment and understanding.
> Grant us the will to study Your Torah,
> To heed its words and to teach its precepts. . . .
> Enlighten our eyes in Your Torah,
> Open our hearts to Your commandments. . . .
> Unite our thoughts with singleness of purpose
> To hold You in reverence and in love. . . .
> You have drawn us close to You;
> We praise You and thank You in truth.
> With love do we thankfully proclaim Your unity.
> And praise You who chose Your people Israel in love.[3]

Here is the way in which revelation takes concrete and specific form in the Judaic tradition: God, the Creator, revealed his will for creation through the Torah, given to Israel his people. That Torah contains the "laws of life."

The Jew, moved to worship by the daily miracle of sunrise and sunset, responds with the prayer that he or she, like nature, may enjoy divine compassion. But what does that compassion consist of? The ability to understand and the will to study *Torah!* This is the mark of the relationship between God and human being, the Jewish person in particular: that a person's eyes are open to Torah and that a person's heart is open to the commandments. These are the means of divine service and of reverence and love for God. Israel sees itself as "chosen"—close to God—because of Torah, and it finds in its devotion to Torah the marks of its chosenness. The covenant made at Sinai—a contract on Israel's side to do and hear the Torah, on God's side to be the God of Israel—is evoked by natural events and then confirmed by the deeds and devotion of men.

In the *Shema,* Torah—revelation—leads Jews to enunciate the chief teaching of revelation:

Hear, O Israel, the Lord Our God, the Lord is One.

This proclamation is followed by three Scriptural passages. The first is
Deuteronomy 6:5–9:

> *You shall love the Lord your God with all your heart, with all your soul, with
> all your might.*

And further, one must diligently teach one's children these words and
talk of them everywhere and always and place them on one's forehead,
doorposts, and gates. The second Scripture is Deuteronomy 11:13–21,
which emphasizes that if Jews keep the commandments, they will enjoy
worldly blessings; but that if they do not, they will be punished and disappear from the good land God gives them. The third is Numbers 15:37–
41, the commandment to wear fringes on the corners of one's garments.
The fringes are today attached to the prayer shawl worn at morning services by Conservative and Reform Jews and worn on a separate under-
garment for that purpose by Orthodox Jews, and they remind the Jew of
all the commandments of the Lord.

The proclamation is completed and yet remains open, for having created humanity and revealed his will, God is not unaware of events since
Sinai. Humanity is frail, and in the contest between the word of God and
the will of humanity, Torah is not always the victor. We inevitably fall
short of what is asked of us, and Jews know that their own history consists of divine punishment for human failure time and again. The theme
of redemption, therefore, is introduced.

Redemption—in addition to creation and revelation, the third element
in the tripartite world view—resolves the tension between what we are
told to do and what we are able actually to accomplish. In the end it is
the theme of God, not as Creator or Revealer but as Redeemer, that concludes the twice-daily drama:

> You are our King and our father's King,
> Our redeemer and our father's redeemer.
> You are our creator. . . .
> You have ever been our redeemer and deliverer.
> There can be no God but You. . . .
> You, O Lord our God, rescued us from Egypt;
> You redeemed us from the house of bondage. . . .
> You split apart the waters of the Red Sea,
> The faithful you rescued, the wicked drowned. . . .
> Then Your beloved sang hymns of thanksgiving. . . .
> They acclaimed the King, God on high,
> Great and awesome source of all blessings,
> The everliving God, exalted in his majesty.
> He humbles the proud and raises the lowly;
> He helps the needy and answers His people's call. . . .
> Then Moses and all the children of Israel
> Sang with great joy this song to the Lord:
> Who is like You O Lord among the mighty?
> Who is like You, so glorious in holiness?
> So wondrous your deeds, so worthy of praise!
> The redeemed sang a new song to You;

They sang in chorus at the shore of the sea,
Acclaiming Your sovereignty with thanksgiving:
The Lord shall reign for ever and ever.
Rock of Israel, arise to Israel's defense!
Fulfill Your promise to deliver Judah and Israel.
Our redeemer is the Holy One of Israel,
The Lord of hosts is His name.
Praised are You, O Lord, redeemer of Israel.[4]

Redemption is both in the past and in the future. That God not only creates but also redeems is attested by the redemption from Egyptian bondage. The congregation repeats the exultant song of Moses and the people at the Red Sea, not as scholars making a learned allusion but as participants in the salvation of old and of time to come. Then the people turn to the future and ask that Israel once more be redeemed.

But redemption is not only past and future. When the needy are helped, when the proud are humbled and the lowly are raised—in such commonplace, daily events redemption is already present. Just as creation is not only in the beginning but happens every day, morning and night, so redemption is not only at the Red Sea but every day, in humble events. Just as revelation was not at Sinai alone but takes place whenever people study Torah, whenever God opens their hearts to the commandments, so redemption and creation are daily events.

The great cosmic events of creation in the beginning, redemption at the Red Sea, and revelation at Sinai—these are everywhere, every day near at hand. The Jew views secular reality under the mythical aspect of eternal, ever-recurrent events. What happens to the Jew and to the world, whether good or evil, falls into the pattern revealed of old and made manifest each day. Historical events produce a framework in which future events will find a place and by which they will be understood. Nothing that happens cannot be subsumed by the paradigm.

The myths of creation, of the Exodus from Egypt, and of the revelation of Torah at Sinai are repeated not merely to tell the story of what once was and is no more but rather to recreate out of the raw materials of everyday life the "true being"—life as it was, always is, and will be forever. Streng says, "Myth and ritual recreate in profane time what is eternally true in sacred reality. To live in the myth is to live out the creative power that is the basis of any existence whatever."[5] We here see an illustration of these statements. At prayer the Jew repeatedly refers to the crucial elements of his or her mythic being, thus uncovering the sacred both in nature and in history. We therefore cannot say that Judaic myth does not emphasize a repetition of a cosmic pattern in cyclical or mythical time, for what happens in the proclamation of the *Shema* is just that: The particular events of creation—sunset, sunrise—evoke in response the celebration of the power and the love of God, of his justice and mercy, and of revelation and redemption.

CHAPTER 13

Coming Together

For the Jew the most intimate occasion—the marriage ceremony—is also intrinsically public. Here a new family begins. Individual lover and beloved celebrate the uniqueness, the privacy of their love. One should, therefore, expect the nuptial prayer to speak of him and her, natural man and natural woman. Yet the blessings that are said over the cup of wine of sanctification are as follows:

> Praised are You, O Lord our God, King of the universe, Creator of the fruit of the vine.
> Praised are You, O Lord our God, King of the universe, who created all things for Your glory.
> Praised are You, O Lord our God, King of the universe, Creator of Adam.
> Praised are You, O Lord our God, King of the universe, who created man and woman in his image, fashioning woman from man as his mate, that together they might perpetuate life. Praised are You, O Lord, Creator of man.
> May Zion rejoice as her children are restored to her in joy. Praised are You, O Lord, who causes Zion to rejoice at her children's return.
> Grant perfect joy to these loving companions, as You did to the first man and woman in the Garden of Eden. Praised are You, O Lord, who grants the joy of bride and groom.
> Praised are You, O Lord our God, King of the universe, who created joy and gladness, bride and groom, mirth, song, delight and rejoicing, love and harmony, peace and companionship. O Lord our God, may there ever be heard in the cities of Judah and in the streets of Jerusalem voices of joy and gladness, voices of bride and groom, the jubilant voices of those joined in marriage under the bridal canopy, the voices of young people feasting and singing. Praised are You, O Lord, who causes the groom to rejoice with his bride.[1]

These seven blessings say nothing of private people and of their anonymously falling in love. Nor do they speak of the community of Israel, as one might expect on a public occasion. In them are no hidden sermons to be loyal to the community and faithful in raising up new generations in it. Lover and beloved rather are transformed from natural to mythical figures. The blessings speak of archetypical Israel, represented here and now by the bride and groom.

Israel's history begins with creation—first, the creation of the vine, symbol of the natural world. Creation is for God's glory. All things speak to nature, to the physical as much as the spiritual, for all things were made by God. In Hebrew, the blessings end, "who formed the *Adam*." All things glorify God; above all creation is Adam. The theme of ancient paradise is introduced by the simple choice of the word *Adam*, so heavy with meaning. The myth of man's creation is rehearsed: Man and woman are in God's image, together complete and whole, creators of life, "life God." Woman was fashioned from man together with him to perpetuate life. And again, "blessed is the creator of Adam." We have moved, therefore, from the natural world to the archetypical realm of paradise. Before us we see not merely a man and a woman but Adam and Eve.

But this Adam and this Eve also are Israel, children of Zion the mother, as expressed in the fifth blessing. Zion lies in ruins, her children scattered:

> If I forget you, O Jerusalem, may my right hand forget its skill . . . if I do not place Jerusalem above my greatest joy.
> **—Psalm 137**

Adam and Eve cannot celebrate together without thought to the condition of the mother, Jerusalem. The children will one day come home. The mood is hopeful yet sad, as it was meant to be, for archaic Israel mourns as it rejoices and rejoices as it mourns. Quickly then, back to the happy occasion, for we do not let mourning lead to melancholy: "Grant perfect joy to the loving companions," for they are creators of a new line in mankind—the new Adam, the new Eve. And their home: May it be the garden of Eden. And if joy is there, then "praised are you for the joy of bride and groom."

The concluding blessing returns to the theme of Jerusalem. This time it evokes the tragic hour of Jerusalem's first destruction. When everyone had given up hope, supposing with the end of Jerusalem had come the end of time, only Jeremiah counseled renewed hope. With the enemy at the gate, he sang of coming gladness:

> Thus says the Lord:
> In this place of which you say, "It is a waste, without man or beast," in the cities of Judah and the streets of Jerusalem that are desolate, without man or inhabitant or beast,
> There shall be heard again the voice of mirth and the voice of gladness, the voice of the bridegroom and the voice of the bride, the voice of those who sing as they bring thank-offerings to the house of the Lord. . . .
> For I shall restore the fortunes of the land as at first, says the Lord.
> **—Jeremiah 33:10–11**

The closing blessing is not merely a literary artifice or a learned allusion to the ancient prophet. It is rather the exultant, jubilant climax of this acted-out myth: Just as here and now there stand before us Adam and Eve, so here and now in this wedding, the olden sorrow having been rehearsed, we listen to the voice of gladness that is coming. The joy of this new creation prefigures the joy of the Messiah's coming, hope for which is very present in this hour. And when he comes, the joy then will echo the joy of bride and groom before us. Zion the bride, Israel the groom, united now as they will be reunited by the compassionate God—these stand under the marriage canopy.

In classical Judaism, who are Jewish men and women? They are ordinary people who live within a mythic structure and who thereby hold a view of history centered upon Israel from the creation of the world to its final redemption. Political defeats of this world are by myth transformed into eternal sorrow. The natural events of human life—here, the marriage of ordinary folk—are by myth heightened into a reenactment of Israel's life as a people. In marriage, individuals stand in the place of mythic figures yet remain, after all, boys and girls. What gives their love its true meaning is the myth of creation, revelation, and redemption, here and now embodied in that love. But in the end, the sacred and the secular are united in most profane, physical love.*

The wedding of symbol and reality—the fusion and confusion of the two—these mark the classical Judaic experience shaped by myths of creation, of Adam and Eve, of the Garden of Eden, and by the historical memory of the this-worldly destruction of an old, unexceptional temple. Ordinary events, such as a political and military defeat or success, are changed into theological categories such as divine punishment and heavenly compassion. If religion is a means of ultimate transformation, rendering the commonplace into the paradigmatic, changing the here and now into a moment of eternity and of eternal return, then the marriage liturgy serves to exemplify what is *religious* in Judaic existence.

---

*In classical times the marriage ceremony included provision for bride and groom to consummate their marriage with sexual intercourse while left in private for an appropriate period. Nowadays the privacy is brief and symbolic, to be sure.

CHAPTER 14

Going Forth

At the festival of Passover, in the spring, Jewish families gather around their tables for a holy meal. There they retell the story of the Exodus from Egypt in times long past. With unleavened bread and sanctified wine, they celebrate the liberation of slaves from Pharaoh's bondage. How do they see themselves?

> *We* were the slaves of Pharaoh in Egypt; and the Lord our God brought us forth from there with a mighty hand and an outstretched arm. And if the Holy One, blessed be He, had not brought our fathers forth from Egypt, then surely we, and our children, and our children's children, would be enslaved to Pharaoh in Egypt. And so, even if all of us were full of wisdom and understanding, well along in years and deeply versed in the tradition, we should still be bidden to repeat once more the story of the exodus from Egypt; and he who delights to dwell on the liberation is a man to be praised.[1]

Through the natural eye, one sees ordinary folk, not much different from their neighbors in dress, language, or aspirations. The words they speak do not describe reality and are not meant to. When Jewish people say of themselves, "We were the slaves of Pharaoh in Egypt," they know they never felt the lash; but through the eye of faith that is just what they have done. It is *their* liberation, not merely that of long-dead forebears, they now celebrate.

To be a Jew means to be a slave who has been liberated by God. To be Israel means to give eternal thanks for God's deliverance. And that deliverance is not at a single moment in historical time. It comes in every generation and is always celebrated. Here again, events of natural, ordinary life are transformed through myth into paradigmatic, eternal, and ever-recurrent sacred moments. Jews think of themselves as having gone forth from Egypt, and Scripture so instructs them. God did not redeem the dead generation of the Exodus alone, but the living too—especially the living. Thus the family states:

Again and again, in double and redoubled measure, are we beholden to God the All-Present: that He freed us from the Egyptians and wrought His judgment on them; that He sentenced all their idols and slaughtered all their first-born; that He gave their treasure to us and split the Red Sea for us; that He led us through it dry-shod and drowned the tyrants in it; that He helped us through the desert and fed us with the manna; that He gave the Sabbath to us and brought us to Mount Sinai; that He gave the Torah to us and brought us to our homeland—there to build the Temple for us, for atonement of our sins.[2]

This is the promise which has stood by our forefathers and stands by us. For neither once, nor twice, nor three times was our destruction planned; in every generation they rise against us, and in every generation God delivers us from their hands into freedom, out of anguish into joy, out of mourning into festivity, out of darkness into light, out of bondage into redemption.[3]

For ever after, in every generation, *every Israelite must think of himself or herself as having gone forth from Egypt* [italics added]. For we read in the Torah: "In that day thou shalt teach thy son, saying: All this is because of what God did for me when I went forth from Egypt." It was not only our forefathers that the Holy One, blessed be He, redeemed; us too, the living, He redeemed together with them, as we learn from the verse in the Torah: "And He brought us out from thence, so that He might bring us home, and give us the land which he pledged to our forefathers."[4]

Israel was born in historical times. Historians, biblical scholars, and archaeologists have much to say about that event. But to the classical Jew, their findings, while interesting, have little bearing on the meaning of reality. The redemptive promise that stood by the forefathers and "stands by us" is not a mundane historical event but a mythic interpretation of historical, natural events. Oppression, homelessness, extermination—like salvation, homecoming, renaissance—are this-worldly and profane, supplying headlines for newspapers. The myth that a Jew must think of himself or herself as having gone forth from Egypt and as being redeemed by God renders ordinary experience into a moment of celebration. If "us too, the living, He [has] redeemed," then the observer no longer witnesses only historical men in historical time, but an eternal return to sacred time.

The "going forth" at Passover is one sort of Exodus. Another comes morning and night when Jews complete their service of worship. Every synagogue service concludes with a prayer prior to going forth, called *Alenu*, from its first word in Hebrew. Like the Exodus, the moment of the congregation's departure becomes a celebration of Israel's God, a self-conscious, articulated rehearsal of Israel's peoplehood. But now it is the end of time, rather than the beginning, that is important.

When Jews go forth, they look forward:

Let us praise Him, Lord over all the world;
Let us acclaim Him, Author of all creation.
He made our lot unlike that of other peoples;
He assigned to us a unique destiny.
We bend the knee, worship, and acknowledge
The King of kings, the Holy One, praised is He.

He unrolled the heavens and established the earth;
His throne of glory is in the heavens above;
His majestic Presence is in the loftiest heights.
He and no other is God and faithful King,
Even as we are told in His Torah:
Remember now and always, that the Lord is God;
Remember, no other is Lord of heaven and earth.
We, therefore, hope in You, O Lord our God,
That we shall soon see the triumph of Your might,
That idolatry shall be removed from the earth,
And false gods shall be utterly destroyed.
Then will the world be a true kingdom of God,
When all mankind will invoke Your name,
And all the earth's wicked will return to You.
Then all the inhabitants of the world will surely know
That to You every knee must bend,
Every tongue must pledge loyalty.
Before You, O Lord, let them bow in worship,
Let them give honor to Your glory.
May they all accept the rule of Your kingdom.
May You reign over them soon through all time.
Sovereignty is Yours in glory, now and forever.
So it is written in Your Torah:
The Lord shall reign for ever and ever.[5]

In secular terms, Jews know that in some ways they form a separate, distinct group. In mythical reality, they thank God that they enjoy a unique destiny. They do not conclude with thanks for their particular "being" but sing of hope merely that he who made their lot unlike that of all others will soon rule as sovereign over all. The secular difference, the unique destiny, is for the time being only. When the destiny is fulfilled, there will be no further difference. The natural eye beholds a social group with some particular cultural characteristics defining that group. The myth of peoplehood transforms *difference* into *destiny*.

The existence of the natural group means little, except as testimony to the sovereignty of the God who shaped the group and rules its life. The unique, the particular, the private now are no longer profane matters of culture but become testimonies of divine sovereignty, pertinent to all people, all groups. The particularism of the groups is for the moment alone; the will of God is for eternity. When that will be done, then all people will recognize that the unique destiny of Israel was intended for everyone. The ordinary facts of sociology no longer predominate. The myth of Israel has changed the secular and commonplace into a paradigm of true being.

CHAPTER 15

*Nourishing Life in
the Here and Now:
The Land and Jerusalem
in the Age to Come*

The public and the private join together, as we see, when we consider
how the Land of Israel and the holy city of Jerusalem are brought to
mind every time the pious Jew eats bread. The story starts way back
with the entry into the land, the conquest of the land by Israel from the
Canaanites.

Israel's history did not end, but rather began, with the entry into the
land of Canaan. That history, in a worldly sense, consisted of the secular
affairs of a seldom important kingdom, able to hold its own only when
its neighbors permitted or could not prevent it. In a mythic context, however, Jews looked back on the history of the people as a continuing revelation of divine justice and mercy. Israel, the people, kept the Torah;
therefore, they enjoyed peace and prospered. Then Israel sinned, so God
called forth instruments of his wrath: the Philistines, Assyrians, Babylonians, Persians, Greeks, Romans—there was no end to the list as time
went on. But when Israel was properly chastised, God restored their
prosperity and brought them back to the land.

Perhaps the single most powerful worldly experience in the history of
Judaism was the destruction of the First Temple in 586 B.C.E., followed by
the restoration of Jews to their land by the Persians approximately a half
century later. The worldly motives of the Persians are of no interest here,
for they never played a role in the interpretation of historical events put
forward by Judaic tradition. What the Jews understood was simply this:
God had punished them, but when they repented and atoned, he had forgiven and redeemed them. And they further believed that the prophets
who had foretold just this pattern of events were now vindicated, so
much else that they said was likely to be true. From the fifth century B.C.E.
to the present, Jews have seen their history within the paradigm of sin,
punishment, atonement, reconciliation, and then restoration.

The land entered the Judaic imagination as a powerful, indeed overwhelming, symbol. It was holy, the state for sacred history. We have already noted numerous references to the land, Jerusalem, Zion, and the like. These references all represent concrete exemplifications of myth. Redemption is not an abstract concept, but rather it is what happened when Moses led the people through the Sea of Reeds or what happened with the return to Zion when the Second Temple was built (ca. 500 B.C.E.) or what will happen when God again shines light on Zion and brings the scattered people back to their homes. In classical Judaism, the sanctity of the land, the yearning for Zion, the hope for the restoration of Jerusalem and the Temple cult are all symbols by which the redemption of the past is projected onto the future. The equivalent of the salvation at the sea will be the restoration of Israel to the land and the reconstruction of the Temple and of Jerusalem: The one stands at the beginning of Israel's history; the other, its counterpart, stands at the end.

How do the several salvific symbols fit together in the larger mythic structure of creation, revelation, and redemption? In the Grace After Meals, recited whenever pious Jews eat bread, we see their interplay. To understand the setting, we must recall that in classical Judaism the table at which meals were eaten was regarded as the equivalent of the sacred altar in the Temple. Judaism taught that each Jew before eating had to attain the same state of ritual purity as the priest in the sacred act of making a sacrifice. So in the classic tradition the Grace After Meals is recited in a sacerdotal circumstance.

On Sabbaths and festivals, times of eternity in time, Jews first sing Psalm 126:

> *When the Lord brought back those that returned to Zion, we were like dreamers.*
> *Our mouth was filled with laughter, our tongue with singing. Restore our fortunes, O Lord, as the streams in the dry land. They that sow in tears shall reap in joy. . . .*

Then they recite the grace:

> Blessed art Thou, Lord our God, King of the Universe, who nourishes all the world by His goodness, in grace, in mercy, and in compassion: He gives bread to all flesh, for His mercy is everlasting. And because of His great goodness we have never lacked, and so may we never lack, sustenance—for the sake of His great Name. For He nourishes and feeds everyone, is good to all, and provides food for each one of the creatures He created.
>
> Blessed art Thou, O Lord, who feeds everyone.
>
> We thank Thee, Lord our God, for having given our fathers as a heritage a pleasant, a good and spacious land; for having taken us out of the land of Egypt, for having redeemed us from the house of bondage; for Thy covenant, which Thou hast set as a seal in our flesh, for Thy Torah which Thou has taught us, for Thy statutes which Thou hast made known to us, for the life of grace and mercy Thou hast graciously bestowed upon us, and for the nourishment with which Thou dost nourish us and feed us always, every day, in every season, and every hour.

For all these things, Lord our God, we thank and praise Thee; may Thy praises continually be in the mouth of every living thing, as it is written, And thou shalt eat and be satisfied, and bless the Lord thy God for the good land which He hath given thee.

Blessed art Thou, O Lord, for the land and its food.

O Lord our God, have pity on Thy people Israel, on Thy city Jerusalem, on Zion the place of Thy glory, on the royal house of David Thy Messiah, and on the great and holy house which is called by Thy Name. Our God, our Father, feed us and speed us, nourish us and make us flourish, unstintingly, O Lord our God, speedily free us from all distress.

And let us not, O Lord our God, find ourselves in need of gifts from flesh and blood, or of a loan from anyone save from Thy full, generous, abundant, wide-open hand; so we may never be humiliated, or put to shame.

O rebuild Jerusalem, the holy city, speedily in our day. Blessed art Thou, Lord, who in mercy will rebuild Jerusalem. Amen.

Blessed art Thou, Lord our God, King of the Universe, Thou God, who art our Father, our powerful king, our creator and redeemer, who made us, our holy one, the holy one of Jacob, our shepherd, shepherd of Israel, the good king, who visits His goodness upon all; for every single day He has brought good, He does bring good, He will bring good upon us; He has rewarded us, does reward, and will always reward us, with grace, mercy and compassion, amplitude, deliverance and prosperity, blessing and salvation, comfort, and a living, sustenance, pity and peace, and all good—let us not want any manner of good whatever.[1]

The context of grace is enjoyment of creation, through which God nourishes the world in his goodness. That we have had this meal, however humble, is not to be taken for granted, but rather as a gift. Whenever one eats, he or she must reflect on the beneficence of the Creator. The arena for creation is the land, which to the ordinary eye is commonplace, small, dry, rocky; but which to the eye of faith is pleasant, good, spacious. The land lay at the end of redemption from Egyptian bondage. Holding it, enjoying it—as we saw in the *Shema*—is a sign that the covenant is intact and in force and that Israel is loyal to its part of the contract and God to his. The land, the Exodus, the covenant—these all depend on the Torah, statutes, and a life of grace and mercy, here embodied in and evoked by the nourishment of the meal. Thanksgiving wells up, and the paragraph ends with praises for the land and its food.

Then the chief theme recurs—that is, redemption and hope for return and then future prosperity in the land: "May God pity the people, the city, Zion, the royal house of the Messiah, the Holy Temple." The nourishment of this meal is but a foretaste of the nourishment of the messianic time, just as the joy of the wedding is a foretaste of the messianic rejoicing.

Still, it is not the messianic time, so Israel finally asks not to depend on the gifts or mortal men but only on those of the generous, wide-open hand of God. And then it asks to "rebuild Jerusalem." The concluding paragraph summarizes the whole, giving thanks for creation, redemption, divine goodness, every blessing.

In some liturgies, creation takes the primary place, as here and in the wedding ceremony. In others, the chief theme is revelation. Redemptive and concrete salvific symbols occur everywhere. So much for the life of the community. What about the life cycle of the year, the events of everyday life? These too, as we shall now see, express in their way that same way of Torah that the public events of worship convey.

PART FOUR

The Torah's Way of Life

CHAPTER 16

Life Under the
Law of the Torah

When people think of the law, they ordinarily imagine a religion for bookkeepers, who tote up the good deeds and debit the bad and call the result salvation or damnation, depending on the outcome. But life under the Torah brings the joy of expressing love of God through a cycle of celebration. In fact, the Judaic way of life joins three separate cycles, one in the rhythm of the year, the second in the rhythm of the week, the third in the rhythm of a person's life.

The Judaic year follows the lunar calendar, so the appearance of the new moon marks the beginning of a month, and that is celebrated. There are two critical moments in the unfolding of the year: the first full moon after the autumnal equinox and the first full moon after the vernal equinox. These mark the time of heightened celebration. To understand how the rhythm of the year unfolds, however, we begin with the new moon of the month of *Tishri*, corresponding to September. That marks the New Year, Rosh Hashanah. Ten days later comes the Day of Atonement, commemorating the rite described in Leviticus 16 and marking God's judgment and forgiveness of humanity. Five days afterward is the full moon, which is the beginning of the festival of Tabernacles, in Hebrew *Sukkot;* that festival lasts for eight days and ends with a day of solemn assembly, Shemini Atzeret, and of rejoicing of the Torah, Simhat Torah. So nearly the whole month of Tishri is spent in celebration: eating, drinking, praying, studying, enjoying, and celebrating God's sovereignty, creation, revelation, redemption, as the themes of the festivals and solemn celebrations of the season work themselves out. The next major sequence of celebration, as we realize, follows the first new moon after the vernal equinox, which begins in the month of *Nisan* and culminates, at its full moon, with Passover, in Hebrew *pesah,* which commemorates the Exodus of Israel from Egypt and celebrates Israel's freedom, bestowed by God. Fifty days thereafter comes the festival of Pentecost, in Hebrew *Shavuot,* which commemorates the giving of the Torah at Mount Sinai.

Other occasions for celebration exist, but apart from the Sabbath, the New Year, Day of Atonement, Tabernacles, Passover, and Pentecost are the main holy days.

Just as the Days of Awe (the New Year and the Day of Atonement) and the festivals of Tabernacles, Passover, and Pentecost mark the passage of the lunar year, so the Sabbath marks the movement of time through the week. The sanctification of the Sabbath, observed on the seventh day, Saturday, is one of the Ten Commandments. It is the single happiest moment in Judaism, and coming as it does every week, the Sabbath sheds its light on the life of every day of the week. On it people do no servile labor, and they devote themselves to sacred activities, including both synagogue worship and study of the Torah, as well as to eating, drinking, relaxing, and enjoying themselves. The song for the Sabbath day, Psalm 92, expresses the spirit of this observance: It is good to give thanks to the Lord. Faithful Jews find in the Sabbath the meaning of their everyday lives.

The passage of the individual's life, from birth to death, marks out the third of the three cycles in the way of Torah, the cycles that convey the spirit of the Torah, or law as the word is translated. The principal points are birth, puberty, marriage, and death. In later chapters we shall review pertinent materials. Birth in the case of males is marked by circumcision on the eighth day. Nowadays in the synagogue the birth of both sons and daughters is celebrated by a rite of naming the child. The celebration of a child's becoming responsible to carry out the religious duties that are called *mitzvot*, or commandments, entering the status known as *bar mitzvah* for the boy and *bat mitzvah* for the girl, takes place in the synagogue in a simple way. The young woman or man is called to the Torah, which she or he reads, and the prophetic passage of the day also is read by the newly responsible young adult. We have already noted the marriage ceremony. Rites of death involve a clear recognition that God rules and is the true and just authority over all humanity. The memorial prayer, or *Kaddish* for mourners, expresses the worshipper's recognition of God's holiness and dominion and states the hope for the coming of the Messiah. In a few words these events of celebration, which one might call "life-style events," define life under the law and explain how Judaists seek to live in accord with God's will, which is that Israel live the holy life in the here and now and await salvation at the end of time.

The word for concrete instruction of one's duty, of the proper way of doing things, is *halakhah*, and when we speak of life under the law, we mean life in accord with the *halakhah*, the rules and regulations of the holy life. The mythic structure built on the themes of creation, revelation, and redemption finds expression not only in synagogue liturgy but especially in concrete, everyday actions or action-symbols—that is, deeds that embody and express the fundamental mythic life of the classical Judaic tradition.

These action-symbols are set forth in *halakhah*. This word, as is clear, is normally translated as "law," for the *halakhah* is full of normative, prescriptive rules about what one must do and refrain from doing in every situation of life and at every moment of the day. But *halakhah* derives

from the root *halakh*, which means "go," and a better translation would
be "way." The *halakhah* is "the way": *the way* man lives his life; *the way* man shapes his daily routine into a pattern of sanctity; *the way* man follows the revelation of the Torah and attains redemption.

For the Judaic tradition, this *way* is absolutely central. Belief without the expression of belief in the workaday world is of limited consequence. The purpose of revelation is to create a kingdom of priests and a holy people. The foundation of that kingdom, or sovereignty, is the rule of God over the lives of humanity. For the Judaic tradition, God rules much as people do, by guiding others on the path of life, not by removing them from the land of living. Creation lies behind, redemption in the future; Torah is for here and now. To the classical Jew, *Torah* means "revealed law or commandment, accepted by Israel and obeyed from Sinai to the end of days."

The spirit of the Jewish way *(halakhah)* is conveyed in many modes, for law is not divorced from values; rather it concretizes human beliefs and ideals. The purpose of the commandments is to show the road to sanctity, the way to God. In a more mundane sense, the following provides a valuable insight:

> Rava [a fourth-century rabbi] said, "When a man is brought in for judgment in the world to come, he is asked, 'Did you deal in good faith? Did you set aside time for study of Torah? Did you engage in procreation? Did you look forward to salvation? Did you engage in the dialectics of wisdom? Did you look deeply into matters?'"
> **—Babylonian Talmud tractate Shabbat, p. 31(a)**

Rava's interpretation of the Scripture *and there shall be faith in thy times, strength, salvation, wisdom and knowledge* (Isaiah 33:6) provides one glimpse into the life of the classical Jew who followed the way of Torah. The first consideration was ethical: Did the man conduct himself faithfully? The second was study of Torah, not at random but every day, systematically, as a discipline of life. Third came the raising of a family, for celibacy and abstinence from sexual life were regarded as sinful; the full use of man's creative powers for the procreation of life was a commandment. Nothing God made was evil. Wholesome conjugal life was a blessing. But fourth, merely living day by day according to an upright ethic was not sufficient. It is true that people must live by a holy discipline, but the discipline itself was only a means. The end was salvation. Hence the pious people were asked to look forward to salvation, aiming their deeds and directing their hearts toward a higher goal. Wisdom and insight—these completed the list, for without them the way of Torah was a life of mere routine rather than a constant search for deeper understanding.

If in this context we have not referred also to women, it is not because they were wholly excluded from the system but because in this setting the principal activities—study of Torah, for example—were done by men only. The *halakhah*, in fact, clearly recognized that there were religious duties incumbent on both men and women, but there were some required only of men. Women were excluded, in particular, from the requirement to perform those religious acts that had to be done at a particular time. The reason was that their responsibilities to their family overrode their responsibilities to heaven. If at the same time a woman had to perform a particular commandment and also take care of her daughter or her son, she could not do the former with a whole heart. Therefore, from the very beginning, the law excluded her. We shall later survey a religious world from which, in point of fact, women were excluded when there was no reason for their exclusion intrinsic to the law and the system. That is a separate problem.

CHAPTER 17

Hear Our Prayer, Grant Us Peace

Life under the law means praying—morning, noon, night, and at meals—both routinely and when something unusual happens. To be a Jew in the classical tradition, one lives his or her life constantly aware of the presence of God and always ready to praise and bless God. The way of Torah is the way of perpetual devotion to God. What is the substance of that devotion? For what do pious Jews ask when they pray?

The answers to these questions tell us about more than the shape and substance of Judaic piety. They tell us, too, what manner of person would take shape, for the constant repetition of the sacred words and moral and ethical maxims in the setting of everyday life is bound to affect the personality and character of the individual and the quality of communal life as well. Prayer expresses the most solemn aspirations of the praying community; it is what gives that community a sense of oneness and of shared hopes; it embodies the values of the community. But if it is the community in its single most idiomatic hour, it also presents the community at its least particular and self-aware, for in praying, people stand before God without the mediation of culture and ethnic consciousness. But, as we shall see, that does not mean in Judaic prayer we do not find an acute awareness of history and collective destiny. These are very present.

In the morning, noon, and evening prayers are found the Eighteen Benedictions. Some of these, in particular those at the beginning and the end, recur in Sabbath and festival prayers. They are said silently. Each individual prays by and for himself or herself, but together with other silent, praying individuals. The Eighteen Benedictions are then repeated aloud by the prayer leader, for prayer is both private and public, individual and collective. To contemplate the meaning of these prayers one should imagine a room full of people, all standing by themselves yet in close proximity, some swaying this way and that, all addressing themselves directly and intimately to God in a whisper or in a low tone. They do not move their feet, for they are now standing before the King of kings, and it is not meet to shift and shuffle. If spoken to, they will not answer. Their attention is fixed upon the words of supplication, praise, and gratitude. When they begin, they bend their knees—so too toward the end—and at the conclusion they step back and withdraw from the presence. These, on ordinary days, are the words they say:

WISDOM–REPENTANCE

> You graciously endow man with intelligence;
> You teach him knowledge and understanding.
> Grant us knowledge, discernment, and wisdom.
> Praised are You, O Lord, for the gift of knowledge.
> *Our Father, bring us back to Your Torah;*
> Our King, draw us near to Your service;
> Lead us back to you truly repentant.
> Praised are You, O Lord who welcomes repentance.

FORGIVENESS–REDEMPTION

> Our Father, forgive us, for we have sinned;
> Our King, pardon us, for we have transgressed;
> You forgive sin and pardon transgression.
> Praised are You, gracious and forgiving Lord.
> *Behold our affliction and deliver us.*
> Redeem us soon for the sake of Your name,
> For You are the mighty Redeemer.
> Praised are You, O Lord, Redeemer of Israel.

HEAL US–BLESS OUR YEARS

> Heal us, O Lord, and we shall be healed;
> Help us and save us, for You are our glory.
> Grant perfect healing for all our afflictions,
> O faithful and merciful God of healing.
> Praised are You, O Lord, Healer of His people.
> O Lord our God! Make this a blessed year;
> May its varied produce bring us happiness.
> Bring blessing upon the whole earth.
> Bless the year with Your abounding goodness.
> Praised are You, O Lord, who blesses our years.

GATHER OUR EXILES–REIGN OVER US

> Sound the great shofar to herald [our] freedom;
> Raise high the banner to gather all exiles;
> Gather the dispersed from the corners of the earth.
> Praised are You, O Lord, who gathers our exiles.
> Restore our judges as in days of old;
> Restore our counsellors as in former times;
> Remove from us sorrow and anguish.
> Reign over us alone with loving kindness;
> *With justice and mercy sustain our cause.*
> Praised are You, O Lord, King who loves justice.

Humble the Arrogant–Sustain the Righteous

103
*Hear Our
Prayer,
Grant Us
Peace*

Frustrate the hopes of those who malign us;
Let all evil very soon disappear;
Let all Your enemies be speedily destroyed.
May You quickly uproot and crush the arrogant;
May You subdue and humble them in our time.
Praised are You, O Lord, who humbles the arrogant.
Let Your tender mercies, O Lord God, be stirred
For the righteous, the pious, the leaders of Israel,
Toward devoted scholars and faithful proselytes.
Be merciful to us of the house of Israel;
Reward all who trust in You;
Cast our lot with those who are faithful to You.
May we never come to despair, for our trust is in You.
Praised are You, O Lord, who sustains the righteous.

Favor Your City and Your People

Have mercy, O Lord, and return to Jerusalem, Your city;
May Your Presence dwell there as You promised.
Rebuild it now, in our days and for all time;
Re-establish there the majesty of David, Your servant.
Praised are You, O Lord, who rebuilds Jerusalem.
Bring to flower the shoot of Your servant David.
Hasten the advent of the Messianic redemption;
Each and every day we hope for Your deliverance.
Praised are You, O Lord, who assures our deliverance.
O Lord, our God, hear our cry!
Have compassion upon us and pity us;
Accept our prayer with loving favor.
You, O God, listen to entreaty and prayer.
O King, do not turn us away unanswered,
For You mercifully heed Your people's supplication.
Praised are You, O Lord, who is attentive to prayer.
O Lord, Our God, favor Your people Israel;
Accept with love Israel's offering of prayer;
May our worship be ever acceptable to You.
May our eyes witness Your return in mercy to Zion.
Praised are You, O Lord, whose Presence returns to Zion.

Our Thankfulness

We thank You, O Lord our God and God of our fathers,
Defender of our lives, Shield of our safety;
Through all generations we thank You and praise You.
Our lives are in Your hands, our souls in Your charge.
We thank You for the miracles which daily attend us,
For Your wonders and favor morning, noon, and night.
You are beneficent with boundless mercy and love.
From of old we have always placed our hope in You.
For all these blessings, O our King,
We shall ever praise and exalt You.
Every living creature thanks You, and praises You in truth.

O God, You are our deliverance and our help. Selah!
Praised are You, O Lord, for Your Goodness and Your glory.

PEACE AND WELL-BEING

Grant peace and well-being to the whole house of Israel;
Give us of Your grace, Your love, and Your mercy.
Bless us all, O our Father, with the light of Your Presence.
It is Your light that revealed to us Your life-giving Torah,
And taught us love and tenderness, justice, mercy, and peace.
May it please You to bless Your people in every season,
To bless them at all times with Your fight of peace.
Praised are You, O Lord, who blesses Israel with peace.[1]

The first two petitions pertain to intelligence. The Jew thanks God for mind: knowledge, wisdom, discernment. But knowledge is for a purpose, and the purpose is knowledge of Torah. Such discernment leads to the service of God and produces a spirit of repentance. We cannot pray without setting ourselves right with God, and that means repenting for what has separated us from God. Torah is the way to repentance and to return. So knowledge leads to Torah, Torah to repentance, and repentance to God. The logical next step is the prayer for forgiveness. That is the sign of return. God forgives sin; God is gracious and forgiving. Once we discern what we have done wrong through the guidance of Torah, we can seek to be forgiven. It is sin that leads to affliction. Affliction stands at the beginning of the way to God; once we have taken that way, we ask for our suffering to end; we beg redemption. This request is then specified. We ask for healing, salvation, a blessed year. Healing without prosperity means we may suffer in good health or starve in a robust body. So along with the prayer for healing goes the supplication for worldly comfort.

The individual's task is done. But what of the community? Health and comfort are not enough. The world is unredeemed. Jews are enslaved, in exile, and alien. At the end of days a great *shofar*, or ram's horn, will sound to herald the Messiah's coming. This is now besought. The Jewish people at prayer ask first for the proclamation of freedom, then for the ingathering of the exiles to the Promised Land. Establishing the messianic kingdom, God needs also to restore a wise and benevolent government, good judges, good counselors, and loving justice.

Meanwhile Israel, the Jewish people, finds itself maligned. As the prayer sees things, arrogant men hating Israel hate God as well. They should be humbled. And the pious and righteous—the scholars, the faithful proselytes, the whole House of Israel that trusts in God—should be rewarded and sustained. Above all, remember Jerusalem. Rebuild the city and dwell there. Set up Jerusalem's messianic king, David, and make him prosper. These are the themes of the daily prayer: personal atonement, good health, and good fortunes; collective redemption, freedom, the end of alienation, good government, and true justice; the final and complete salvation of the land and of Jerusalem by the Messiah. At the end comes a prayer that prayer may be heard and found acceptable; then an expression of thanksgiving, not for what may come but for the miracles and mercies already enjoyed morning, noon, and night. And at the end is the prayer for peace, a peace that consists of wholeness for the sacred community.

People who say such prayers do not wholly devote themselves to this world. True, they ask for peace, health, and prosperity. But these are transient. At the same moment they ask, in so many different ways, for eternity. They arise in the morning and speak of Jerusalem. At noon they make mention of the Messiah. In the evening they end the day with talk of the *shofar* to herald freedom and the ingathering of the exiles. Living here in the profane, alien world, they constantly talk of going to the Holy Land and its perfect society. They address themselves to the end of days and the Messiah's time. The praying community above all seeks the fulfillment and end of its, and humanity's, travail.

CHAPTER 18

Sabbaths for Rest, Festivals for Rejoicing

The classical Jew keeps the Sabbath both as a memorial of creation and as a remembrance of the redemption from Egypt. The primary liturgy of the Sabbath is the reading of the Scripture lesson from the Torah in the synagogue service. So the three chief themes—creation, revelation, and redemption—are combined in the weekly observance of the seventh day, from sunset Friday to sunset Saturday.

The Sabbath is protected by negative rules: One must not work; one must not pursue mundane concerns. But the Sabbath is also adorned with less concrete but affirmative laws: One must rejoice; one must rest.

The Sabbath comes at sunset Friday and leaves when three stars appear Saturday night. How do pious Jews keep the Sabbath? All week long they look forward to it, and the anticipation enhances the ordinary days. By Friday afternoon they have bathed, put on their Sabbath garments, and set aside the affairs of the week. At home, the family—husband, wife, children—will have cleaned, cooked, and arranged their finest table. It is common to invite guests for the Sabbath meals. After a brief service the family comes together to enjoy its best meal of the week, a meal at which particular Sabbath foods are served. In the morning comes the Sabbath service—including a public reading from the Torah, the Five Books of Moses, and prophetic writings—and an additional service in memory of the Temple sacrifices on Sabbaths of old. Then the family returns home for lunch and very commonly a Sabbath nap, the sweetest part of the day. As the day wanes, the synagogue calls for a late-afternoon service, followed by Torah-study and a third meal. Then comes a ceremony, *havdalah* (separation)—effected with spices, wine, and candlelight—between the holy time of the Sabbath and the ordinary time of weekday.

This simple, regular observance has elicited endless praise. To the Sabbath-observing Jew, the Sabbath is the chief sign of God's grace:

> For thou hast chosen us and sanctified us above all nations, in love and favor has given us thy holy Sabbath as an inheritance.[1]

So states the sanctification of the Sabbath wine. Likewise in the Sabbath morning liturgy:

> You did not give it [Sabbath] to the nations of the earth, nor did you make it the heritage of idolators, nor in its rest will unrighteous men find a place.
>
> But to Israel your people you have given it in love, to the seed of Jacob whom you have chosen, to that people who sanctify the Sabbath day. All of them find fulfillment and joy from your bounty.
>
> For the seventh day did you choose and sanctify as the most pleasant of days and you called it a memorial to the works of creation.

Here again we find a profusion of themes, this time centered upon the Sabbath. The Sabbath is a sign of the covenant. It is a gift of grace, which neither idolators nor evil people may enjoy. It is the testimony of the chosennesss of Israel. And it is the most pleasant of days. Keeping the Sabbath *is* living in God's kingdom:

> Those who keep the Sabbath and call it a delight will rejoice in your kingdom.

So states the additional Sabbath prayer. Keeping the Sabbath now is a foretaste of the redemption: "This day is for Israel light and rejoicing." The rest of the Sabbath is, as the afternoon prayer affirms, "a rest granted in generous love, a true and faithful rest. . . . Let your children realize that their rest is from you, and by their rest may they sanctify your name."

That people need respite from the routine of work is no discovery of the Judaic tradition. That the way in which they accomplish such a routine change of pace may be made the very heart and soul of their spiritual existence is the single absolutely unique element in Judaic tradition. The word *Sabbath* simply renders the Hebrew *Shabbat;* it does not translate it, for there is no translation. In no other tradition or culture can an equivalent word be found. Certainly those who compare the Sabbath of Judaism to the somber, supposedly joyless Sunday of the Calvinists know nothing of what the Sabbath has meant and continues to mean to Jews.

In his account of the Sabbath, Abraham J. Heschel builds his theology around the meaning of the Sabbath day. He reflects:

> Judaism is a religion of time aiming at the sanctification of time. . . . Judaism teaches us to be attached to holiness in time, to be attached to sacred events, to learn how to consecrate sanctuaries that emerge from the magnificent stream of a year. The Sabbaths are our great cathedrals, and our Holy of Holies is a shrine that neither the Romans nor the Germans were able to burn. . . . Jewish ritual may be characterized as the art of significant forms in time as architecture of time.[2]

Heschel finds in the Sabbath "the day on which we are called upon to share in what is eternal in time, to turn from the world of creation to the creations of the world."[3]

From this brief description of what the Jew actually does on the seventh day, we can hardly derive an understanding of how the Sabbath can have meant so much as to elicit words such as those of the Jewish Prayerbook and of Rabbi Heschel. Those words, like the laws of the Sabbath—not to mourn, not to confess sins, not to repent, not to do anything that might lead to unhappiness—describe something only the participant can truly comprehend and feel. Only a family whose life focuses on the Sabbath week by week, year by year, from birth to death, can know the sanctity of which the theologian speaks, the sacred rest to which the prayers refer. As the heart and soul of the Judaic tradition, the Sabbath cannot be described, only experienced. For the student of religions, it stands as that element of Judaism that is absolutely unique and therefore a mystery.

The festivals mark the passage of time, not of the week but of the seasons. Earlier we took note of the festivals as expressions of life under the law. Let us now consider precisely how people live out those seasons of sanctification and celebration.

Sukkot, the Feast of Tabernacles, is the autumnal festival. It marks the end of agricultural toil. The fall crops by then were gathered in from the fields, orchards, and vineyards. The rainy season was about to begin. It was time both to give thanks for what had been granted and to pray for abundant rains in the coming months. Called festival of the ingathering, it was the celebration of nature par excellence. The principal observance is still the construction of a frail hut, or booth, for temporary use during the festival. In it Jews eat their meals. The huts are covered over with branches, leaves, fruit, and flowers, but light shows through and, at night, the stars. We do not know the origin of the practice. Some have held that during the harvest it was common to build an ordinary shack in the fields for shelter from the heat of the day. In any event, the ancient practice naturally was given a historical context: When the Jews wandered in the wilderness, they lived not in permanent homes but in frail booths. At a time of bounty it is good to be reminded of man's travail and dependence on heavenly succor.

Passover is the Jewish spring festival, and the symbols of the Passover *seder*—hard-boiled eggs and vegetable greens—are not unfamiliar in other spring rites. But here the spring rite has been transformed into a historical commemoration. The natural course of the year, while important, is subordinated to the historical events remembered and relived in the festival. Called the Feast of Unleavened Bread and the season of our freedom, the Passover festival preserves very ancient rites in a new framework.

It is, for example, absolutely prohibited to make use of leavened, fermented dough and the like. The agricultural calendar of ancient Canaan was marked by the grain harvest, beginning in the spring with the cutting of barley and ending with the reaping of the wheat approximately seven weeks later.[4] The farmers would get rid of all their sour dough, which they used as yeast, and old bread as well as any leaven from last year's crop. The origins of the practice are not clear, but that the Passover taboo against leaven was connected with the agricultural calendar is beyond doubt. Just as the agricultural festivals were historicized, likewise much of the detailed observance connected with them was supplied with historical "reasons" or explanations. In the case of the taboo against leaven, widely observed today even among otherwise unobservant Jews, the "reason" was that the Israelites had to leave Egypt in haste and therefore had to take with them unleavened bread, for they had not time to permit the bread to rise properly and be baked. Therefore we eat the *matzah*, unleavened bread.

The Feast of Weeks, *Shavuot* or Pentecost, comes seven weeks after Passover. In the ancient Palestinian agricultural calendar, it marked the end of the grain harvest and was called the Feast of Harvest. In Temple times, two loaves of bread were baked from the wheat of the new crop and offered as a sacrifice, the firstfruits of wheat harvest. So *Shavuot* came to be called the Day of the Firstfruits. Pharisaic Judaism added a historical "explanation" to the natural ones derived from the land and its life. The rabbis held that the Torah was revealed on Mount Sinai on that day and celebrated it as "the time of the giving of our Torah."[5] Nowadays, confirmation and graduation ceremonies of religious schools take place on *Shavuot*.

The three historical-agricultural festivals pertain, in varying ways and combinations, to the themes we have already considered. Passover is the festival of redemption and points toward the Torah-revelation of the Feast of Weeks; the harvest festival in the autumn celebrates not only creation but especially redemption.

The New Year, Rosh Hoshanah, and the Day of Atonement, Yom Kippur, together mark the Days of Awe, of solemn penitence, at the start of the autumn festival season; they are followed by *Sukkot*. These are solemn times. In the myth of classical Judaism, at the New Year humanity is inscribed for life or death in the heavenly books for the coming year, and on the Day of Atonement the books are sealed. The synagogues on that day are filled with penitents. The New Year is called the birthday of the world: "This day the world was born." It is likewise a day of remembrance on which the deeds of all creatures are reviewed. On it God asserts his sovereignty, as in the New Year Prayer:

> Our God and God of our Fathers, Rule over the whole world in Your honor . . . and appear in Your glorious might to all those who dwell in the civilization of Your world, so that everything made will know that You made it, and every creature discern that You have created him, so that all in whose nostrils is breath may say, "The Lord, the God of Israel is king, and His kingdom extends over all."[6]

The themes of the liturgy are divine sovereignty, divine memory, and divine disclosure. These correspond to creation, revelation, and redemption. Sovereignty is established by creation of the world. Judgment depends on law: "From the beginning You made this, Your purpose known. . . ." And therefore, since people have been told what God requires of them, they are judged:

> On this day sentence is passed upon countries, which to the sword and which to peace, which to famine and which to plenty, and each creature is judged today for life or death. Who is not judged on this day? For the

remembrance of every creature comes before You, each man's deeds and destiny, words and way. . . .

The theme of revelation is further combined with redemption; the ram's horn, or *shofar,* which is sounded in the synagogue during daily worship for a month before the Rosh Hashanah festival, serves to unite the two:

> You did reveal yourself in a cloud of glory. . . . Out of heaven you made them [Israel] hear Your voice. . . . Amid thunder and lightning You revealed yourself to them, and while the shofar sounded You shined forth upon them. . . . Our God and God of our fathers, sound the great shofar for our freedom. Lift up the ensign to gather our exiles. . . . Lead us happily to Zion Your city, Jerusalem the place of Your sanctuary.

The complex themes of the New Year, the most "theological" of Jewish holy occasions, thus weave together the central mythic categories we have already discovered elsewhere.

The most personal, solemn, and moving of the Days of Awe is the Day of Atonement, Yom Kippur, the Sabbath of Sabbaths. It is marked by fasting and continuous prayer. On it, the Jew makes confession:

> Our God and God of our fathers, may our prayer come before You. Do not hide yourself from our supplication, for we are not so arrogant or stiff-necked as to say before You . . . we are righteous and have not sinned. But we have sinned.
> We are guilt laden, we have been faithless, we have robbed. . . .
> We have committed iniquity, caused unrighteousness, have been presumptuous. . . .
> We have counseled evil, scoffed, revolted, blasphemed. . . .

The Hebrew confession is built upon an alphabetical acrostic, as if by making certain every letter is represented, God, who knows human secrets, will combine them into appropriate words. The very alphabet bears witness against us before God. Then:

> What shall we say before You who dwell on high? What shall we tell You who live in heaven? Do You not know all things, both the hidden and the revealed? You know the secrets of eternity, the most hidden mysteries of life. You search the innermost recesses, testing men's feelings and heart. Nothing is concealed from You or hidden from Your eyes. May it therefore be Your will to forgive us our sins, to pardon us for our iniquities, to grant remission for our transgressions.

A further list of sins follows, built on alphabetical lines. Prayers to be spoken by the congregation are all in the plural: "For the sin which we have sinned against You with the utterance of the lips. . . . For the sin which we have sinned before You openly and secretly. . . ." The community takes upon itself responsibility for what is done in it. All Israel is part of one community, one body, and all are responsible for the acts of each. The sins confessed are mostly against society, against one's fellow men; few pertain to ritual laws. At the end comes a final word:

O my God, before I was formed, I was nothing. Now that I have been formed, it is as though I had not been formed, for I am dust in my life, more so after death. Behold I am before You like a vessel filled with shame and confusion. May it be Your will . . . that I may no more sin, and forgive the sins I have already committed in Your abundant compassion.

So the Jew in the classical Judaic tradition sees himself or herself before God, possessing no merits yet hopeful of God's love and compassion. To be a classical Jew is to be intoxicated by faith in God, to live every moment in God's presence, and to shape every hour by the paradigm of Torah. The day with its worship in the morning and evening, the week with its climax at the Sabbath, the season marked by nature's commemoration of Israel's sacred history—all shape life into rhythms of sanctification and thus make all of life an act of worship. How does an individual enter into and leave that life? That is the question we answer in the next chapter.

CHAPTER 19

Birth, Maturity, Death

The covenant between God and Israel is not a mere theological abstraction, nor is it effected only through laws of community and family life. It is quite literally engraved on the flesh of every male Jewish child through the rite of circumcision, *brit milah* (the covenant of circumcision).

Circumcision must take place on the eighth day after birth, normally in the presence of a quorum of ten adult males. Elijah, the prophet of scriptural record, is believed to be present. A chair is set for him, based on the legend that Elijah complained to God that Israel neglected the covenant (I Kings 19:10–14).[1] God therefore ordered him to come to every circumcision so as to witness the loyalty of the Jews to the covenant. The *mohel*, or circumciser, is expert at the operation. The traditional blessing is said: "Praised are You . . . who sanctified us with Your commandments and commanded us to bring the son into the covenant of Abraham our father." The wine is blessed: "Praised are You, Lord our God, who sanctified the beloved from the womb and set a statute into his very flesh, and his parts sealed with the sign of the holy covenant. On this account, Living God, our portion and rock, save the beloved of our flesh from destruction, for the sake of his covenant placed in our flesh. Blessed are You . . . who makes the covenant."

The advent of puberty is marked by the *bar mitzvah* rite for a young man and the *bat mitzvah* rite for a young woman, at which the young person becomes obligated to keep the commandments; *bar* means "son" and *bat* means "daughter," with the sense that one is subject to, and *mitzvah* means "commandment." The young person is called to pronounce the benediction over a portion of the Torah-lection in the synagogue and is given the honor of reading the prophetic passage as well. In olden times it was not so important an occasion as it has become in modern America.

Only when a Jew achieves intelligence and self-consciousness, normally at puberty, is he or she expected to accept the full privilege of *mitzvah* (commandment) and to regard himself or herself as *commanded* by God. Judaism perceives the commandments as expressions of one's acceptance of the yoke of the kingdom of heaven and submission to God's will. That acceptance cannot be coerced but requires thoughtful and complete affirmation. The *bar* or *bat mitzvah* thus represents the moment that the young Jew first assumes full responsibility before God to keep the commandments.

At the onset of death, the dying Jew says a confession:

> My God and God of my fathers, accept my prayer. . . .
> Forgive me for all the sins which I have committed in my lifetime. . . .
> Accept my pain and suffering as atonement and forgive my wrong-
>   doing for against you alone have I sinned. . . .
> I acknowledge that my life and recovery depend on You.
> May it be Your will to heal me.
> Yet if You have decreed that I shall die of this affliction,
> May my death atone for all sins and transgressions which I have com-
>   mitted before You.
> Shelter me in the shadow of Your wings.
> Grant me a share in the world to come.
> Father of orphans and Guardian of widows, protect my beloved
>   family. . . .
> Into Your hand I commit my soul. You redeem me, O Lord God of truth.
> Hear O Israel, the Lord is our God, the Lord alone.
> The Lord He is God.
> The Lord He is God.[2]

The corpse is carefully washed and always protected. The body is covered in a white shroud, then laid in a coffin and buried. Normally burial takes place on the day of death or on the following day. Once the body has been placed in the grave, three pieces of broken pottery are laid on eyes and mouth as signs of their vanity. A handful of dirt from the Land of Israel is laid under the head.[3] The family recites the *kaddish*, an eschatological prayer of sanctification of God's name that looks forward to the messianic age and the resurrection of the dead. The prayer expresses the hope that the Messiah will soon come, "speedily, in our days," and that "he who brings harmony to the heavens will make peace on earth." The mourners remain at home for a period of seven days and continue to recite the memorial *kaddish* for eleven months. The life cycle for the private individual is simple, but for the individual as part of Israel, God's holy people, it is rich, absorbing, and encompassing. Life is lived with people, God's people, in God's service.

CHAPTER 20

The Center of Life: Study of Torah

If you have accomplished much in the study of the Torah, do not take pride on that account, for it was to that end that you were created.
—**Rabban Yohanan ben Zakkai**

In the world of Judaism today, and for long centuries past, the study of the Torah forms the central action of the religious virtuosi, the elite, of the faith. These people, until very recently all of them males, spent all day, all week, all month, all year engaged in the recitation and analysis of the holy books of Judaism, with special reference to "the Talmud"—that is, the Talmud of Babylonia—and its codes, commentaries, and the like. They formed an intellectual class that shaped the beliefs and values of everyone else: the models of what it means, in this world, to live life like Moses our rabbi, whom God instructed when God gave the Torah. While the secular world of the Jewish people, in the United States and Europe as much as in the state of Israel, appeals to politicians and business people, the holy world of "Israel," the eternal people of God, appeals to those who form their lives, every day, around and in response to Torah-study. You may encounter few of such people, because they spend their lives in the cloisters of the *yeshivas*, or Torah-study academies, but they are universally understood to represent the authentic model of the Judaic human being. The politicians and the businesspeople decide trivial questions of this world; the masters of Torah spend their lives in the service of God through the study of Torah, and they decide the eternal questions of the holy way of life in the here and now and of the road to salvation at the end of time.

The central myth of classical Judaism, the world view of the Torah, is the belief that the ancient Scriptures constituted divine revelation, but only a part of it. At Sinai God had handed down a dual revelation: the written part known to one and all but also the oral part preserved by the great scriptural heroes, passed on by prophets to various ancestors in the obscure past and finally and most openly handed down to the rabbis who created the Palestinian and Babylonian Talmuds. The "whole Torah" thus consists of both written and oral parts. The rabbis taught that that "whole Torah" was studied by David, augmented by Ezekiel, legislated by Ezra, and embodied in the schools and by the sages of every period in Israelite history from Moses to the present. It is a singular, linear conception of a revelation preserved by the few, pertaining to the many, and in time capable of bringing salvation to all.

The Torah-myth further regards Moses as "our rabbi," the first and prototypical figure of the ideal Jew. It holds that whoever embodies the teachings of Moses "our rabbi" thereby conforms to the will of God—and not to God's will alone but also to his *way.* In heaven, God and the angels study Torah just as rabbis do on earth. God dons phylacteries like a Jew. He prays in the rabbinic mode. He carries out the acts of compassion called for by Judaic ethics. He guides the affairs of the world according to the rules of Torah, just as does the rabbi in his court. One exegesis of the creation legend taught that God had looked into the Torah and therefrom had created the world.

The myth of Torah is multidimensional. It includes the striking detail that whatever the most recent rabbi is destined to discover through proper exegesis of the tradition is as much a part of the way revealed to Moses as is a sentence of Scripture itself. It therefore is possible to participate even in the giving of the law by appropriate, logical inquiry into the law. God himself, studying and living by Torah, is believed to subject himself to these same rules of logical inquiry. If an earthly court overruled the testimony, delivered through miracles, of the heavenly one, God would rejoice, crying out, "My sons have conquered me! My sons have conquered me!"

In a word, before us is a mythical-religious system in which earth and heaven correspond to each other, with Torah as the nexus and model of both. The heavenly paradigm is embodied on earth. Moses "our rabbi" is the pattern for the ordinary sage of the streets of Jerusalem, Pumbedita, Mainz, London, Lvov, Bombay, Dallas, or New York. And God himself participates in the system, for it is his image that, in the end, forms that cosmic paradigm. The faithful Jew constitutes the projection of the divine on earth. Honor is due to the learned rabbi more than to the scroll of the Torah, for through his learning and logic he may alter the very content of Mosaic revelation. He *is* Torah, not merely because he lives by it but because at his best he forms as compelling an embodiment of the heavenly model as does a Torah scroll itself.

The final element in the rabbinic Torah-myth concerns salvation. It takes many forms. One salvific teaching holds that had Israel not sinned —that is, disobeyed the Torah—the Scriptures would have closed with the story of the conquest of Palestine. From that eschatological time, the sacred community would have lived in eternal peace under the divine law. Keeping the Torah was therefore the veritable guarantee of salvation. The opposite is said in many forms as well. Israel had sinned; therefore God called the Babylonians in 586 B.C.E. and the Romans in C.E. 70 to destroy the Temple of Jerusalem; but in his mercy he would be equally faithful to restore the fortunes of the people when they, through their suffering and repentance, had expiated the result and the cause of their sin.

So in both negative and positive forms, the Torah-myth tells of a necessary connection between the salvation of the people and the salvation of the world and the state of Torah among them. For example, if all Israel would properly keep a single Sabbath, the Messiah would come. Of special interest here is the rabbinic saying that the rule of the pagans depends on the sin of Israel. If Israel would constitute a full and complete replication of "Torah"—that is, of heaven—then pagan rule would come to an end. It would end because all Israel then, like some few rabbis even now, would attain to the creative, theurgical powers inherent in Torah. Just as God created the world through Torah, so saintly rabbis could now create a sacred community. When Israel makes itself worthy through its embodiment of Torah—that is, through its perfect replication of the heavenly way of living—then the end will come.

Learning thus finds a central place in a classical Judaic tradition because of the belief that God revealed his will to mankind through the medium of a written revelation given to Moses at Mount Sinai, accompanied by oral traditions taught in the rabbinical schools and preserved in the Talmuds and related literature. The text without the oral traditions might have led elsewhere than into the academy, for the biblicism of other groups yielded something quite different from Jewish religious intellectualism. But belief in the text was coupled with the belief that oral traditions were also revealed. The books composed in the rabbinical academies, as much as in the Hebrew Bible itself, contained God's will for man.

The act of study, memorization, and commentary upon the sacred books is holy. The reason is that, when studying Torah, the faithful Jew hears God's word and will. The study of sacred text therefore assumes a *central* position in Judaism. Other traditions had their religious virtuosi whose virtuosity consisted in knowledge of a literary tradition; but few held, as does Judaism, that everyone must become such a virtuoso.

Traditional processes of learning are discrete and exegetical. Creativity is expressed not through abstract dissertation but rather through commentary on the sacred writings or, more likely in later times, commentary on earlier commentaries. One might also prepare a code of the laws, but such a code represents little more than an assemblage of authoritative opinions of earlier times, with a decision being offered on those few questions the centuries have left unanswered.

The chief glory of the commentator is his *hiddush* (novelty). The *hiddush* constitutes a scholastic disquisition upon a supposed contradiction between two earlier authorities chosen from any period, with no concern for how they might in fact relate historically, and upon a supposed harmonization of their "contradiction." Or a new distinction might be read into an ancient law, upon which basis ever more questions might be raised and solved. The focus of interest quite naturally is law rather than theology, history, philosophy, or other sacred sciences. But within the law it rests on legal theory, and interest in the practical consequences of the law is decidedly subordinated.

The devotion of the Jews to study of the Torah, as here defined, is held by them to be their chief glory. This sentiment is repeated in song and prayer and shapes the values of the common society. The important Jew is the learned man. The child many times is blessed, starting at birth: "May he [or in today's world, she] grow in Torah, commandments, good deeds."

One central *ritual* of the Judaic tradition, therefore, is study. Study as a natural action entails learning traditions and executing them—in this context, in school or in court. Study becomes a *ritual action* when it is endowed with values *extrinsic* to its ordinary character—that is, when set into a mythic context. When a disciple memorizes his master's traditions and actions, he participates in that myth. His study is thereby endowed with the sanctity that ordinarily pertains to prayer or other cultic matters. Study loses its referent in intellectual attainment. The *act* of study itself becomes holy, so that its original purpose, which was mastery of particular information, ceases to matter much. What matters is piety, expressed through the rites of studying. Repeating the words of the oral revelation, even without comprehending them, produces reward, just as imitating the master matters, even without really being able to explain the reasons for his actions.

The separation of the value, or sanctity, of the act of study from the natural, cognitive result of learning therefore transforms study from a natural to a ritual action. That separation is accomplished in part by myth and in part by the powerful impact of the academic environment itself. A striking illustration of the distinction between mere learning and learning as part of ritual life derives from the comment of Mar Zutra, a fifth-century C.E. Babylonian rabbi, on Isaiah 14:5:

> *The Lord has broken the staff of the wicked, the scepter of rulers.* He said, "These are disciples of the sages who teach public laws to boorish judges."
> **—Babylonian Talmud Shabbat, p. 139(a)**

The fact that the uncultivated judge would know the law did not matter, for he still was what he had been—a boor, not a disciple of the sages. Mere knowledge of the laws does not transform an ordinary person, however powerful, into a sage.

Learning carried with it more than naturalistic valence, as further seen in the saying of Amemar, a contemporary of Mar Zutra:

> A sage is superior to a prophet, as Scripture [Psalm 90:12] says, *And a prophet has a heart of wisdom."*
> **—Talmud, b. Bava Batra, p. 12(a)**

The sense is that what made a prophet credible was his knowledge of wisdom, and wisdom, in sages' speech, stood for Torah-learning. What characterized the prophet was, Amemar said, sagacity. Since the prophet was supposed to reveal the divine will, it was not inconsequential that his revelation depended not on gifts of the spirit but on *learning.*

The talmudic rabbis' emphasis on learning as a ritual act ought not to obscure their high expectations of actual accomplishment in learning. While they stressed the act of study without reference to its achievement, they also possessed very old traditions on how best to pursue their task. These traditions included much practical advice on how to acquire and preserve learning. Another Babylonian sage, R. Mesharsheya, advised his sons:

> When you wish to come before your teacher to learn, first review your Mishnah and then go to your teacher. When you are sitting before your teacher look at the mouth of your teacher, as it is written, *But thine eyes shall see they teacher* [Isaiah 30:20]; and when you study any teaching, do so by the side of water, for as the water is drawn out, so your learning may be prolonged. Be on the dustheaps of Mata Mehasia [a great center of learning] rather than in the palaces of Pumbedita [where Torah was lacking].
>
> **—Babylonian Talmud tractate Keritot, p. 6(a)**

Part of that advice was perfectly reasonable. Reviewing before classes, concentrating on the teacher, staying near the great schools would make sense anywhere. On the other hand, his advice to study by a body of water, "so that your learning may be prolonged," has little to do with the practical problems of memorizing and reasoning. Rather, it reflects the rabbis' view of a correspondence between their own study and those aspects of nature that the rabbis looked on as symbolic of their activities, and they many times compared Torah to living waters.

No role whatever was assigned to women. They did not study in the schools, and the life of Torah effectively was closed to them. On the other hand, mothers would encourage their sons to study Torah. Rabina, a late fourth-century master, explained how study of the Torah applied to women: Women acquired merit when they arranged for their sons' education in Scripture and Mishnah and when they waited for their husbands to return from the schools. Since that return was often postponed by months or even years, it was no small sacrifice. But the schools were entirely male institutions, and no equivalent religious life was available for women, as we saw when we considered women in the system of the Mishnah: systemically central but also inert. It is only in our own day that women have entered the world of Torah-study in the ways in which men have carried on that enterprise. There are now yeshivot in the state of Israel and in Europe and America in which women study Torah; women also complete doctorates in Judaic studies, including Talmudic studies, and take up professorships in both universities and Reform and Conservative rabbinical schools.

From the study of the Torah, we turn to the figure of the sage, or rabbi ("my lord"). The rabbi functioned in the Jewish community as judge and administrator. But he lived in a society in some ways quite separate from that of Jewry as a whole. The rabbinical academy was, first, a law school. Some of its graduates served as judges and administrators of the law. But the rabbinical school was by no means a center for merely legal study. It was, like the Christian monastery, the locus for a peculiar kind of religious living. Only one of its functions concerned those parts of the Torah to be applied in everyday life through the judiciary. In ancient, medieval, and modern times these activities and institutions remained remarkably stable.

The school, or yeshiva (literally, session), was a council of Judaism, a holy community. In it men learned to live a holy life, to become saints. When they left, sages continued to live by the discipline of the school. They invested great efforts in teaching that discipline by example and precept to ordinary folk. Through the school, classical Judaism transformed the Jewish people into its vision of the true replica of Mosaic revelation.

The schools, like other holy communities, imposed their own particular rituals, intended in the first instance for the disciples and masters. Later, it was hoped, all Jews would conform to those rituals and so join the circle of master and disciples.

As with study, the schools' discipline transformed other ordinary, natural actions, gestures, and functions into rituals, the rituals of "being a rabbi." Everyone ate. Rabbis did so in a "rabbinic" manner. That is to say, what others regarded as matters of mere etiquette, formalities and conventions intended to render eating aesthetically agreeable, rabbis regarded as matters of "Torah," something to be *learned*. It was "Torah" to do things one way, and it was equally "ignorance" to do them another way (although not heresy, for theology was the issue).

The master of Torah, whether disciple or teacher, would demonstrate his mastery not merely through what he said in the discussion of legal traditions or what he did in court. He would do so by how he sat at the table, by what ritual formulas he recited before eating one or another kind of fruit or vegetable, by how he washed his hands. Everyone had to relieve himself. The sage would do so according to "Torah." The personality traits of men might vary. Those expected of, and inculcated into, a sage were of a single fabric.

We must keep in mind the fundamental difference between the way of Torah and ways to salvation explored by other holy men and sacred communities. The rabbi at no point would admit that his particular rites were imposed on him alone, apart from all Israel. He ardently "spread Torah" among the Jews at large. He believed he had to, because Torah was revealed to all Israel at Sinai and required of all Israel afterward. If he was right that Moses was "our rabbi" and that even God kept the commandments as he did, then he had to ask of everyone what he demanded of himself: conformity to the *halakhah*, the way of Torah. His task was facilitated by the widespread belief that Moses had indeed revealed the Torah and that some sort of interpretation quite naturally was required to apply it to everyday affairs. The written part of the Torah generally shaped the life of ordinary pious folk. What the rabbi had to accomplish was to persuade the outsider that the written part of the Torah was partial and incomplete, requiring further elaboration through the oral traditions he alone possessed and embodied.

The central human relationship in the schools was between the disciple and the master. Long ago it was taught that the master took the place of the father. The father brought the son into this world; the master would lead him into the world to come. Whatever honor was due the father was all the more owing to the master. But the master did not merely replace the father. He also required the veneration and reverence owing to the Torah. The extreme forms of respect that evolved over the centuries constitute the most striking rituals attached to "being a rabbi." If study was an act of piety, then the master was partly its object. That is not to suggest that the master, although a saint, was regarded as in any sense divine. But the forms of respect reserved for the divinity and for the Torah were not too different, in appropriate circumstances, from those owing to the master.

The forms of respect for the master constituted part of the ritual of being a rabbi. The service of the disciples separated the true sage from the merely learned man. It had earlier been taught that if one had studied Scripture and Mishnah but did not attend upon the sages, he was regarded as a boor, an *Am haarez.* To these epithets, a fourth-century rabbi added: "Behold, such a one is a Magus." The talmudic discussion then cited a popular saying:

> The Magus mumbles and does not know what he is saying, just as the Tanna [the professional memorizer and reciter of Mishnah] who has not attended on the sages recites and does not know what he is saying.
> —b. Sotah, p. 22(a)

The sage claimed to see no difference between a learned Jew and a learned Zoroastrian except that the disciple served the sages. That service—meaning not merely personal attendance but imitation and study of the *master* as much as of the Torah—constituted a vital part of the Torah. The master exemplified the whole Torah, including the oral part of it. Scripture and Mishnah, written and oral Torah, meant little without observation and imitation of the sage. The whole Torah was not in books nor in words to be memorized. Torah was to be found in whole and complete form in the master. That is why the forms of respect for the master were both so vital and so unique to the mythic life of the schools.

Ordinary folk could reasonably be expected to carry out most of the rites we have called characteristic of the rabbinical estate. True, common people were supposed to honor all rabbis, but that honor was quite different from the perpetual humility displayed by a disciple before his particular master. The real difference was not the depth of submission but the constant attendance and attention. On the rare occasions when a great rabbi appeared in public, the ordinary people could be just as humble as his private entourage. But the one thing they could not do was keep it up, wait on him constantly, and so learn all his ways. They just did not have the time. Of all human relationships open to rabbis, therefore, the one between master and disciple was most thoroughly ritualized, most utterly divorced from natural forms of human intercourse. If the master is a living Torah, source of revelation of the oral tradition given at Sinai and embodied now in the master himself, then the disciple had best humbly imitate each and every gesture of that living Torah and so prepare himself as the nexus of the transmission of this same oral tradition to the coming generation.

Submission to the master produced several sorts of tensions. First, the master's knowledge, so much greater than the disciple's, must have intimidated the latter. As this phenomenon reproduced itself one generation after the other, it led to exaggerating the attainments of the ancients and denigrating one's own.

> Rava said, "We are like a finger in wax as regards reasoning." R. Ashi said, "We are like a finger in the well as regards forgetting"—that is to say, "just as a finger cannot bring up water from a well, so easily do we forget what we have learned."
> —b. 'Eruvin, p. 53(a)

Both similes come at the end of a long line of sayings on the glories of the ancients and the limitations of the moderns. It was an attitude inculcated by the schools, inherent in the belief that perfection had been revealed at Sinai, only to be slowly but inevitably forgotten, to suffer attrition through the ages.

CHAPTER 21

The Philosopher

Up to now we have dealt with those enduring formations of the Judaism of the dual Torah that had come into being in late antiquity, the first seven centuries of the Common Era, from the destruction of the Temple in 70 to the Muslim conquest of the Near and Middle East from 640 onward. But as we recall, the Judaism of the dual Torah not only survived the historical changes represented by the shift from Christian to Muslim rule of territories in which Jews lived, such as the Land of Israel and Babylonia. The rise of Islam brought important intellectual changes, because of the character of Islamic culture. Specifically, Muslim theologians, who could read Greek or Greek philosophy translated into Arabic, developed a philosophical mode of thought that was rigorous, abstract, and scientific, with special interest in a close reading of Aristotle. In ancient times a school of Judaic philosophy in the Greek-speaking Jewish world, represented by Philo of Alexandria, read Scripture in the light of such philosophical modes, but the sages of the Talmud did not follow that generalizing and speculative model. They read Scripture within a different framework altogether. But as the Judaic intellectuals of Islam faced the challenge of Muslim rationalism and philosophical rigor, they read Scripture and the oral Torah as well in a new way. The task at hand was to reconcile and accommodate the one with the other. For just as today most Judaists, faithful believers all, cannot imagine denying the established truths of science while affirming the revelation of the Torah—no one thinks the world is flat, for instance, and the story of a seven-day-creation is set aside as well—so in medieval Islam no Judaic intellectuals could rest easy in the admission that Scripture and science, in its philosophical form, came into conflict.

That is why alongside study of Torah—meaning spending one's life in learning the Babylonian Talmud and later codes, commentaries, and rabbinical court decisions—a different sort of intellectual-religious life flourished in classical Judaism. It was the study of tradition through the instruments of reason and the discipline of philosophy.

For the whole history of the classical tradition, "study of Torah" predominated. The philosophical enterprise attracted small numbers of elitists and mainly served their specialized spiritual and intellectual needs. That does not mean the philosophical way was unimportant. Those who followed it included the thoughtful and the perplexed, those who took the statements of the tradition most seriously and, through questioning and reflection, intended to examine and then effect them. Moreover, the philosophers were not persons who limited their activities to study and teaching; they frequently occupied high posts within the Jewish community and served in the high society of politics, culture, and science outside the community as well. Although not numerous, the philosophers exercised considerable influence, particularly in an age that believed reason and learning, not wealth and worldly power, were what really mattered.

The philosophical way proved attractive only at specific times and under unique circumstances, whereas the way of Torah was always and everywhere characteristic in premodern times. Philosophy proved uniquely important to Jews living in close contact with other cultures and traditions, like those of Hellenistic Alexandria in the first century C.E., of ninth-century Muslim Baghdad, of Spain in the eleventh and twelfth centuries, of Christian Germany in the nineteenth century, and of twentieth-century America. In such settings, Jews coexisted in an open society with Gentiles—pagans, Muslims, Christians, Zoroastrians. They did not live isolated from or in ignorance of the dominant spiritual currents of the day. On the contrary, each particular group felt called on to explain its chief ideas and doctrines in terms accessible to all others. Reason was conceived as the medium for such discourse.

All groups in the day-to-day encounter of differing cultures and traditions, therefore, attained a high degree of self-consciousness, so that something called Judaism or Christianity or Islam could be defined by contrast to—against the background of—other sorts of "isms" and "ities." The total, all-encompassing world view of Torah, on the other hand, quite unselfconsciously spoke of "person," in the assumption that people were much alike because they were Jews. "The good way" for a human being could be defined in a homogeneous setting. The doctrines of Judaism had to be defined because of the heterogeneous situation.

But the heterogeneity was only one of detail. Philosophy flourished in a world of deep religious conviction, which was common to several disparate communities. The issues of philosophy were set not by lack of belief but by deep faith. Few, if any, denied providence, a personal God, and a holy book revealed by God through his chosen messenger.[1] Everyone believed in reward and punishment, in a last judgment, and in a settling of accounts.

The Jewish philosopher had to cope with problems imposed not only by the classical faith but also by the anomalous situation of the Jews themselves. What was the meaning of the strange, unfortunate history of the Jews? How was philosophy to account reasonably for the homelessness of God's people, who were well aware that they lived as a minority among powerful, prosperous Christian and Muslim majorities? If Torah were true, why did different revelations claiming to be based on it—but to complete it—flourish, while the people of Torah suffered?

Why, indeed, ought one to remain a Jew when every day one was confronted by the success of the daughter religions? Conversion was always a possibility, an inviting one even under the best of circumstances, for a member of a despised minority.[2]

These problems pressed particularly on the philosopher, a marginal figure both in Jewry and in the urban civilization of the day. For him, the easy answers—we are still being punished for our sins or we suffer now but our reward will be all the greater later on—were transparent, self-serving, and unsatisfactory because they were too easy. He was further concerned with the eternal questions facing all religious people: Is God just? What is the nature of humanity? What is the meaning of revelation? Where are answers to be found?

The search was complicated by the formidable appeal of Greek philosophy to medieval Christian and Islamic civilization. Its rationalism, its openness, its search for pure knowledge challenged all revelations. Philosophy called into question all assertions of truth verifiable not through reason but only through appeals to a source of truth not universally recognized. Reason thus stood, it seemed, against revelation. Mysterious divine plans came into conflict with allegations of the limitless capacity of human reason. Free inquiry might lead anywhere and so would not reliably lead to the synagogue, church, or mosque. And not merely traditional knowledge, but the specific propositions of faith and the assertions of a holy book had to be measured against the results of reason. Faith *or* reason—this seemed to be the choice.

For the Jews, moreover, the very substance of faith—in a personal, highly anthropomorphic God who exhibited traits of character not always in conformity with humanity's highest ideals and who in rabbinic hands looked much like the rabbi himself—posed a formidable obstacle. Classical conundrums of philosophy were further enriched by the obvious contradictions between belief in free will and belief in divine providence. Is God all-knowing? If so, how can people be held responsible for what they do? Is God perfect? If so, how can he change his mind or set aside his laws to forgive people?

No theologian in such a cosmopolitan, rational age could begin with an assertion of a double truth or a private, relative one. The notion that something could be true for one party and not for another, or that faith and reason were equally valid and yet contradictory, were ideas with little appeal. And the holy book had to retain the upper hand: "Scripture as the word of God contained, of course, absolute truth, while philosophy as a human activity could find its truth only in reasoning."[3] The two philosophers we shall now consider represent the best efforts of medieval Judaic civilization to confront these perplexities.

The first is Moses Maimonides (1141–1205), who was at the same time a distinguished student of the Talmud and of Jewish law in the classical mode, a community authority, a great physician, and a leading thinker of his day. His achievement was to synthesize a neo-Platonic Aristotelianism with biblical revelation. His *Guide to the Perplexed,* published in 1190, was intended to reconcile the believer to the philosopher and the philosopher to faith. For him philosophy was not alien to religion but identical with it, for truth was in the end the sole issue. Faith is a form of knowledge; philosophy is the road to faith.

His proof for the existence of God was Aristotelian. He argued from creation to Creator but accepted the eternity of the world. Julius Guttmann describes Maimonides's view as follows:

> Since, in addition to bodies which are both moving and moved, there are other bodies which are moved and yet are not causes of movement, there must also exist a being which moves without being moved. The second proof is based not on the movement of bodies but on their transition from potency to act: the transition presupposed the existence of an actualizing principle which is external to the being thus changed. The impossibility of an infinite regression of causes, just as it led in the first proof to prime mover, now serves to establish the existence of a first actualizing principle, free of all potentiality and hence also immaterial in nature. . . . Maimonides can prove the origin of the world as a whole, from God, only by deduction from the contingent existence of things.[4]

God becomes, therefore an "absolutely simple essence from which all positive definition is excluded."[5] One can say nothing about the attributes of God. He is purged of all sensuous elements. One can say only that God is God, nothing more, for God can only be *known* as the highest cause of being.

What then of revelation? Did God not say anything about himself? And if he did, what need for reasonings such as these? For Maimonides, prophecy, like philosophy, depends on the Active Intellect. But in the case of the prophets, "the Active Intellect impresses itself especially upon their imaginative faculty, which is why they express their teachings in a poetic or literary form, rather than in the ratiocinative form of the philosophers."[6] Prophecy is a gift bestowed by God upon man. The Torah and commandments are clearly important but are not ultimately beyond question or reasonable inquiry. Yet they survive the inquiry unimpaired. The Torah fosters a sound mind and body:

> All its precepts and teachings conspire to guide a man to the greatest benefits, moral and intellectual. Everything in the Torah, whether it be a law or a narrative or genealogy, is significant . . . intended to inculcate a moral or intellectual truth, to wean men away from wrong beliefs, harmful excesses, or dangerous indulgences. In its entirety, the Law is the supreme means whereby man realizes himself most fully.[7]

The greatest good, however, is not to study Torah in the sense described earlier but rather to know God—that is, to worship and love him. Piety and knowledge of Torah serve merely to prepare people for this highest achievement. Study of Torah loses its character as an end in itself and is rendered into a means to a philosophical goal. This was the most striking transformation of the old values. Philosophical knowledge of physical and metaphysical truths "culminates in a purified conception of the nature of God. It is this kind of understanding that engenders the longing for God and the love of him."[8]

Maimonides provided a definition of Judaism, a list of articles of faith that he thought obligatory for every faithful Jew. These are as follows: (1) the existence of God, (2) his unity, (3) his incorporeality, (4) his eternity, (5) the obligation to worship him alone, (6) prophecy, (7) Moses as the greatest of the prophets, (8) the divine origin of Torah, (9) the eternal validity of Torah, (10) God's knowledge of man's deeds, (11) his punishment of evil and rewarding of goodness, (12) his promise to send a Messiah, and (13) his promise to resurrect the dead. These philosophical principles were hotly debated and much criticized, but ironically, they achieved a place in the life of Judaic piety. Although subjected to debate and criticism, in the end they were sung as a prayer in a hymn, *Yigdal*, which is always sung at the conclusion of synagogue prayer:

1. The living God we praise, exalt, adore
   He was, he is, he will be evermore.
2. No unity like unto his can be
   Eternal, inconceivable is he.
3. No form or shape has the incorporeal one
   Most holy he, past all comparison.
4. He was ere aught was made in heaven or earth
   But his existence has no date or birth.
5. Lord of the Universe is he proclaimed
   Teaching his power to all his hand has framed.
6. He gave his gift of prophecy to those
   In whom he gloried, whom he loved and chose.
7. No prophet ever yet has filled the place
   Of Moses, who beheld God face to face.
8. Through him (the faithful in his house) the Lord
   The law of truth to Israel did accord.
9. This Law of God will no alter, will not change
   For any other through time's utmost range.
10. He knows and heeds the secret thoughts of man:
    He saw the end of all ere aught began.
11. With love and grace doth he the righteous bless,
    He metes out evil unto wickedness.
12. He at the last will his anointed send
    Those to redeem who hope and wait the end.
13. God will the dead to life again restore.
    Praised by his glorious name for evermore.[9]

The esoteric words of the philosopher were thus transformed into a message of faith, at once sufficiently complex to sustain critical inquiry according to the canons of the day and simple enough to bear the weight of the faith of ordinary folk and to be sung. The "God without attributes" is still guide, refuge, stronghold. It is a strange and paradoxical fate for the philosopher's teachings. Who would have supposed at the outset that the way of the philosopher would lead to the piety of the people?

Many, indeed, came to no such supposition. They found the philosophers presumptuous, inadequate, and incapable of investigating the truths of faith. But the critics of "philosophy" were themselves philosophers. The greatest was Judah Halevi (1080–1141), who produced *not* a work of sustained philosophical argument and analysis but a set of dialogues between a king (the king of the Khazars, a kingdom that did, in fact, adopt Judaism several centuries earlier) in search of true religion and the advocates of the several religious and philosophical positions of the day, including Judaism. Halevi, poet and mystic, objected to the indifference of philosophy to the comparative merits of the competing traditions. In philosophy's approach, "the ultimate objective is the knowledge of God. Religion is recommended because it inculcates the proper moral qualities in men, but no attention is paid to the question of *which* system of religious morality one ought to follow."[10] For the majority religions in the West, Islam and Christianity, such an indifference may have been tolerable, but it was not tolerable for a minority destined any day to have to die for the profession of faith.

Martyrdom will not be evoked by the unmoved mover, the God anyone may reach either through revelation or through reason. Only for the God of Israel will a Jew give up his or her life. By its nature, philosophy is insufficient for the religious quest: "It starts with assumptions and ends with mere theories."[11] It can hardly compete with, let alone challenge, the *history* of the Jewish people, which records extraordinary events starting with revelation. What has philosophy to do with Sinai, with the land, with prophecy? On the contrary, the Jew, expounding religion to the king of the Khazars, begins not like the philosopher with a disquisition on divine attributes, nor like the Christian who starts with the works of creation and expounds the Trinity, nor like the Moslem who acknowledges the unity and eternity of God, but as follows:

> I believe in the God of Abraham, Isaac, and Israel, who led the Israelites out of Egypt with signs and miracles; who fed them in the desert and gave them the Land, after having made them traverse the sea and the Jordan in a miraculous way; who sent Moses and His Torah and subsequently thousands of prophets, who confirmed His law by promises to those who observed and threats to the disobedient. We believe in what is contained in the Torah—a very large domain.[12]

The king then asks why the Jew did not say he believed in the creator of the world and in similar attributes common to all creeds. The Jew responds that the evidence for Israel's faith is *Israel*, the people, its history and endurance, and not the kinds of reasonable truths offered by other traditions. The *proof* of revelation is the testimony of those who were *there* and wrote down what they heard, saw, and did.

If so, the king wonders, what accounts for the despised condition of Israel today? The Jew compares Israel to the dry bones of Ezekiel:

> . . . these bones, which have retained a trace of vital power and have once been the seat of a heart, head, spirit, soul, and intellect, are better than bones formed of marble and plaster, endowed with heads, eyes, ears, and all limbs, in which there never dwelt the spirit of life.[13]

God's people is Israel; he rules them and keeps them in their present status:

Israel amid the nations is like the heart amid the organs: it is the most sick and the most healthy of them all. . . . The relationship of the Divine power to us is the same as that of the soul to the heart. For this reason it is said, *You only have I known among all the families of the earth, therefore I will punish you for all your iniquities* [Amos 3:2]. . . . Now we are oppressed, while the whole world enjoys rest and prosperity. But the trials which meet us serve to purify our piety, cleanse us, and to remove all taint from us.[14]

The pitiful condition of Israel is, therefore, turned into the primary testimony and vindication of Israel's faith. That Israel suffers is the best assurance of divine concern. The suffering constitutes the certainty of coming redemption. In the end, the Jew parts from the king to undertake a journey to the Land of Israel. There he seeks perfection with God:

The invisible and spiritual *Shekhinah* [presence of God] is with every born Israelite of pure life, pure heart, and sincere devotion to the Lord of Israel. And the Land of Israel has a special relation to the Lord of Israel. Pure life can be perfectly lived only there.[15]

To this the king objects. He thought the Jew loved freedom, but the Jew finds himself in bondage because of the duties imposed on those residing in the Land of Israel. The Jew replies that the freedom he seeks is from the service of men and the courting of their favor. He seeks the service of one whose favor is obtained with the smallest effort: "His service is freedom, and humility before him is true honor." He therefore turns to Jerusalem to seek the holy life. He closes his remarks:

Thou shalt arise and have mercy upon Zion; for it is time to favor her, the moment is come. For thy servants love her stones and pity her dust [Psalm 102:14–15]. This means, Jerusalem can only be rebuilt when Israel yearns for it to such an extent that we sympathize even with its stones and its dust.[16]

Here we find no effort to identify Judaism with rational truth. Rather we find the claim that the life of the pious Jew stands above, indeed constitutes the best testimony to, truth.

The source of truth is biblical revelation, which was public, complete, fully in the light of history. History, not philosophy, testifies to the truth and in the end constitutes its sole criterion. Philosophy claims reason can find the way to God. Halevi says only God can show the way to God, and God does so through revelation and therefore in history. For the philosopher, God is the object of knowledge.[17] For Halevi, God is the subject of knowledge: "The yearning heart seeks the god of Abraham; the labor of the intellect is directed toward the God of Aristotle."[18] And Israel has a specifically religious faculty that mediates the relationship to God, as we have seen in references to the role of Israel among the nations as similar to the role of the heart among the limbs.

Halevi seeks to explain the supernatural status of Israel. The religious faculty is its peculiar inheritance and makes it the core of humanity. He thus "predicates . . . the supernatural religious faculty."[19] But while the rest of humanity is subject to the laws of nature, Israel is subject to super-

natural, divine providence, manifested in reward and punishment. The
very condition of the Jews, in that God punishes them, verifies the particular and specific place of Israel in the divine plan. The teaching of
prophecy thus returns in Halevi's philosophy.

Maimonides and Halevi were among the important thinkers who attempted to meet the challenge of philosophy and reason by constructing
a comprehensive theological system. But the uses of reason were not exhausted by the philosophical enterprise. Reason played a central role in
the study of Torah. The settings, however, were vastly different. Still, insofar as reasoning power "is one of the modes of human awareness
through which man constructs human experience,"[20] the classic Judaic
tradition fully explored this mode.

If, in Judaic tradition, salvation was never reduced to a "confession of
a creed or theological agreement," important efforts were still made, as
by Maimonides, to produce just such a creed. It is not, as often asserted,
that Judaism had (or has) no theology. Such a statement is obviously ab-
surd. It is simply that the theological idiom of the Judaic tradition often
diverged from that of the Christian West. In Maimonides we meet a theological mind quite capable of addressing itself to the issues confronting
any religious tradition perplexed by philosophical reason. But Halevi, so
much more private, subjective, and particularistic, ends up in a supra-
rationalist position not far divorced from neo-Platonism.

Although they were like the Muslim and Christian intellectuals in
mentality, the Jewish philosophers had more in common with the
talmudic rabbis. The rabbis accepted the Bible and the Talmud as "the
whole Torah," and so did the Jewish philosophers. Both groups devoted
themselves to the articulation of the role of Torah in the life of Israel, to
the meaning of the fate of Israel and to the effort to form piety and shape
faith. And for both, *reason* was the means of reaching into Torah, of re-
covering and achieving truth. For both, therefore, the "unique, personal
situation in which a person is receptive to a dimension of meaning," as
Streng says,[21] can indeed be exposed through linguistic and conceptual
relationships. Both agreed that words could contain and convey the sacred and therefore that reason, the examination of the meaning and refer-
ents of words, was the golden measure. They differed only in the object
of reason; the one studied law, the other philosophy. Yet Maimonides, the
complete and whole Jew, studied both and made a lasting impact on the
formation of both sorts of Judaic tradition as well as on the pious imagination of the ordinary Jew.

CHAPTER 22

The Mystic

The Judaism of the dual Torah, in ancient times and in the medieval and modern ages, welcomed and placed a high value on mystical experience attained through prayer, asceticism, and devotion to godly service. It furthermore made a place within Torah for holy books of mystical doctrine. In ancient times, it is clear, a mystical experience involving visions of God in the levels of the firmament was available to some sages. A continuing tradition of speculation about matters of mystical knowledge and experience flourished from late antiquity forward. That tradition came to its zenith in the most important work of mystical speculation and experience, the *Zohar*, a thirteenth-century work of immense proportions and commensurate influence. It suffices to say that the dual Torah of Judaism encompassed not only Scripture and the Mishnah and other writings of the oral tradition of the ancient rabbis, but also yet a third powerful and important "torah" as well, the Torah of religious experience of an intense and mystical confrontation with the living God. The *Zohar* is that third component of the Judaism of the dual Torah.

We know that Moses de Leon wrote the *Zohar* in Spain between 1281 and 1286, but we cannot be surprised that de Leon speaks in the name of important second-century rabbis. The mystics before and after the *Zohar* took for granted that their doctrines were Torah and were derived from the same authorities who gave them Mishnah and other parts of the oral Torah. The intense inner life of direct encounter through prayer, observance of the commandments, and study of Torah thus strengthened the power of the rabbinic Torah-myth in the life of the Jewish people and indeed generated fructifying, creative forces in the way of Torah.

Especially important was the conviction that every deed of a human being on earth has its counterpart in invisible reality in heaven. The talmudic stress on practical action elevated concrete deeds into the highest mode of religious expression. What a Jew did affected the profound reality. Before performing a commandment, a mystic would say, "Thus I

do this *mitzvah* for the sake of the unity of the Holy One, blessed be He."
These words indicate that the mystic was able to help effect the greater
unity of the one God. The social effect was to stress the performance of
deeds that formed a pattern of religious living, deeds that the nonmystic
performed habitually in a more mundane spirit and in an attitude of
mere conformity. The mystic knew that one does things for a deeper,
transcendent reason. The mystic therefore brought new devotion to the
old, established way of life. He joined the community ever more concerned to do precisely what everyone else was doing anyhow, but for his
own reason.

It is no accident that the greatest lawyers and Talmudists also were
among the most profound and influential mystics. For example, the author of the code of Jewish law *(Shulhan Arukh)*, Joseph Karo, believed
that he received heavenly visitations from the Mishnah incarnate. A
great biblical commentator, Nachmanides, introduced into his commentary on the Pentateuch important mystical considerations. The greatest
genius of the talmudic tradition—Elijah, the Gaon of Vilna, who lived at
the end of the eighteenth century—was a paragon of rabbinic rationality
who also gave his best efforts to the study of the *Zohar* and other mystical writings. We cannot in fact locate a major legal authority who, after
mystic literature became available, did not also devote himself in some
measure to the study of mysticism. The reason is that the law and the inner life of the believing Jew were understood to express one and the
same pattern. The former was the body and the latter the spirit; the
former was the outer capsule and the latter the inner meaning. So when
the mystics, for their part, undertook ascetic behavior, it was in the form
of moral behavior. Ascetic renunciation led less to hair shirts and fasting, although there assuredly was self-torture, than to moral action—
that is, giving up one's rights in favor of another's. Because the Jewish
mystic wanted to love God, he had also to love his neighbor.

This is how the practical expression of ascetic mysticism is described
in a thirteenth-century book of mysticism, the *Book of the Pious:*

> At all times you should love your Creator with all your heart and all your
> soul and take council with your heart and a lesson from man who is but
> worms; if a person give you ten gold pieces or more, how deeply en-
> graved would his love be in your heart. And if he provides your support
> and the support of your children and of your household you would cer-
> tainly think, "This man which I have never seen and who has extended
> to me such kindness I would not be able to repay for all the goodness he
> has shown me should I live a thousand years. I would love him with all
> my heart and with all my soul; he could not command me to do anything
> that I would not do for him, because both my wealth and my being are
> his." As with the love of man so with the love of the Holy One, blessed
> be He, raised and exalted be His fame. It is He who gives sustenance to
> all, how much better that we should cleave to the love of the Creator, fear
> Him, nor transgress His commands whether great or small. For we do not
> know the reward of each commandment, and the punishment for trans-
> gressions though they appear light in our eyes, as it is written, *When the
> iniquity of my supplanters compasseth me about* (Psalm 49:6). The transgres-
> sions to which a man becomes habituated in this world will encompass

him on the Day of Judgement. If he is deserving his good deeds will bear witness for him. True and firm it is that we are not to transgress the commandments of our Creator even one of the small ones for a house full of gold and silver. If an individual says, "I will transgress a commandment and with the gold and silver they give me I will fulfill the difficult commandments. With this I will support the poor, invite wayfarers, I will do very many favors." These are the futile thoughts, for perhaps soon after the transgression he will die and not succeed to the gift. Moreover, if he should not die the money would soon be dissipated so that he dies in his sin. Come and see how much you should love your Creator and who does wonderful kindnesses with you, He creates you from a decayed drop, He gives you a soul, draws you forth from the belly, then gives you a mouth with which to speak, a heart to understand, ears to hear the pure words of His mouth, which are refined as silver and pure gold. It is He who leads you on the face of earth, who gives sustenance to all, who causes death and gives life to all. In His hand are the souls of all the living. It is He who distributes your share of bread. What is there to say? For the mouth is unable to speak, the ear unable to hear, for to Him all praise is as silence, there is no end to the length of His days, His years will have no end, He is the King of kings, the Holy One, blessed be His name and His fame. It is He who has created the heavens and earth, sea, and all that is therein. He is the provider of all, for His eyes are open upon all men's paths recompensing each according to his ways and the fruit of his deeds, whether good or bad. Behold it is He who sets forth before men two paths, the path of life and the path of death and says to you, *Choose life* (Deuteronomy 30:19). In spite of all this, we who are filled with worms do not think and do not set our hearts but to fill our appetites freely. We do not think that man's days are numbered, today he is here, tomorrow in the grace, that suddenly he dies. For no man rules over his spirit retaining it (forever). Therefore it is good for man to remove himself from all appetites and direct his heart to love and fear the Lord with all his heart at all times and revile the life of vanity. For we will not be able to humble ourselves and subdue our passion which thrusts us from the land of the living, except through subduing our heart and returning to our Maker in complete repentance, to serve Him and to do His will with a whole heart. Our sages have said, "Bread and salt shalt thou eat and water in measurement shall you drink and beware of gazing at women which drives a person from the world. Love humans and judge all people in the scale of merit." And this is what the Torah has said, *But in righteousness shalt thou judge thy neighbor* (Leviticus 19:15). Be humble before all, busy yourself with Torah, which is whole, pure and upright and do not praise yourself for it, because for this were you created.[1]

Some may ask how this intense religious experience is particularly mystical, since the generality of religious people seek to attain that same unity of life and thought with God. Indeed, the main purpose of mysticism for Judaism is that God is very real, and the desire of the mystic is "to feel and to enjoy Him; not only to obey but to approach Him." So says Abraham J. Heschel, the greatest theologian of Judaism in the twentieth century, who goes on: "They want to taste the whole wheat of spirit before it is ground by the millstones of reason. They would rather be overwhelmed by the symbols of the inconceivable than wield the definitions

of the superficial."[2] What, then, is the mystic doctrine of God in Judaism?
This is how Heschel answers that question:

Mystic intuition occurs at an outpost of the mind, dangerously detached from the main substance of the intellect. Operating as it were in no-mind's land, its place is hard to name, its communications with critical thinking often difficult and uncertain and the accounts of its discoveries not easy to decode. In its main representatives, the cabbala teaches that man's life can be a rallying point of the forces that tend toward God, that this world is charged with His presence and every object is a cue to His qualities. To the cabbalist, God is not a concept, a generalization, but a most specific reality; his thinking about Him full of forceful directness. But He who is "the Soul of all souls" is "the mystery of all mysteries." While the cabbalists speak of God as if they commanded a view of the Beyond, and were in possession of knowledge about the inner life of God, they also assure us that all notions fail when applied to Him, that He is beyond the grasp of the human mind and inaccessible to medita-tion. He is the *En Sof*, the Infinite, "the most Hidden of all Hidden." While there is an abysmal distance between Him and the world, He is also called All. "For all things are in Him and He is in all things. . . . He is both manifest and concealed. Manifest in order to uphold the all and concealed, for He is found nowhere. When He becomes manifest He projects nine brilliant lights that throw light in all directions. So, too, does a lamp throw brilliance in all directions, but when we approach the bril-liance we find there is nothing outside the lamp. So is the Holy ancient One, the Light of all Lights, the most Hidden of all Hidden. We can only find the light which He spreads and which appears and disappears. This light is called the Holy Name, and therefore All is One."

Thus, the "Most Recondite One Who is beyond cognition does reveal of Himself a tenuous and veiled brightness shining only along a narrow path which extends from Him. This is the brightness that irradiates all." The *En Sof* has granted us manifestations of His hidden life: He had de-scended to become the universe; He has revealed Himself to become the Lord of Israel. The ways in which the Infinite assumes the form of finite existence are called *Sefirot*. These are various aspects or forms of Divine action, spheres of Divine emanation. They are, as it were, the garments in which the Hidden God reveals Himself and acts in the universe, the channels through which His light is issued forth.[3]

Obviously, in so fresh and original a system, all the antecedent sym-bols and conceptions of Judaism are going to be revised and given new meanings. The single most striking revision is in the very definition of *Torah*. We know that for classical Judaism *Torah* means "revelation," and revelation is contained in various documents, some of them written down and handed on from Sinai, others transmitted orally from Sinai. But for the mystic, Torah also becomes a "mystic reality," as Heschel explains:

The Torah is an inexhaustible esoteric reality. To enter into its deep, hid-den strata is in itself a mystic goal. The Universe is an image of the Torah and the Torah is an image of God. For the Torah is "the Holy of Holies"; it consists entirely of the name of the Holy One, blessed be He. Every let-ter in it is bound up with that Name.

The Torah is the main source from which man can draw the secret wisdom and power of insight into the essence of things. "It is called Torah (lit.: showing) because it shows and reveals that which is hidden and unknown; and all life from above is comprised in it and issues from it." "The Torah contains all the deepest and most recondite mysteries; all sublime doctrines both disclosed and undisclosed; all essences both of the higher and the lower grades, of this world and of the world to come are to be found there." The source of wisdom is accessible to all, yet only few resort to it. "How stupid are men that they take no pains to know the ways of the Almighty by which the world is maintained. What prevents them? Their stupidity, because they do not study the Torah; for if they were to study the Torah they would know the ways of the Holy One, blessed be He."

The Torah has a double significance: literal and symbolic. Besides their plain, literal meaning, which is important, valid and never to be overlooked, the verses of the Torah possess an esoteric significance, "comprehensible only to the wise who are familiar with the ways of the Torah." "Happy is Israel to whom was given the sublime Torah, the Torah of truth. Perdition take anyone who maintains that any narrative in the Torah comes merely to tell us a piece of history and nothing more! If that were so, the Torah would not be what it assuredly is, to wit, the supernal Law, the Law of truth. Now if it is not dignified for a king of flesh and blood to engage in common talk, much less to write it down, is it conceivable that the most high King, the Holy One, blessed be He, was short of sacred subjects with which to fill the Torah, so that He had to collect such commonplace topics as the anecdotes of Esau, and Hagar, Laban's talks to Jacob, the words of Balaam and his ass, those of Balak, and of Zimri, and such-like, and make of them a Torah? If so, why is it called the 'Law of Truth'? Why do we read *The Law of the Lord is perfect. . . . The testimony of the Lord is sure. . . . The Ordinances of the Lord are true. . . . More to be desired are they than gold, yea, than much fine gold* (Psalm 19:8–11). But assuredly each word of the Torah signifies sublime things, so that this or that narrative, besides its meaning in and for itself, throws light on the all-encompassing Rule of the Torah."[4]

In Heschel's statement we see how it was that the long and influential tradition of mysticism in Judaism was able to reinforce and vivify rabbinic Judaism in its talmudic mode. It is clear that the mystic finds in Torah meanings and dimensions not perceived in the earlier phases of talmudic Judaism. In many ways the mysterious power of the mystic is to see what lesser eyes cannot perceive. But the perception is there, and to the mystic and his audience it was very real. So Torah took on a richer meaning than it had had, even for the rabbi. Thus Torah came to include both the literal meaning of the words and the deeper or symbolic meaning, the level of meaning far more profound than meets the eye. Torah was made to yield the meanings not solely of its sentences but now of each and every individual letter.

The essence of the mystic way is not contained within the notion of the deeper layers of meaning to be found within Torah. Rather, the essence of mysticism is the inquiry into the very essence of God. What made mysticism a powerful force in Judaism is the vivid encounter with God made possible in mysticism as it was not in any other mode of Judaism or Judaic religiosity. This is how Gershom C. Scholem explains the mystic encounter with God:

> The mystic strives to assure himself of the living presence of God, the God of the Bible, the God who is good, wise, just and merciful and the embodiment of all other positive attributes. But at the same time he is unwilling to renounce the idea of the hidden God who remains eternally unknowable in the depths of His own Self, or, to use the bold expression of the Kabbalists "in the depths of his nothingness." This hidden God may be without special attributes—the living God of whom the Revelation speaks, with whom all religion is concerned, must have attributes, which on another plane represent also the mystic's own scale of moral values: God is good, God is severe, God is merciful and just. . . . The mystic does not even recoil before the inference that in a higher sense there is a root of evil even in God. The benevolence of God is to the mystic not simply the negation of evil, but a whole sphere of divine light, in which God manifests Himself under this particular aspect of benevolence to the contemplation of the Kabbalist.[5]

In many ways, then, mysticism must be seen as the ultimate, logical conclusion of that mode of Judaism taking shape in the aftermath of the messianic disasters of the first and second century. For the encounter with God outside history and time—the direct realization of the knowledge of God, who in some measure is hidden and unknowable in the depths of His nothingness—removes the mystic from the one thing that rabbinic Judaism proposed to neutralize—namely, the vagaries of history. The essentially ahistorical quality of mystical thinking accounts for the ready home provided to mysticism by the form of Judaism that began with the Mishnah and the Talmud and, we now see, came to fruition and fulfillment, in the minds of many great Talmudists, in the mystical realization of the encounter with God's hidden self.

To what degree did the values of the rabbis of the Talmud and the values of the great philosophers and mystics actually influence the lives of ordinary folk? Were Jews truly the "people of Torah" that the rabbis, philosophers, and mystics wanted them to be? Next we turn to an ordinary man, and then we shall look at the spiritual traits of an ordinary woman —both of whom lived in the long centuries during which Judaism in its classical form predominated. At the end, when we discover in the writing of a pious and traditional woman an essentially fresh aspiration, we shall know that it is time to ask what has changed in the modern period of Judaism and why that change has taken place.

CHAPTER 23

An Ordinary Man

Christian anti-Semites have described life under the law—that is, under the Torah—in derogatory terms, denying that any true piety can emerge under the burden of so many petty rules and regulations. But the prayers we have studied contradict that judgment. Not only so, but when we examine the statements of ordinary people, we find rich evidence of a profound ethical life with God: women and men devoted to the holy way of life because they love God and want to live their lives and form their communities in accord with the covenant that God made with Israel at Mount Sinai. Life under the law has rightly been characterized by the New Testament scholar E. P. Sanders as a life of "covenantal nomism," meaning that Israel keeps the Torah in obedience to the covenant made by God with the holy people through the Torah.

So we come to ask, what of the common folk who lived out their days in a community shaped by the values of the Torah? What were their ideals? One insight is to be derived from the "ethical wills" written by fathers for their children. In the ethical will, the legator divides not his earthly property but his highest ideals. He asks his heirs to carry out those ideals. Such wills obviously present the father at his best, for, facing the prospect of death and judgment, the father hopes to show his best side and urge upon his children the highest and noblest ideals. The fact that ethical wills mirror ordinary folk ideals at an extraordinary moment is what makes them so interesting. The ideals of an average Jew are represented by the testament of Eleazar of Mainz, who died in 1357:

> These are the things which my sons and daughters shall do at my request. They shall go to the house of prayer morning and evening, and shall pay special regard to the Prayer and the *Shema*. So soon as the service is over, they shall occupy themselves a little with the Torah, the Psalms, or with works of charity.
>
> Their business must be conducted honestly, in their dealing both with Jew and gentile.

They must be gentle in their manners, and prompt to accede to every honorable request. They must not talk more than is necessary, by this will they be saved from slander, falsehood and frivolity.

They shall give an exact tithe of all their possessions; they shall never turn away a poor man empty-handed, but must give him what they can, be it much or little. If he beg a lodging overnight, and they know him not, let them provide him with the wherewithal to pay an innkeeper. Thus shall they satisfy the needs of the poor in every possible way.

My daughters must obey scrupulously the rules applying to women; modesty, sanctity, reverence, should mark their married lives. Marital intercourse must be modest and holy, with a spirit of restraint and delicacy, in reverence and silence. They shall be very punctilious and careful with their ritual bathing. They must respect their husbands, and must be invariably amiable to them. Husbands, on their part, must honor their wives more than themselves, and treat them with tender consideration. If they can by any means contrive it, my sons and daughters should live in communities, and not isolated from other Jews, so that their sons and daughters may learn the ways of Judaism. Even if compelled to solicit from others the money to pay a teacher, they must not let the young, of both sexes, go without instruction in the Torah. Marry your children, O my sons and daughters, as soon as their age is ripe, to members of respectable families.

Every Friday morning, they shall put themselves in careful trim for honoring the Sabbath, kindling the lamps while the day is still great, and in winter lighting the furnace before dark, to avoid desecrating the Sabbath (by kindling fire thereon). For due welcome to the Sabbath, the women must prepare beautiful candles.

In their relation to women, my sons must behave continently, avoiding mixed bathing and mixed dancing and all frivolous conversation, while my daughters ought not to speak much with strangers, nor jest nor dance with them. They ought to be always at home, and not be gadding about. They should not stand at the door, watching whatever passes. I ask, I command, that the daughters of my house be never without work to do, for idleness leads first to boredom, then to sin. But let them spin, or cook, or sew.

I earnestly beg my children to be tolerant and humble to all, as I was throughout my life. Should cause for dissension present itself, be slow to accept the quarrel; seek peace and pursue it with all the vigor at your command. Even if you suffer loss thereby, forbear and forgive, for God has many ways of feeding and sustaining His creatures. To the slanderer do not retaliate with counter-attack; and though it be proper to rebut false accusations, yet is it most desirable to set an example of reticence. You yourselves must avoid uttering any slander, for so will you win affection. In trade be true, never grasping at what belongs to another. For by avoiding these wrongs—scandal, falsehood, money-grubbing—men will surely find tranquility and affection. And against all evils, silence is the best safeguard. . . .

Whatever happiness befalls you, be it in monetary fortune or in the birth of children, be it some signal deliverances of any other of the many blessings which may come to you, be not stolidly unappreciative, like dumb cattle that utter no word of gratitude. But offer praises to the Rock who has befriended you, saying: "O give thanks unto the Lord, for He is good, for His mercy endureth for ever. Blessed art Thou, O Lord, who are good and dispenses good." Besides thanking God for His bounties at the moment they occur, also in your regular prayers let the memory of these personal favors prompt your hearts to special fervor during the utterance of the communal thanks. When words of gratitude are used in the liturgy, pause to reflect in silence on the goodness of God to you that day. And when ye make the response: "May Thy great Name be blessed," call to mind your own personal experiences of the divine favor.

Be very particular to keep your houses clean and tidy. I was always scrupulous on this point, for every injurious condition, and sickness and poverty, are to be found in foul dwellings. Be careful over the benedictions; accept no divine gift without paying back the Giver's part; and His part is man's grateful acknowledgment.

Every one of these good qualities becomes habitual with him who studies the Torah; for that study indeed leads to the formation of a noble character. Therefore, happy is he who toils in the Law! For this gracious toil fix daily times, of long or short duration, for it is the best of all works that a man can do. . . .

Be of the first ten in Synagogue, rising betimes for the purpose. Pray steadily with the congregation, giving due value to every letter and word, seeing that there are in the *Shema* 248 words, corresponding to the 248 limbs in the human body.

I beg of you, my sons and daughters, my wife and all the congregation, that no funeral oration be spoken in my honor. Do not carry my body on a bier but in a coach. Wash me clean, comb my hair, trim my nails, as I was wont to do in my life-time, so that I may go clean to my eternal rest, as I went clean to Synagogue every Sabbath day. If the ordinary officials dislike the duty, let adequate payment be made to some poor man who shall render this service carefully and not perfunctorily. At a distance of thirty cubits from the grave, they shall set my coffin on the ground, and drag me to the grave by a rope attached to the coffin. Every four cubits they shall stand and wait awhile, doing this in all seven times, so that I may find atonement for my sins. Put me in the ground at the right hand of my father, and if the space be a little narrow, I am sure that he loves we well enough to make room for me by his side. If this be altogether impossible, put me on his left, or near my grandmother, Yuta. Should this also be impractical, let me be buried by the side of my daughter.[1]

Where did the "way of Torah" lead? The human being before us clearly shapes his life and values by what Torah was supposed to mean. He stresses a life of prayer, study, and good deeds. A disciple of the sages should not bring Torah into disrepute by false dealing, and no distinction is made between Jew and Gentile. The disciple must be gentle and modest, not talk too much, and be careful to avoid slander. He must tithe and generously receive the poor man. Daughters must be modest and sons solicitous. Jews must live with other Jews, so as to sustain one another during the long exile. Living as a nation within other nations, governed by their own laws and under their own administrations, Jews had best seek one another out. Above all, one should borrow, even impoverish himself, to make certain his children study Torah. The Sabbath comes next in order of interest and then again an appeal for modesty, sobriety, and tolerance. Life is to be lived as a gift from God. Whatever happens, one must thank God, in public and private worship, on every possible occasion. The difference between man and beast is *gratitude*. And once more, all these virtues are the habits of the student of Torah. Study leads not to learning but to nobility. As to the rituals of death, they should be humble, even degrading, so that penance on earth may produce felicity in heaven.

You may well doubt that any ordinary person could live up to these high ideals. Indeed, the homely touch at the end of Eleazar's testament reminds us of his humanity: "Put me in the ground at the right hand of my father . . . he loves me well enough to make room . . . or near my grandmother . . . [or] by the side of my daughter." Life under Torah law was meant to produce a saint. Being men of flesh and blood, Jews cannot be thought everywhere and always to have replicated the values of the Torah; but what is important is that these values set the standard.[2] Until modern times, no others were widely adopted. Studying Torah, living in the traditional community, following the stable and serene way of life from Sabbath to Sabbath and from season to season—these were what it meant to be a Jew. It was a sweet life, sweeter than honey, full of piety, reverence, and beauty. So the pious Jew prayed, and continues to pray, day by day: "How good our lot! How pleasant our portion!"

CHAPTER 24

Two Extraordinary Women

At the end of our description of the way of Torah explored by Jews from the second to the nineteenth century, we return to the position of women. This is for two reasons. First, the matter is intrinsically important. We cannot understand a religion unless we make some sense of the role and position that religion accords half its adherents—women—just as we must attend to the values and ideals shaped for that religion's male adherents. Second, and still more importantly, one of the principal traits of the new era in the history of Judaism will be a shift in the status and role of women, along with women's aspirations for such a shift to take place.

We may point to important roles taken by women in Israelite politics, culture, and religion in biblical times. The Hebrew Scriptures speak of women who were important political figures, such as general, head of state, prophet. Women form the center of important biblical narratives from that of Miriam, the sister of Moses, through Deborah to Ruth, Esther, Bathsheba, and others. So there is no doubt that, within the complexities of a mosaic of biblical documents, one continuing trait is that women may come to the center of the stage and play a leading role. That this was so in exceptional circumstances—that men generally were the heads of state, prophets, generals, and other important political figures—is beside the point. Women could and did attain prominence.

There was one institution in ancient times in which women were afforded no role whatsoever and from which, in point of fact, they were essentially excluded. That was the Temple and with it the priesthood, which was no mean exclusion. The priestly law codes contained within Leviticus and Numbers take women very seriously and devote much attention to the status of women within the priesthood. But women's status was solely dependent on the priests, all of whom were males, and it was principally a vehicle for the sanctification of the priesthood. While some rites (for example, those performed after childbirth) were defined for women, no rites could be performed by women, who were not permitted into the holier part of the Temple buildings and were kept outside in a women's courtyard. By contrast, the royal house could put forward queens as well as kings, the prophetic movement could put forward a Hulda along with a Jeremiah, and the great writers could pay attention to a Ruth and an Esther as much as to a David and a Solomon. We cannot now speculate on why the priesthood should have excluded all roles for women; we must only recognize that exclusion from Temple and priesthood as a fact.

In the first and second centuries, when movements took shape out of the priesthood and around the priestly ideals, the consequence of that fact became clear. Just as the priesthood excluded women, so its successor, the rabbinate, found little place for women. After the second century, we hear of a few if any women in the all-male society of the rabbinical schools (yeshivot). And for the next eighteen hundred years there is not a *single* woman associated with the writing of a commentary to the Talmud, the conduct of a rabbinical court, or the administration of the Jewish community as a rabbinical authority. The exclusion of women from the centers of learning and leadership does not, of course, mean that women were abused or disgraced. The contrary is the case. Every effort was made to preserve the rights, property, and dignity of women. But women could not preserve their own rights, property, or dignity. They formed a subordinated caste within the community of Judaism.

Now we must ask ourselves: Does the fact of their subordination mean women were alienated by the system? In the writings of Glückel of Hameln (1646–1724) we find that was not so. Indeed, if we now compare Glückel's letter to her children with the ethical will of Eleazar of Mainz— written three hundred years earlier!—we find much the same beliefs and ethical values. Glückel's message is the same and expresses precisely the same religious world view as Eleazar's.

> In my great grief and for my heart's ease I begin this book in the year of Creation 5451—God soon rejoice us and send us His redeemer soon. Amen.
>
> With the help of God, I began writing this, my dear children, upon the death of your good father in the hope of distracting my soul from the burdens laid upon it, and the bitter thought that we have lost our faithful shepherd. In this way I have managed to live through many wakeful nights, and springing from my bed have shortened the sleepless hours.
>
> I do not intend, my dear children, to compose and write for you a book of morals. Such I could not write, and our wise men have already written many. Moreover, we have our holy Torah in which we may find and learn all that we need for our journey through this world to the world to come. Of our beloved Torah we may seize hold. . . . We sinful men are in the world as if swimming in the sea and in danger of being drowned. But our great, merciful and kind God, in His great mercy, has thrown ropes into the sea that we may take hold of them and be saved. These are our holy Torah where is written what are the rewards and punishments for good and evil deeds. . . .
>
> I pray you this, my children: be patient, when the Lord, may He be praised, sends you a punishment, accept it with patience and do not

cease to pray to Him; perhaps He will have mercy upon you. . . . Therefore, my dear children, whatever you lose, have patience, for nothing is our own, everything is only a loan. . . . We men have been created for nothing else but to serve God and to keep His commandments and to obey the Torah, "for that is thy life, and the length of thy days."

The kernel of the Torah is: "Thou shalt love thy neighbour as thyself." But in our days we seldom find it so, and few are they who love their fellowmen with all their heart. On the contrary, if a man can contrive to ruin his neighbour nothing pleases him more. . . .

The best thing for you, my children, is to serve God from your heart without falsehood or deception, not giving out to people that you are one thing while, God forbid, in your heart you are another. Say your prayers with awe and devotion. During the time for prayers do not stand about and talk of other things. While prayers are being offered to the Creator of the world, hold it a great sin to engage another man in talk about an entirely different matter—shall God Almighty be kept waiting until you have finished your business?

Moreover, set aside a fixed time for the study of the Torah, as best you know how. Then diligently go about your business, for providing your wife and children with a decent livelihood is likewise a mitzwah—the command of God and the duty of man. We should, I say, put ourselves to great pains for our children, for on this the world is built, yet we must bear in mind that if children did as much for their parents, the children would quickly tire of it.

A bird once set out to cross a windy sea with its three fledglings. The sea was so wide and the wind so strong that the father bird was forced to carry his young, one by one, in his claws. When he was half-way across with the first fledgling the wind turned to a gale, and he said: "My child, look how I am struggling and risking my life in your behalf. When you are grown up, will you do as much for me and provide for my old age?" The fledgling replied: "Only bring me to safety, and when you are old I shall do everything you ask of me." Whereat the father bird dropped his child into the sea, and it drowned, and he said: "So shall it be done to such a liar as you." Then the father bird returned to the shore, set forth with his second fledgling, asked the same question, and receiving the same answer, drowned the second child with the cry "You, too, are a liar!" Finally he set out with the third fledgling, and when he asked the same question, the third and last fledgling replied: "My dear father, it is true you are struggling mightily and risking your life in my behalf, and I shall be wrong not to repay you when you are old, but I cannot bind myself. This though I can promise: when I am grown up and have children of my own, I shall do as much for them as you have done for me." Whereupon the father bird said: "Well spoken, my child, and wisely; your life I will spare and I will carry you to shore in safety."

Above all, my children, be honest in money matters, with both Jews and Gentiles, lest the name of Heaven be profaned. If you have in hand money or goods belonging to other people, give more care to them than if they were your own, so that, please God, you do no one a wrong. The first question put to a man in the next world is, whether he was faithful in his business dealings. Let a man work ever so hard amassing great wealth dishonestly, let him during his lifetime provide his children fat dowries and upon his death a rich heritage—yet woe, I say, and woe again to the wicked man who for the sake of enriching his children has lost his share in the world to come! For the fleeting moment he has sold Eternity.[1]

If we look in vain for evidence that Glückel is discontented with her status as a woman, it is because within the system her work is as important as her husband's. She shapes and transmits Judaism, as much as her husband. But she does it in a different context; she has a different job to do. And she carries out her work unselfconsciously and in a thoroughly accepting spirit.

A dramatic and profound shift took place in the consciousness and culture of the Jewish people of Europe and America in the nineteenth and twentieth centuries. That shift is captured in a letter written by one woman in 1906. One symptom of the great changes of modern times is the fact that women became conscious of their subordinated and secondary role in Judaism and undertook to change that role. One of the earliest and most effective leaders in this movement was Henrietta Szold, who founded the Women's Zionist Movement (Hadassah) and formed it into the single most important organization in American and world Zionism. When her mother died, she insisted on saying the memorial prayer *(kaddish)* in her mother's memory and refused the offer of a well-meaning male to say it on her behalf. This is what she replied in her letter:

> It is impossible for me to find words in which to tell you how deeply I was touched by your offer to act as *"Kaddish"* for my dear mother. I cannot even thank you—it is something that goes beyond thanks. It is beautiful, what you have offered to do—I shall never forget it.
>
> You will wonder, then, that I cannot accept your offer. Perhaps it would be best form not to try to explain to you in writing, but to wait until I see you to tell you why it is so. I know well, and appreciate what you say about, the Jewish custom; and Jewish custom is very dear and sacred to me. And yet I cannot ask you to say *Kaddish* after my mother. The *Kaddish* means to me that the survivor publicly and markedly manifests his wish and intention to assume the relation to the Jewish community which his parent had, and that so the chain of tradition remains unbroken from generation to generation, each adding its own link. You can do that for the generations of your family, I must do that for the generations of my family.
>
> I believe that the elimination of women from such duties was never intended by our law and custom—women were freed from positive duties when they could not perform them, but not when they could. It was never intended that, if they could perform them, their performance of them should not be considered as valuable and valid as when one of the male sex performed them. And of the *Kaddish* I feel sure this is particularly true.
>
> My mother had eight daughters and no son; and yet never did I hear a word of regret pass the lips of either my mother or my father that one of us was not a son. When my father died, my mother would not permit others to take her daughters' place in saying the *Kaddish,* and so I am sure I am acting in her spirit when I am moved to decline your offer. But beautiful your offer remains nevertheless, and, I repeat, I know full well

that it is much more in consonance with the generally accepted Jewish tradition than is my or my family's tradition. You understand me, don't you?[2]

It would not be possible to adduce a more eloquent statement of the shift toward modernity, represented for us by the change in the consciousness and aspirations of Jewish women, than this simple, deeply traditional statement. In the modern age some women would no longer accept the role, assigned to them in classical Judaism, of silent partner and member of a protected but subordinated caste. It is time to ask: What other changes took place? And how shall we account for them?

PART FIVE

The Torah in Modern Times: Continuity and Change

CHAPTER 25

The Historical Setting

When the Messiah comes, as the prayer says, he will sound a great trumpet to call the scattered people of Israel out of the four corners of creation and bring them back to Zion. In the past three hundred years the Jews have looked hopefully toward two Messiahs: one in the seventeenth century, Sabbatai Zevi, and the other in the twentieth century, Theodor Herzl, founder of Zionism. The contrast between the two provides a striking symbol of how classical Judaism has changed while remaining constant in the process of modernization. Sabbatai Zevi, with his apostle, Nathan of Gaza, proclaimed a messianic mission in 1664. Although in a crisis he renounced Judaism for Islam, his movement had by then spread like wildfire throughout the entire Jewish world. As a result, in the words of G. G. Scholem: "An emotional upheaval of immense force took place among the mass of the people, and for an entire year [1665–66] men lived a new life which for many years remained their first glimpse of a deeper spiritual reality."[1] In 1897 Theodor Herzl convened at Basel a world Zionist congress, there predicting that within fifty years a Jewish state would become a reality, as indeed it did.

What is striking about these two movements is their universal impact within Jewry: Both evoked a broad and international experience and set the issues for discussion among Jews from the Vistula to the Atlantic. Sabbatianism was the last such international movement before Zionism, and since the fulfillment of Zionism, no similarly worldwide movement has affected all Jewry. The contrast between the two is also instructive. Sabbatianism was religious and mystical; it phrased its message in strictly theological, kabbalistic terms. Sabbatai Zevi was "the Messiah" and played a central role in the metaphysical drama created by tensions within the godhead itself. Zionism was worldly, practical, and spoke in political and thoroughly secular terms. It identified the Jewish problem with sociological, economic, and cultural matters—not with sin and the need to atone, believe, or adopt a new mystical Messiah. Herzl was never "the Messiah," although Zionism used the ancient messianic Scriptures and images of Jewish messianism. The contrast is, therefore, between theological and ideological messianism. Nevertheless, it is rendered significant because both spiritual experiences, apart from the verbal explanations associated with them, exhibit striking features in common: an emotional, millennarian upheaval dividing friend from friend, leading some to despair and others to unworldly hope, and moving a great many to act in new ways.

What we understand by the process or phenomenon of modernization is illustrated in messianism; yet we must not be bound by the limitations of our illustration. The passage from religion and theology to politics and ideology marks only one way among many leading in much the same direction. Similar contrasts of tradition and modernity may be drawn between sacred revelation and secular enlightenment; between revealed law, guiding every action from heaven and lending supernatural significance to workaday behavior, and simple rules of accepted conduct; between Torah-study and research; between the life of the corporate community of the village, in which most Jews in Eastern European countries lived at the turn of the twentieth century, and that of the cold and impersonal city, in which most Jews in the West and in the state of Israel lived by the end of the same century. One may likewise point to the internationalization of "culture," in which appeals to singular revelation carry less weight than the demands of reason and in which parochialism, tribalism, and self-sustaining realms of discourse and meaning are set aside in favor of a single, universal language of thought and technology.

Let us first consider the two events in the modern history of the Jews that most decisively shaped the modern history of Judaism. The first was political "emancipation"—that is, the extension to Jews of the rights and privileges of full citizenship in the various countries in which they lived.[2] The first country to do so was the United States. Its Constitution extended full and equal rights to all Americans. Shortly thereafter, and of greater immediate consequence, came the emancipation of French Jewry in the aftermath of the Revolution of 1789. Later on, in the nineteenth century, British, German, and other Western European Jews achieved the same rights. The process was not smooth or easy, and the Jews were never really fully integrated into the political life of Western European countries. But it marked an immense change in Jews' status and condition.

What in fact had changed? Medieval society was organized by estates into a corporate society. Each estate had a specific status in law and life. As we have seen, that fact conformed to the realities of Jewish life. Jews had no reason to reject recognition as a particular class or estate among other such "corporations." If Jews as individuals were later on given "equality," they thereby lost their ethnic-religious autonomy.[3] The modern state demanded the abolition of corporate distinctions, seeking to make all men (and later, all women) equal under the law and therefore equally obligated to serve the state.

Emancipation in the form of the provision of equal rights, therefore, was a mixed blessing, especially because of the universal failure fully to realize those rights and to construct a society of equal opportunity and responsibility. As a result, Jewry lost more in security and autonomy than it gained in liberty and freedom. Traditional religious values were undermined; new values and ideals that took their place tended to separate the Jew from the classical tradition but to provide no certain ideals at all. Jews indeed were expected to "assimilate"—that is, to cease being Jews at all as a condition of their "acceptance" by Gentiles. It is clear that emancipation posed the most serious challenge to the Jews and their religious tradition since the destruction of the First Temple in 586 B.C.E. The modern crisis compares in novelty and depth to the crisis represented by the destruction of the first Temple and the removal of the Jewish population of Jerusalem to Babylonia. The premise of Jewish existence before the nineteenth century—that the Jews constituted a recognized entity, a group and a polity—now came under question. We have to look backward to 586 to find a comparable crisis of political consciousness.

Second, the crisis was greatly intensified by the growing racist and political anti-Semitism in Western countries, culminating in what Jews universally call the Holocaust. By this they refer to the destruction of approximately six million European Jews between 1933 and 1945, particularly in death factories built during the war after 1939. This historical event dominates Judaic theology today, just as it shapes the imagination of the Jewish people in many lands. To understand why, one must keep in mind the difference between the Holocaust and all former massacres, riots, expulsions, and other calamities suffered by Jewry over millennia. The first difference was quantitative: Six million Jews represented one out of every three Jews in the world in 1939. In all of human history, only the massacre of two million of the four million Armenian people by the Turks in World War I is comparable. And of all Jews alive in lands conquered by Germany after 1939, nearly 90 percent died. The second difference was the racist character of the massacres. When Christians killed Jews, they would spare those who converted to Christianity; but the Nazis spared no one, regarding as a Jew someone who had only a single Jewish grandparent. Formerly, Jews might be expelled. Now no one was permitted to escape. As Raul Hilberg puts it: "The missionaries of Christianity had said in effect, You have no right to live among us as Jews. The secular rulers who followed had proclaimed, You have no right to live among us. The German Nazi at last decreed, You have no right to live."[4] The third and most important difference was that the Holocaust was the achievement of an efficient, modern industrial state, prepared to invest vast efforts and sums in the creation of an industry producing one thing only: dead Jews. Nothing episodic, sporadic, or occasional characterized the Holocaust. On the contrary, it was systematic, orderly, well planned, and superbly carried out. Despite the need for war transport for troops, train schedules were drawn up to move hundreds of thousands of human beings, eventually millions; despite the scarcity of men and material, great concentration camps were built and staffed; gas chambers were manufactured even in preference to war production; corpses were carefully devoted to useful ends. True, Nazi special forces would also gather

Jewish communities in front of large ditches and then machine-gun the whole lot; but these special actions, carried out mainly in newly conquered territories in the east, could not in a few years have accounted for millions of people. The great bureaucracy required for this task, "operating with accelerating speed and ever-widening destructive effect, proceeded to annihilate the European Jews."[5]

To understand the impact of the Holocaust on the contemporary Jewish mind, you need only imagine yourself a Jew living with the knowledge and the nightmare that had you been in Europe at that time, you would have died. There was no way out. The nations of the world did practically nothing after 1939 and little enough before then. Nor did salvation come from another place.

Modern Judaism was the creation of European Jewry. And European Jewry was moving inexorably to destruction. Its creations lived on in various ways in America, Britain, Israel, and elsewhere, so that there is hardly an idea or an institution of contemporary Jewry whose roots do not go deep into nineteenth-century Europe. The historical foundation of modern Judaism is, therefore, deeply flawed. Raul Hilberg writes: "Jewry is faced with ultimate weapons. It has no deterrent. The Jews can live more freely now. They can also die more quickly. The summit is within sight. An abyss has opened below."[6] If what happened to the ancient Israelites bore heavy implications for the shape of Israelite religion, the same is so today. If the Exodus led to Sinai, then where does Auschwitz lead? What are its religious implications? One who broods on that perplexity has entered the contemporary Jewish situation.[7]

We shall study the history of Judaism in modern times through a consideration of what we mean by "modernization" and how we may ask the right questions about Jews' experience of modernity. Then in Chapter 26 we shall examine the process by which the traditional community disintegrated and the internal forces that produced its destruction. Third, in Chapters 27, 28, 29, and 30 we shall review four aspects of the tradition—theology, messianism, social ethics, and the study of Torah—and how they changed in modern times. Finally, Chapter 31 is a summary and Chapter 32 a prospect of what I see for the twenty-first century.

CHAPTER 26

For Some, the End of Traditional Society

Two powerful European movements, one intellectual, the other political, shook the foundations of the received social structure of the Judaism of the dual Torah. The intellectual movement was the Enlightenment, a movement of intellectuals who maintained that reason was the measure of all things and that, through rational planning, action, and its own best efforts, humanity could attain perfection. All things then had to withstand the test of reason. The political movement closely allied to the Enlightenment was the Emancipation, which recognized the rights of individuals as citizens, not differentiated by reason of ethnic or religious origin, but which did not recognize the standing of the caste or ethnic group or quasi-official community that the Jewish community had enjoyed for so long.

Jacob Katz, an Israeli historian, provides a comprehensive account of "traditional Judaism" on the threshold of modernization.[1] Defining "traditional society" as "a type of society which regards its existence as based upon a common body of knowledge and values handed down from the past," Katz stresses the commonalities of religion, nationhood, and messianic hope and traces the disintegrative effect on them of religious charisma in Hasidism and of rationalism in the Jewish Enlightenment.

To the end of the eighteenth century, when the "modern period" of the history of Judaism begins, Jewish society was corporate, segregated, and collective in emphasis. Jews in Europe spoke a common language, Yiddish, and regarded themselves as a separate nation, living within other nations and awaiting their ultimate return to their own land. The central social ideal was study of Torah, which would result in heavenly reward. The obligation to study the Torah, leading to an intense appreciation for intellectualism, prevented the sanctification of economic activity as an ultimate goal and ensured tradition's effective control over the people's value structure. Indeed, the study of tradition was the chief purpose of living. The community itself was governed by its own classical legal tradition, with the rabbi as judge and community official.

The *kehillah* (structure of community government) controlled economic activities, relations with non-Jews, family and social life, and matters of religion—including, of course, all aspects of culture and education. It was the structural embodiment of the corporate community.

How did this community disintegrate so that the focus of Judaism came to be the individual and the emphasis of Jewish thought the individual's personal religious needs and convictions? *It was not the result of external catastrophes.* Jewish society was badly shaken by the massacres of 1648–49, but the response of the community, as Katz points out, did not deviate from the traditional pattern: "There is no record of any program of action being instituted to prevent the recurrence of such an event . . . no political or social conclusions were drawn from the historical experience. As a matter of fact, the realistic explanations were overshadowed by the traditional view of divine providence, so that the lesson that emerged from the stocktaking was a religious-moral one."[2] It took the form of fasting, prayer, severe sumptuary laws, and rededication to study and observance of the Torah.

During the eighteenth century, Hasidism in Eastern Europe and *Haskalah* (Enlightenment) in the West undermined traditional society. These movements shattered the framework of the community, which had formerly been able to reconstitute itself following banishments and migrations, in the several localities.

Hasidism, a pietist movement recalling the contemporary Methodism of Britain and the Great Awakening of mid-eighteenth-century New England, weakened the fidelity of the people to the rabbinic lawyer's leadership by stressing the importance *not* of learning in the law but of religious charisma, the capacity to say particularly effective prayers, tell evocative stories, and engage in acts of a theurgic character. Existing institutions seemed to have lost their hold on large numbers of people. The situation was ripe for new social groups to take shape among people who had lost faith in the old ones. The Hasidic rabbi, called *tzaddik* (literally, righteous one), won the loyalty of such people through the force of his personality. He was regarded not as a mere wonder worker but as an intermediary between heaven and earth.

Hasidism was more than an adjustment to new social conditions or a movement of protest. In content, value, and structure, it was a revolution that set in a new light all preceding faith. One achieved holiness through Torah or through the *tzaddik* (by celebrating his holiness), but not through both. A movement within the community, Hasidism created sects in the traditional corporate society. Some followed the charismatic leader; others did not. The consequence of these doctrines and policies was a religious and social revolution based on a new requirement for leadership: not learning but personality. It resulted in the formation, within the body of the old community, of new and limited societies; in consequence, the traditional *kehillah* was destroyed.

The second force for modernization of traditional society was the Emancipation, which in France and Germany altogether revolutionized the basis of Jewish society by destroying both its legal and its philosophical foundation. External rather than internal in its impact, the Emancipation withdrew the political basis of Jewry by extending to the Jews the rights of citizens and at the same time denying Judaism the authority over Jews it had formerly exercised. It furthermore encouraged the development within Jewry of a new type of person, the *maskil* (illumined man), who mastered areas of human erudition formerly thought to be irrelevant to Jews. So the Enlightenment's processes of intellectual dissolution and the Emancipation's revision of the Jews' political status and condition reinforced one another. On account of the Emancipation, the *kehillah* lost its legal standing, and on account of the Enlightenment, some of its subjects opted out of the *kehillah* at the same time.

Now individual members of Jewish society began to interest themselves in the opinion of the Gentile world and to seek the esteem of non-Jews on the basis of Gentile values. Had Jews merely converted to Christianity, they would hardly have affected traditional society; but many left that society and yet chose to remain Jews. They plunged into a crisis of identity that has yet to find resolution.

As part of the Jewish community, although perhaps on its fringes, the *maskilim* held up to the tests of reason, intelligence, and nature the artifacts of the tradition that had formerly been accepted as part of the given, the revealed reality, of the world. And they did so aggressively and derisively. The values they projected were those of the neutral society, which they saw as the wave of the future. They criticized the economic structure of Jewish society, its occupational one-sidedness, the traditional organizations (whose compulsory authority they rejected), and the traditional system of education, which did nothing to prepare young people to participate in the new world then seen to be opening up.

They did not propose to abandon Jewish society but to "modernize" it. Values formerly held to be ends in themselves now came to be evaluated in terms of their usefulness and rationality—a usefulness measured not within the Jewish framework at all. The synagogue was seen as the locus of assemblage of the faithful for prayer rather than as the focus of community life, society, and culture, as in former times. The content and language of prayer, the architecture of the synagogue, and its ritual were among the earliest objects of a reformation. Most significantly, the traditional modes of social control, denunciation and excommunication, ceased to operate effectively. Deviants no longer saw themselves as sinners. They did not justify themselves by traditional values at all.

Modernization was hardly a broad, widespread phenomenon. It mattered in only a few places, and even there unevenly, to almost the present time. Although the *kehillah* in its late medieval form underwent vast changes, Jews' traditional personality and traditional pattern of living in many places did not. The Enlightenment's impact was limited to the upper classes, even in Germany until well into the nineteenth century. Hasidism was a mostly regional phenomenon, and after two generations, its fervor was directed into more or less traditional channels. Today, while remaining highly sectarian, it has become a bastion of "the tradition," in its least malleable forms.

More broadly still, the Jews in Moslem countries—apart from the gallicized urban upper classes—remained deeply a part of the traditional culture, not so much affirming intellectual *reasons* for remaining so as *practicing* the faith in its classical forms into the twentieth century. For many, arriving in the state of Israel also signified arrival in the twentieth century as we know it. The political changes we associated under the title of Emancipation had hardly reach Polish, Rumanian, and Russian Jewry before the Holocaust of 1933 to 1945. Furthermore, for many Jews in Western countries, the experience of modernization was objectionable; as we shall see, many rejected it. If a tradition changes, it is only for some; it never disintegrates for all.

It would be impossible to offer a fully adequate delimitation of the modernization of Judaism, for three reasons. First of all, substantial parts of the Jewish people never underwent such a process, including not only the Jews in Moslem countries but also very large segments of Eastern European Jewry. Second, even in the great cities, to which the majority of Central and Western European Jews had come by 1900, significant populations of traditionalists existed to the time of the Holocaust during World War II; in the Western countries, groups of traditionalists have continued to exist to the present day. Whether they are traditional in the way in which the seventeenth-century Jew was traditional is not the issue. The fact is that those qualities we have associated with traditionalism apply without qualification to large parts of Jewry and therefore to significant segments of Judaism in Israel, the United States, Great Britain, continental Europe, and elsewhere. Third, the inner dynamism of a living tradition is such that at no point may we arbitrarily arrest its development for purposes of definition and conclude that a given form is the tradition from which all that changes thereby deviates and therefore constitutes "modernization." Within the circles of the most traditional Jews, cultural phenomena are today accepted that a century ago would have been regarded as unacceptable; and yet, should we call such Jews modernists, the term would be deprived of any meaning whatever. In context, they think of themselves and are thought of by others as living within the classical tradition.

By this point in the discussion, we can begin to see some of the complexity of the problem of modernity. On the one hand, we have reviewed some of the climactic moments and experiences of the life of the Jew. We have seen that the Judaic religious tradition exercises a majestic force, a power, over the imagination and feeling, the mind and the soul, of the Jew. So we must ask how it was possible for large numbers of people to break the bonds that tied them to so glorious a world as that constructed by Judaism.

On the other hand, we have examined the immense changes in political and social life that overtook Jews in Western Europe and America in the nineteenth and twentieth centuries. The political status of the Jew radically changed; the Jews no longer formed a fairly closed social group but wanted to relate to non-Jews and get to know and live with them. In Western countries—the United States, Britain, France, Holland, Belgium, Canada, and Germany—Jews were granted full civil rights and were able to exercise them in some measure. The wonder is, then, why anyone should have held to the old way of life at all. How could anyone have resisted the appeal of the new age?

This is the paradox: the power of tradition and the force of modernity. The two spent themselves, to be sure, in the disasters of World War II. But by then the changes were pretty well in place. Western Jews (in the United States, France, Britain, and Canada, for example) clearly had found their way into the larger societies in which they were born and grew up. Few of them wanted to live on the fringes of culture and in tight little communities of faith. On the other hand, these same Jews clearly wanted not only to remain Jewish but also to remain Jewish in a religious way. Many of them aspired to regain access to that which their grandparents and great-grandparents had rejected. Indeed, as the great historian of American immigration, Marcus Lee Hansen, put it: "What the child [the first-generation American] wants to forget, the grandchild [the third generation] tries to remember."[3] To state Hansen's perception in terms of the religious history of contemporary Jews: The native-born Jew of the third and fourth and fifth generations past immigration (or "Emancipation") are fully acculturated, so much so that they too are in search of their roots.

The question becomes, then, whether the majesty of an alien world view may once more exert its reality-constructing power. To phrase the question in the language with which we began: Has the context, the natural system, of the Jewish people so vastly changed that the old, world-constructing system—Judaism—that made sense for so long can make sense no longer? Are the ecological data so new and unprecedented that a way of seeing the world that worked for so many generations of moderately skeptical, moderately optimistic people today can work no more? These are the issues.

But we have again moved ahead of ourselves. In stressing the paradox of modernity, we should not forget the complexity of the facts. What we shall now see is that wherever we turn, we find a very genuine question of how modern are the modern expressions of classical Judaic institutions, ideas, and ideals. Upon first glance, nothing is the same; upon second glance, nothing seems to have changed. Clearly, the problem is that there are continuities and there are changes. So we are puzzled at how to interpret what it is that we are, in fact, observing. But such puzzlement is, of course, natural to the study of religions.

In the four chapters that follow, we shall examine four significant themes within the Jewish tradition. In each instance we shall ask how the tradition has changed and how it has preserved continuities with the past. In no instance shall we be able to locate simple or obvious examples of modernization. In each we shall see that much has changed but much has remained the same. Nothing standing by itself is an adequate instance of pure, one-way modernization.

The four structures are not easily compared. The first, *theology*, Chapter 27, comprehends the ways in which thoughtful Jews have explained to themselves the central propositions of Judaism as a religious tradition. The modern consequences, in Reform and Orthodoxy, were intellectual and are here treated as mostly so; yet the social results of changes of mind are at least as significant. Different theological affirmations produced different social, economic, and cultural ideals and thus different styles of life. The changes at hand affected thought but also life-style: world view and way of life, just as with the received Judaic system of the dual Torah.

The second theme, *messianism,* Chapter 28, produced the Zionist movement—a chief formative factor in creating the state of Israel—so the direct consequence of the new messianism lay in political life instead of religious or cultural life. Yet here, too, we shall see important theological and cultural results.

The third theme, *social ethics,* Chapter 29, produced the most "secular" of all movements in modern Judaism: Jewish socialism in Eastern Europe and the United States. Jewish socialism was a movement of workers committed both to socialist ideology and ideals and to the improvement of the condition of Jews as part of the working class. In Europe the movement took the shape of the General Jewish Workers Bund (alliance) in Poland; this title was a contradiction in terms, for a party calling itself Marxist could hardly propose to solve a particular nationality problem and to limit its constituency to a single persecuted national minority. In the United States the movement created labor unions, supported social legislation, and joined in the struggle to achieve a decent standard of living for the vast majority of Jews and others who lived by their own labor. The Jewish socialists held classic Marxist views on religion, especially Judaism; but that most secular movement seems to have preserved the most profoundly religious theme of Jewish tradition—the primacy of morality—and hence to have revealed the most ambiguous result.

The fourth theme, *scholarship,* Chapter 30, is peculiarly Jewish, for the traditional impulse, which so dominated Jewish life, was to study the Torah. The highest virtues were those of the master of the Torah, and no value more deeply informed Jewish culture. Yet traditional learning and modern scholarship are by no means congruent .

These four facets of the Jewish tradition reveal changes in religious, political, historical, social, and intellectual ways of being Jewish. In the past century and a half, the Jews have endured a lingering crisis of identity, for they have not agreed since the eighteenth century on the most basic propositions of self-definition, as we saw at the outset. Some Jews have found it possible to exhaust the meaning of Jewishness in religion, narrowly construed as the West defines *religion*—that is, faith and cult—while some have expressed it in nationalism, equally narrowly defined in terms of sovereignty, state, and flag. Some expressed their Jewishness in socialism, the new homeland for an international folk; and some few in scholarship, understood in the university way as the detached and open-minded, nonprotagonistic study of a past long dead and gone.

These have not been the only options. Vast numbers of Jews have found a satisfying expression of their Judaism through philanthropic, nonsectarian enterprises; others through clinging close to an ethnic group, in ghettos of the assimilated in all but name; and still others in intense participation, largely with other Jews, in the most advanced cultural enterprises of the day. And of course we cannot ignore the fact that, for many Jews, modernization signified the end of Jewishness altogether. In the nineteenth and twentieth centuries, as the changes of modernity affected Jews of the first generation of the new age, many converted to the dominant religion of their own society, by becoming Anglican, Lutheran, Roman Catholic, Greek Orthodox—or, in the Soviet bloc, by joining the Communist party. Other Jews lapsed into a curious condition in which they did not practice Judaism but also did not become "something else." Of these, some simply walked out of the Jewish world. Others abandoned Judaism but developed a mode of life deemed in their setting to be distinctively Jewish. So modernization not only ended "Jewishness"; more interestingly, it vastly complicated the modes by which people who were Jewish interpreted for themselves and in the contexts of their own lives just what, if anything, that fact was supposed to mean.

CHAPTER 27

Theology: Reform and Orthodoxy

Since the nineteenth century, the efforts of Judaic theologians have been devoted to formulating a "modern" statement of the faith, congruous with contemporary philosophy. In this regard, the theologians resumed that philosophical mode of thought and expression that the medieval philosophers had undertaken, in the tradition of Halevi and Maimonides. But the issue now has shifted. Earlier, the philosophers asked how to reconcile reason and science, represented by Aristotle, with the faith of the Torah. Now the philosopher-theologians address the political rather than the intellectual challenges of the hour. One chief issue faced by these thinkers has been this: Having abandoned what I conceive to be "the traditional faith," do I thereby cease to be a Jew?

It is a very slight step from such a question to a sociological, rather than a theological, reply. Many have not hesitated to take that step: Your "Jewish identity" remains valid. Each of us may supply whatever reasons we choose, but none of us is likely to conceive of a more striking transformation of theological into ideological language than the very question with which such discourse begins. The issue of "identity," then, is sociological, not theological. Nor are the concomitant issues—survival, consensus, commitment—less secular. Central issues of the Judaic tradition have, therefore, taken on a secular character in the hands of modern Judaic theologians.

The most interesting cases of theological modernization are Reform Judaism and Orthodox Judaism. We shall concentrate on these groups, even though numerous individual thinkers would also have supplied interesting examples.

Reform Judaism, as its name implies, began as an effort to reform the classical tradition. The "Judaic Reformation" proceeded on two levels: that of the virtuosi and that of the masses.

Large numbers of Jews in the great cities of Germany—and later on in France, Britain, and the United States—responded to the new situation of

Emancipation by acculturation. They thereby sought to meet the requirements of the world to which they supposed they were invited. Accepted
as citizens, they abandoned any pretense of separate nationality. Granted
full economic equality, they shaped their own economic ideals to conform
to those of the majority. They were desperately eager to deserve the
promises of cultural emancipation. Like the *maskilim* (enlightened ones) a
generation or two earlier, they examined their cult to discover those practices that were alien to the now interested world and determined to do
away with them.

These were *not* Jews who would choose the road of assimilation
through conversion, perfunctory or otherwise. They chose to remain Jews
and retain Judaism. One might say they wanted to be Jews but not too
"Jewish"—not so "Jewish" that they could not be ordinary people achieving a place in the undifferentiated society. This they wanted so badly that
they saw and eagerly seized upon a welcome that few Gentiles, if any,
really proffered.

The religious virtuosi—those who had a better European education, a
richer family experience, a deeper involvement in the tradition to begin
with—had the task of mediating between "the tradition" and the changes
they saw about them and enthusiastically approved. For them, change
became *reform*. The direction of the people proved to be providential. As
Solomon Freehof wrote: "It was the Reformers who hailed the process
and believed in it."[1] They founded their reformation on the concept that
"essential Judaism" in its pure form required none of the measures that
separated the Jew from other enlightened people but consisted rather of
beliefs and ethics, beliefs that were rational and destined in time to con-
vince all mankind and ethics that were universal and far in advance of
any available from other sources. Freehof commented: "Reform Judaism
is the first flaming up of direct world-idealism in Judaism since the days
of Second Isaiah."

Isolating the prophets as the true exponents of Judaism, the reformers
chose within the messages of the prophets those texts that best served as
useful pretexts for the liberalism of the age. The reformers looked back
on the "golden age" when Judaism spoke to all mankind of the obligations of justice and mercy. It was the message they saw to be essential.
All else was expendable. So the social ideals of the masses, who yearned
for a liberal society in which even Jews would find acceptance, and those
of "essential Judaism" were identical. The necessary changes would indeed constitute a reformation and return to *that time* of the true and un-
adorned faith.

But more than this, the reformers turned not only back to a golden age
of "uncorrupted Judaism" but also forward to a golden age in the future,
that time when bigotry and injustice would cease. They exhibited an idealism, an almost otherworldly confidence in mankind, that suggests a
radical disjuncture between their fantasies on the one hand and reality on
the other. Jews were excluded from the universities, ridiculed in the pul-
pits, libeled in the newspapers, insulted in private life. Yet they saw humanity as God's partners in the rebuilding of creation. They had the ef-
frontery even to see themselves as bearers of a mission to mankind: God's

dominion would be realized only through Judaism. The Jews had, they believed, an inherited, innate ability to give the world an ethical consciousness. In the symphony of the nations (so common a metaphor in these decades) Jews would play the ethical melody.

Orthodoxy is a creation of the reformation of Judaism, for only in response to the reformers did traditionalists self-consciously formulate what they regarded as orthodox about Judaism.

The earliest organized expression of Reform Judaism came to light after the turn of the nineteenth century. It was only four or five decades later that Orthodoxy in Germany came to self-conscious expression. Reformism precipitated the creation of Orthodoxy, since Orthodox organizations were founded approximately a half century after the Reform movement took shape—not only in Germany, but also in the United States. Orthodoxy, too, accepted the premises of the reformation: that the Jews were going to live not only *among* Gentiles but *with* them and that therefore they had better learn the languages and adopt the culture of the West. But Orthodoxy settled on a different interpretation of what living with Gentiles must mean, a different ideal for modern Judaism. Orthodoxy stood for the tradition first, last, and always; it accepted, but only grudgingly affirmed, the conditions of modern life. Modernism was to be judged the criterion of Torah, not the contrary. What was up-to-date was, standing by itself, no source of truth, let alone revelation.

Underlying this presupposition, nonetheless, is a vast reformation in traditional attitudes. Before the Jews could conceive of themselves in such a new situation, they had to accept living with Gentiles as a good thing. They had to affirm it as the will of heaven, in a way in which they never had accepted or affirmed the high cultures of medieval and ancient times. Modernization long antedated both the modernist movement *and its opposition.* But the opposition at first was at a deep disadvantage, for it had to debate the issues already set by the reformation and to take a negative view where, in a more congenial situation, it might have found the grounds for affirming natural change as within the spirit of the Torah. That is to say, the Orthodox had to fight on the battlefield selected by the Reformers. The Reformers appealed to history as the court of judgment: Historical facts would settle issues of a theological character. They therefore called into doubt certain (although not all) principles of the Judaic system of the dual Torah, beginning with divine revelation of the Oral Torah itself. The Orthodox affirmed that the oral Torah, as much as the written Torah, came from God at Sinai. That profound and penetrating claim for the unity of all revelation was not readily explained within the positivist framework of the day, nor was it possible (or pertinent) to appeal to (mere) historical facts to validate it. But facts were at issue, and faith could scarcely compete. Still, not all the advantages favored Reform.

Favoring the Orthodox party were four factors. First was the natural conservatism of religious people who, within Judaism, followed not only the path of their parents but also the ways of God in heaven. These ways were set by traditional parents, who lent powerful psychic support to the Orthodox viewpoint.

Second, the Orthodox claimed that they represented the true and authentic Judaism. This claim was strengthened by the fact that the Orthodox were more like the preceding generations than were the reformers. The reformers' claim that they were "the true Judaism" had to be based upon a highly sophisticated, historicistic argument—namely, that if the prophets or the Pharisees were alive in the nineteenth century, they would have been Reform Jews; therefore, Reform Judaism was authentic and Orthodox Judaism was not. But that argument persuaded only those who believed in it to begin with. For the rest, the claim of Orthodoxy to historical authenticity seemed reasonable, for it conformed to their own observations of religious life.

Third, the virtuosi of Reform Judaism were concerned about authenticity, but the Reform laity were not. The Orthodox continued to attract those Jews most serious about Judaism. Orthodoxy therefore benefited from the high level of commitment of its lay men and women, people prepared to make every sacrifice for the faith. In a measure, reform was attractive not only to reformers but also to assimilationists. That is to say, whatever the virtuosi's intent, for lay followers the Reform movement was a vehicle of their own convenience, used by the passengers to reach a point quite outside the itinerary of the driver. Two sorts of Jews participated in the creation of the Reform movement. One was the virtuoso, the Jew who not only was raised in a traditional environment but took seriously the propositions of the tradition and therefore made changes on the basis of commitment and reflection. The other was the ordinary person who, while intending to remain a faithful Jew, could see no reason to preserve what he thought were outdated, "medieval," or simply outlandish habits of dress, nourishment, speech, prayer, and the like. For such people the Reform movement offered a satisfactory way to continue with the Judaic faith; they felt not the slightest interest in the rationalizations for that way. Thus, for example, praying in the manner of Protestant Christians—that is, in the vernacular, in decorous manner, with organ music and choirs, with men and women sitting together—was a sort of public worship with great appeal to German Jews eager to find acceptance among Gentiles not only for themselves as individuals but also for their faith. But those responsible for such changes needed to persuade themselves that greater, more solemn truths than merely aping the Gentile were expressed through the reform of the liturgy.

The fourth factor favoring Orthodox Judaism was that, with development of the Orthodox claim to constitute the one legitimate form of Judaism and to measure by itself the "authenticity" of all "deviant" forms, Orthodoxy came to offer a security and a certainty unavailable elsewhere. Its concept of a direct relationship between the individual's conformity to the tradition and the will of the Creator of the universe bore a powerful attraction for those seeking a safe way in the world and feeling less concerned with the golden age to come, although still hoping for it.

Just as not all Europeans were liberals, some preferring another way, so too not all Jews—not even most Jews, in many places—responded to the liberal message of the reformation. And many who did were in time won back to the "tradition"—in its Central European "cultured" form, to be sure—when Orthodoxy addressed itself to them in good German rather than in good Yiddish. What some wanted was merely to dress like Gentiles and speak like them—but to live, nonetheless, by patterns they believed were revealed at Sinai. The achievement of the Orthodox thinkers was to offer reassurance that certain parts of life were truly neutral; in so saying, they accomplished the grandest reformation of all.

Sampson Raphael Hirsch (1808–1888), the chief spokesman for Western European Orthodoxy, was raised in Germany. His knowledge of the traditional learning was acquired mainly through his own efforts. The chief influence on his thought about contemporary Judaism was Jacob Ettlinger, who stated: "Let not him who is engaged in the war of the Lord against the heretics be held back by the false argument that great is peace and that it is better to maintain the unity of all designated as Jews than to bring about disruption."[2] Such an affirmation of the sectarian option represents a strange attitude indeed among those who would lay claim to "sole legitimacy."

Hirsch, by contrast, in his *Nineteen Letters*,[3] issued no threats of excommunication but stressed the affirmative requirement to study the Torah, with the rationalistic, perhaps ironic, certainty that knowledge would yield assent. His optimism was different in form but not in substance from that of the reformers. When he settled in Frankfurt, he found a community dominated by the Reformation. At his death, he left it a bastion of Orthodoxy, originally established in separation from the "community"—that is, the government-recognized *Gemeinde*—which was Reform Judaism.

Hirsch accomplished this radical change chiefly by founding a school. He designed the curriculum so that the next generation would conform to the ideal by which he lived: "Torah and *Derekh Eretz*"—that is, traditional science combined with general secular enlightenment. Judaism, he held,

> . . . encompasses all of life, in the synagogue and in the kitchen. . . . To be a Jew—in a life which in its totality is borne on the world of the Lord and is perfected in harmony with the will of God—this is the scope and goal of Judaism. . . . In so far as a Jew is a Jew, his views and objectives become universal. He will not be a stranger to anything which is good, true, and beautiful in art and in science, in civilization and in learning. . . . He will hold firmly to this breadth of view in order to fulfill his mission as a Jew and to live up to the function of his Judaism in areas never imagined by his father.[4]

Hirsch therefore proposed a model of "the Jewish-man," who fears God, keeps the commandments, and looks at the "wonders of the Lord in nature and the mighty deeds of the Lord in history." He added, however, that "Jewish-man" brings about not only the redemption of Israel but also the redemption of all mankind. No less than the reformers', Hirsch's Reformation spoke of a "mission of Israel" and aimed at the "redemption of mankind"—both hallmarks of the liberal, enlightened German of the day.

Both Reform and Orthodox Judaism represent, therefore, modes of response to modernization. For both, the constants were Scriptures, concern for the religious dimension of existence, concentration on the historical traditional sciences (although in different ways) and concern for the community of Jews. These persisted, but in new forms. Hirsch's "Torah and *Derekh Eretz*," no less than the "science of Judaism" *(Wissenschaft des Judentums)* produced within the Reform movement, constituted a strikingly new approach to the study of the Torah. The rhetoric of Israel's mission, now focusing in both movements on the private person, reflected the new social datum of Jewish living—no longer as a nation but as individuals—and concealed, in both instances, the utter decay of the traditional social context. For both, concentration on the community and its structures, policies, and future involved considerable use of sociological language. For neither were the traditional categories of covenant and sacred community any longer characteristic of a broad and catholic concern for *all* Jews in a given place. Both addressed themselves, because the times required it, to German- or French- or English-speaking Jews.

Neither Orthodox nor Reform Judaism could conceive of a parochial and self-sustaining language of Jewish discourse. Both spoke of a mission of Israel to the world and conceived of redemption in terms at least relevant to the Gentile. This is not to suggest that the tradition in its earlier formulations was here misrepresented; but both Orthodox and Reform Judaism were very different from contemporary, premodern, archaic Judaism in Eastern Europe, North Africa, and elsewhere. Both were far more sophisticated, intellectual, articulate, and self-conscious than traditional Judaisms outside Western Europe.

The religious virtuosi of Reform and Orthodoxy were already prepared for a new formulation of the tradition long before either made an appearance. Indeed, in significant ways both represent a very considerable lag. One Orthodox rabbi said, "The New is forbidden by the Torah." Made in a polemical context, that statement conveyed a rather rigid and uncharacteristically negative position. The rigidity of Orthodoxy, moreover, is peculiarly modern and was called forth by changes in the quality of the Jews' way of living. We can hardly locate, in earlier times, an equivalent rejection of contemporary learning. Still, we have to recognize that contemporary learning, conducted by the Reform scholars, for its part served to validate Reform and discredit Orthodoxy. We can find only a few premodern examples of such paralysis in the face of the need to update legal doctrines. But in an age of change without discipline, any concession could lead no one knew where.

Quite obviously, it was a fearful inability to cope with changes that produced the claim that change was, for the most part, undesirable and even impossible. Change not only was *not* reform; it was the work of the devil. Similarly, the sectarianism of both Reform and Orthodox groups—their abandonment of the ambition to struggle with all Jews for the achievement of universal goals within a single, united community—constitutes a failure of nerve in the face of the diversities and inconstancies of the modern situation.

Modernization called forth many changes indeed, but those were produced by a tradition already much in flux and by men and women who had come a long way toward the modern situation before the challenges

CHAPTER 28

Nationality and Peoplehood: Messianism and Zionism

Throughout their history, from the exile to Babylonia in 586 B.C.E. onward, the Jews sustained the hope of returning to the homeland, and the very heart of their messianic belief—its symbols and fantasies—was shaped by that hope. Some Jews always remained in the Land of Israel, but all Jews until the nineteenth century expected to assemble to witness the resurrection of the dead there. Judaic messianism was, as Professor Joseph L. Blau emphasizes, invariably supposed to be a political phenomenon by contrast to the restorationism of non-Jews, in which Zion was in heaven, not on earth.[1] William Blake's "Jerusalem" could perhaps be built in England; the Zion of Jewish piety could *only* be the earthly, specific place. For this reason the early reformers found messianism an embarrassment.

When Napoleon asked the French Rabbinical Sanhedrin of 1807 whether those Jews born in France regarded France as their native country, the answer of the rabbis could only have been in the affirmative. Yet such an answer could not possibly have been a true one, except during the Reformation. Ludwig Philippson wrote:

> Formerly the Jews had striven to create a nation . . . but now their goal was to join other nations. . . . It was the task of the new age to form a general human society which would encompass all peoples organically. In the same way, it was the task of the Jews not to create their own nation . . . but rather to obtain from the other nations full acceptance into their society.[2]

Similarly, the West London Synagogue of British Jews heard from its first rabbi in 1845: "To this land [England] we attach ourselves with a patriotism as glowing, as with a devotion as fervent, and with a love as ardent and sincere as any class of our British non-Jewish fellow citizens."[3] One could duplicate that statement—and with it, its excessive protest—many times.

The Reformation emphasized that Judaism could eliminate the residue of its nationalistic phase, which survived in traditional doctrine and liturgy. The reformers saw messianism not as Zionist doctrine but as a call to the golden age in which a union of nations into one peaceful realm to serve their one true God would take place. The happy optimism that underlay these hopes and affirmations survived among some even after the murder of six million Jews in Europe during the Holocaust.

But for the assimilated Western Jews of Paris, Vienna, and London, the rise of virulent scientific and political anti-Semitism during the last third of the nineteenth century raised significant doubts. Nor did the political situation of Eastern Europe Jewry—characterized by pogroms, repression, and outright murder—provide reassurance. Mankind did not seem to be progressing very quickly toward that golden day.

Modern Zionism, the movement to establish a Jewish state in Palestine, represented a peculiar marriage of Western romantic nationalism and Eastern Jewish piety. The virtuosi of the movement were mostly Western, but the masses of followers were in the East. The Western Jewish intellectuals found that European culture barred them. Fustel de Coulanges's saying, "True patriotism is not love of the soil, but love of the past, reverence for the generations which have preceded us," in his book *The Ancient City*, at once excluded Jews (who were newcomers to French culture and could hardly share love for a French past that included banishment of their ancestors) and invited some of them to rediscover their own patriotism—that is, Zionism. The Jews could not share the "collective being" and could not be absorbed into a nation whose national past they did not share. The Dreyfus trial of 1893–94 involved one of the handful of Jewish officers in the French army; he was falsely accused of selling military secrets to Germany. Because of widespread anti-Semitism, Dreyfus was represented as an example of the bigoted notion that Jews were not loyal citizens. When he was publicly disgraced, the crowds shouted not "Down with the traitor!" but "Down with the Jews!" That fact forced upon the Viennese reporter Theodor Herzl a clear apprehension that the "Jewish problem" could be solved only by complete assimilation or complete evacuation. It occurred to no one in the West that extermination was an option, although the czarist Russians thought of it.

After and, it is generally held, in response to the Dreyfus trial, Herzl published *Der Judenstaat (The Jewish State)*. Its appearance in 1896, with the consequent founding of the World Zionist Organization in Basel in 1897, is conventionally dated the beginning of modern Zionism (although there were some earlier movements as well). One can hardly overemphasize the secularity of Herzl's vision. He did not appeal to religious sentiments but to modern secular nationalism. His view of anti-Semitism ignores the religious dimension altogether and stresses only economic and social causes. Modern anti-Semitism grows out of the emancipation of the Jews and their entry into competition with the middle classes. The Jews cannot cease to exist as Jews, for affliction increases their cohesiveness.

Herzl's solution was wholly practical: Choose a country to which Jews could go, perhaps Argentina. In fact, Uganda was made available by the British government a few years later, but the Zionist Congress of the day rejected that possibility, opting for Palestine alone. What was important to Herzl was a rational plan. The poor would go first and build the infrastructure of an economy; the middle class would follow to create trade, markets, and new opportunity. The first Zionist Congress was not a gathering of messianists but of sober women and men. Herzl's statement, "At Basel I founded the Jewish state," was not, however, a sober statement; nor was his following one: "The State is already found in essence, in the will of the people of the State." All that remained were mere practicalities.

Herzl's disciple, Max Nordau, held that Zionism resulted from nationalism and anti-Semitism. Had Zionism led to Uganda, one could have believed it. When Herzl proposed Uganda, he was defeated. The masses in the East had been heard from. They bitterly opposed any "Zion" but Jerusalem. To them, Zionism could mean only Zion; Jerusalem was in one place alone. The classical messianic language, much of which was already associated with Zion in the messianic era, was taken over by the Zionist movement, and it evoked a much more than political response in the Jewish hearts. After the murder of European Jewry, Zionism swept the field, and in the mid-twentieth century even the Reform movement affirmed it and contributed some of its major leaders. Only small groups within extreme Reform and Orthodox circles resisted. In the state of Israel today there are, in addition to the Orthodox religious-political parties like Mizrashi, also Orthodox religious-political parties that are not Zionist and do not affirm the Jewish state.

Calling a land-colonization fund, known in English as the Jewish National Fund, by the Hebrew words *Keren Kayemet Le-Yisrael* (the Eternal Fund of Israel) was a deliberate effort to evoke the talmudic *Keren Kayemet le-Olam HaBa* (Eternal Fund for the World to Come), which consisted of acts of merit, piety, or charity designed to produce a heavenly reward. To the doggedly religious ear, such a title was nothing less than blasphemy, for it made use of sacred language in a secular sense. But that represents the very ambiguity of Zionism: a strange marriage between Western, assimilated leaders, on the one hand, and Eastern traditionalists on the other.

The history of Zionism has not here been adumbrated, let alone exhausted; but for our purposes, its peculiarity has become clear. As Rabbi Arthur Hertzberg stated:

> Zionism cannot be typed, and therefore easily explained as a "normal" kind of national risorgimento [reorganization]. . . . From the Jewish perspective, messianism, and not nationalism, is the primary element in Zionism. . . . Writers too numerous to mention here have characterized the modern movement as "secular messianism," to indicate at once what is classical in Zionism—its eschatological purpose; and what is modern— the necessarily contemporary tools of political effort.

Hertzberg rejects this characterization as too simple. Rather, he sees as the crucial problem of Zionist ideology "the tension between the inherited messianic concept and the radically new meaning that Zionism, at its most modern, was proposing to give it."[4]

Hertzberg's analysis is very searching, but it seems to be precisely this tension that is acknowledged by those who have seen Zionism as a modernized, if not wholly secularized, messianism. Hertzberg greatly deepens the discussion when he says that the crisis is "not solely in the means but in the essential meaning of Jewish messianism . . . it is the most radical attempt in Jewish history to break out of the parochial molds of Jewish life in order to become part of the general history of man in the modern world. Hence we are face to face with a paradoxical truth: for the general historian finds it hard to define because it is too general."[5]

But insofar as Zionism aspired to create a state like other states and to normalize the existence of the Jews, it represented a massive movement toward assimilation. Its goal was to end the particular and peculiar Judaic way of living and to substitute for it the commonplace and universal modern mode of life. So while Zionism was expressive of the unique and special aspects of Judaic messianism and bound up with the most private hopes of Jewry, it served paradoxically as the means for ending the unique and making public what had been private. In creating the largest Jewish neighborhood in the world, where Jews lose a sense of being different, it broke Judaic existence out of its parochial mold and placed the Jews in the mainstream of international life.

CHAPTER 29

The Prophetic Tradition in Modern Times: The Torah and Ethics

Among the most influential ideologies in late nineteenth- and twentieth-century Jewry in Eastern Europe and the United States, and in the Zionist movement in both places, was Jewish socialism. If Reform and Orthodoxy are heirs to the traditional theology and Zionism to the traditional eschatology, then one must see Jewish socialism, a deeply secular movement by conviction and orientation, as the heir of the ethical and moral idealism that in traditional society had found expression in the vast legal enterprise of *halakhah* that lay at the heart of Jewish existence. Evidence of the popular appeal of Jewish socialism is found in the Jewish unions—for example, in the needle trades—with their social-democratic ideology and their powerful program of improving the lot of the working classes. These unions were mass movements among the Jews. The New York Jews also elected a socialist, Meyer London, to Congress and formed one of the principal constituencies of the New York Democratic party, particularly in the time of the New Deal.

No less than Zionism, Jewish socialism exhibited the many ambiguities and eccentricities of a modernized tradition: the psychic and emotional continuities and the formal differences. Zionism chose to restore the Hebrew language; Jewish socialism chose to use Yiddish. Zionism turned to the ancient land; Jewish socialism saw all lands as equally sacred in the struggle for humanity. Zionism's impact in practical terms proved significant mainly in the Middle East—that is, in the founding of the Jewish state—although, of course, the Zionist movement from 1897 to 1939 enjoyed massive support in Europe as well. For its part, Jewish socialism left its mark on the vast American Jewish community—a product far more directly the heir of Jewish socialism than of any other single force in modern Judaism—as well as on the state of Israel, with its socialist orientation over the first thirty years of its history. As we near the twenty-first century, Jewish socialism appears to recede into the past. The state of Israel moves in a different direction, and Jewish Americans find a comfortable place in the Republican Party as much as in the Democratic Party. But in its day, Jewish socialism formed a world view and provided a way of life for masses of Jews, both in Poland and Russia and also in the United States.

Nowadays, most people, Jews and non-Jews, regard Judaism as the foundation of American Jewish life. "We are Americans by nationality and Jews by religion" is frequently said. Although today's American Jews explain their difference from other Americans in terms of religious convictions, the earlier generations of Jews in this country did not. They regarded themselves as an ethnic group, and what was important about that ethnic group was not uniquely religion but also culture, language, and, especially, social ideals. The immigrant generation, to be sure, founded synagogues; but what excited them was the formation of trade unions, political movements, social welfare agencies—instrumentalities to create a better world. Their social idealism was perhaps born in the classical tradition, particularly in the prophetic teachings about the centrality of ethics and morality, but the Jewish socialists of the day did not regard themselves as within that tradition or as religious.

American Jewry now looks back on the supposed orthodoxy of its grandfathers, but the life of the Jewish neighborhoods, which the current generation would like to either idealize or forget, was socialist. Charles S. Liebman makes this quite clear.[1] The immigrants, he says, simply did not give their children a religious education. In 1908, only 28 percent of the Jewish children in New York City received any Jewish education at all. "The immigrants flocked instead to the public schools, to night classes, and to adult-education courses—not only for vocational purposes but for general cultural advancement."

It was only in the 1920s, after the wave of emigration from Eastern Europe spent itself, that traditional Judaism revived in Eastern Europe. Those who migrated before then were the least religious. Liebman calls their piety "situational or environmental" rather than personal, theological, or traditional. It was a matter of habit and culture, not faith. They had been told America was simply not *kosher*; yet they came. One can hardly turn back now and praise their piety. Renowned rabbis warned against emigration. If the immigrant generations were not Orthodox nor, quite evidently, Reform, what were they? Some of them were indeed traditional and observant, even though they braved the new world; others were socialists; the large mass of workers fell somewhere in between.

For a fair number, particularly in New York City, where masses settled, socialism replaced Judaism. The radicals, seeing "religion" as the opiate of the masses and its exponents as agents of reaction, could not but conceive of themselves as more truly heirs of prophecy and ethical rabbinism than others who made more vociferous claim to the legacy. What is it, then, that they affirmed, and how shall we assess it by "the tradition"? A poem by J. L. Kantor provides a testament to the radicals' faith:

We believe
—that misdeeds, injustice, falsehood, and murders will not reign forever, and a bright day will come when the sun will appear

—men will not die of hunger and wealth not created by its own labor
will disappear like smoke

—people will be enlightened and will not differentiate between man and
man; will no longer say, "Christian, Moslem, Jew," but will call each
other "Brother, friend, comrade"

—the secrets of nature will be revealed and people will dominate nature
instead of nature dominating them

—man will no longer work with the sweat of his brow; the forces of
nature will serve him as hands.[2]

Many of them marginal Jews, the radicals harbored sentiments that bore
so strong an affinity to the eschatological visions of Isaiah and other
prophets that one hardly knows how to interpret them. Obviously, they
did not set out to paraphrase prophetic vision and did not do so. Yet
how far away have they strayed from a tradition that both saw in a
starving child an affront to heaven and contained a grand variety of
proof texts for precisely the kind of social revolution espoused by the
radicals?

It is here that the complexity of our problem poses the severest challenges. It would be inviting to identify the new social idealism with the
elements within Jewish tradition that seem so obviously similar to it—for
example, the ethical will of Eleazar of Mainz (see Chapter 23). The radicals never offered a Jewish equivalent of Christian socialism. The radicals
delighted in conducting dances on the evening of the Day of Atonement.
They aroused consternation precisely among those who were held to be
"religious."

Our problem is not simplified, moreover, by the Jewish secularist ide-
ologists, who offer a statement of the "secularity" of the Jewish socialists
that is hardly irreligious. The secularists to whom I refer are the so-
called Yiddishists, who seek to preserve and enhance the Yiddish language as a major vehicle for Jewish creativity. In "Who Needs Yiddish?
A Study in Language and Ethics,"[3] Joseph C. Landis describes the Yiddish language as the embodiment of the ethic of European Jewry: "Jewish value and Jewish sense of life are embodied in the repatterned sentence style and structure, in the altered pronunciation and word order,
in the reshaped inflectional forms, and their derivatives, in the enlarged
vocabulary, in the created folk expressions and sayings, in the metaphors and allusions."

Yiddish's capacity to express man's obligation to be his brother's
keeper, to convey human relatedness, to express tenderness, endearment,
sentimentality, and, more than that, morality renders a language (surely
the most secular of all phenomena) into the instrument, as Landis says,
"in which Jewish *mentschlekhkayt* (humanity) expresses its religious
yidishkayt (Jewishness, Judaism)."

Yiddish, he adds, "is . . . the voice of Jewish ethic, the voice of Judaism
as a religiously centered pattern of life . . . the voice of Jewish loyalty and
self-acceptance, the voice of Jewish rejoicing in Jewishness." Even addressing the secular Jewish values of a language, therefore, an exponent
of the secular viewpoint returns very unashamedly to the religious core
of Jewish existence. Religious ethics and morality become embedded in a
language. The secular proponents of that language, even as they firmly

oppose piety and religion in commonplace forms, cannot for one instant truly divorce themselves from the religious tradition, and in the end they do not really want to.

It is this fact that renders our inquiry so delicate and tentative. On the one hand, Judaic theologians have been willing to argue that religion has functional value because it contributes to the survival of the Jewish people or is the bearer of certain values or ideas. On the other hand, secularists affirm values and ideas that in any other context would mark them as deeply pious Jews.

In modern times, the classical tradition evolved into an exceptionally complex phenomenon, so that an ethnic religion, dividing like an amoeba, became an ethnicism and a religion in the Western sense. The "religious" part of the tradition, narrowly construed, focused on the theological component. The "ethnic" part centered on the messianic and ethical component, if our understanding of Zionism and Jewish socialism makes sense.

As a concept, Judaism, understood to mean the Jewish religion (a datum to be studied by reference to creed, cult, liturgy, and even law), thus appears as the most modern phenomenon of all. The disintegration of Jewish tradition into Judaism, on the one hand, and Jewishness or culture, on the other, is the direct consequence of the modern experience. However, the tradition did not reveal the impact of modernization. Rather, the tradition grew and changed in a growing and changing context.

What has happened to the religiousness of men who either do not express their religiousness formally at all or, if they do, express it in new, supposedly untraditional ways? In so stating the question, we evoke a clear response. The tradition persisted in the very same patterns of the past. Its emphasis on learning was secularized, so that the Jews, who at the end of the nineteenth century were commonly believed to be unable to produce mathematicians and physicists, by the middle of the twentieth century had produced at least a few significant names. More broadly, the intellectual devotion was still present but had entered new channels. Study remained central, but *Torah* became a narrow corpus of books rather than a way of life. Intellectualism applied everywhere else.

The messianic hopefulness persisted, but in new ways. The strong stress on ethical and moral conduct received renewed emphasis. The theological suppleness continued; the traditional hesitation to spell out in great and rigid detail what, precisely, it had to say about God characterized modern religious thought as well. Theology, messianism, and ethics—the three pillars of Jewish tradition in earlier ages—continued strong and firm. But with substantial differences! In Jewish socialism, the ethical and messianic impulses were divorced from theology. In Reform and Orthodoxy alike, theology parted company from messianism by so reconstituting the messianic hope as to render it something entirely different from what it had been. Ancient, supernatural messianism was transformed into a rather secular nineteenth-century optimistic affirmation of the progress and infinite perfectibility of *this* world. In Zionism, as Hertzberg so trenchantly argued, the name remained the same, but all else changed. So, depending on how we interpret matters, we see the persistence of forms with changed content and of attitudes with a drastically reshaped rationale and even focus. From one perspective nothing seems to have changed, but from another nothing is the same.

CHAPTER 30

The Study of Torah in Modern Times: Yeshiva, Seminary, and University

The fourth case proves the most subtle. In the earlier ones, what was really modern and what was traditional seemed fairly clear. We could isolate the classical forms and the modern substance. In the realm of Jewish intellectualism, by contrast, the powerful impetus of the tradition, which laid tremendous stress on the study and transmission of sacred texts as an act of religious consequence, and the equally powerful influence of modern Western culture never ceased to play on each other. The reason the subject matters is very simple. From what has happened to the study of Torah in modern times we see how complex matters have become. The old endures. But alongside, new forms grow up. The received form of study of Torah in yeshivot flourishes in the United States, Europe, and the state of Israel. But alongside, in all three continents where Judaism is well represented, new forms of the study of the same holy books, as well as of other topics concerning Judaism and the Jews, have taken shape. One of these is the very classroom in which you are engaged in study about Judaism, among other religions—a place in which, until nearly this morning, the study of Judaism and its holy books was simply not known. Lines of this textbook are studied in yeshivot, in rabbinical schools, and also, now, in the university. Understanding that fact allows us to grasp how diverse Judaism, represented by its intellectual life, has become—and how interesting it now is.

Had we stood at the threshold of the nineteenth century with a vision of what was to come, we should have felt some confidence in predicting that the Jews would remain literate in their own holy books. Learning was so important in their lives and values that, whatever would happen, they would continue to place the highest value upon the educated person. So it would surely have seemed likely to any observer that whatever else would change, Jewish learning would remain a vital enterprise.

We could not have foreseen what actually happened: The Jews remained deeply devoted to all forms of learning, *except* to Jewish learning. They entered each field of modern science and scholarship as it opened to them, from natural and social science to classics, Romance languages, and finally English. Their children and grandchildren attended universities and entered the professions if they were able. Their great-grandchildren became professors in the very universities that fifty years earlier had excluded Jews.

At the same time, the traditional devotion to learning so changed that the one thing Jews ceased to study was the Jewish tradition. In the history of Judaism, we cannot locate a comparable situation in which the Jews so resolutely studied everything but their own sacred texts. The Jews were not all great talmudic scholars, but they ordinarily could participate in public prayer and in Torah study. The great Jewish physicians of the Middle Ages were also noted doctors of the law. The Jewish astronomers of Babylonia were also, and mainly, teachers of Torah. The masses of every age could read the Hebrew Bible in the original language; read a book of Jewish thought, broadly construed; and look respectfully upon those who wrote it. In the Jewish communities of the West today, "the people of the book" have long since forgotten the language in which it is written. The libraries of "the people of the book" contain the great literatures of the world but only the most banal and philistine examples of Jewish writing, if any at all. The expansion of taste came to everything but the Jewish tradition, which was rendered trivial and bourgeois. Experts in many subjects hardly even comprehended the profundity of their ignorance of Judaism in its historical forms. So one may suppose that the tradition of scholarship exhibits, in the end, the most striking phenomenon: the perfect and continuing viability of the intellectual tradition, along with its absolute de-Judaization.

But that is not the whole story of what has happened to Jewish learning. If among the masses the tradition of learning directed itself away from the holy books of Judaism, among the virtuosi a more interesting change took place in the development of the "science of Judaism."

Modern Jewish scholarship emerged first of all in Germany, where the nascent Reform movement, for essentially theological reasons, committed itself to *Wissenschaft* (science, learning). The motive of the reformers was originally to substantiate their claim that if no one could discover the "essence" of Judaism, if no one could reach back to the golden time in which the faith was pure and unembellished, then one might find the true *authority* for a reformation—namely, historical precedent. Against the legal precedent of the Orthodox, it was a powerful argument. It motivated the adoption of German science and its methodologies in the service of Jewish theology. Leopold Zunz, an early reformer, made this point quite clear in a letter to M. A. Stern, 8 December 1857: "I have discovered the one correct method which will both pave the way for historical insight and truly initiate a continued development based on firm foundation."

A second motive was the eagerness of the reformers for Gentile acceptance, so powerful a concern of their followers. That acceptance seemed to them more likely in the universities, which were supposedly centers of reason and enlightenment. Hence the adoption of university methods of study was important. Zunz never complained that the Orthodox did not read his books. But he did write to Theodor Nöldeke, a great professor of Semitics, that it was strange that the Christian scholars of Germany did not cite his works, that the *Zeitschrift* he edited was not even received by the University of Göttingen library. Zunz rightly saw this as "startling evidences of the narrowest kind of prejudice." Whatever tension characterized the early generations of Reform scholars, however, had resolved itself by the end of the nineteenth century, to be replaced by a phenomenon persisting even to this day: the transit from classical *yeshiva,* where Torah is studied as revelation, to university.

That transit, at first characteristic of the Reform movement alone, persisted throughout the whole era of modernization and became *the* shaping force in modern Jewish learning from about 1180 to the end of World War II. One generation after another of *yeshiva*-trained students went through the spiritual crisis of deciding that the Talmud did not encompass all worthwhile learning. There were other things worth knowing and doing and better ways to do them.

Of course, many who made such a decision went into other areas of learning entirely; but some (and these are most interesting for our purposes) sought to add to their *yeshiva* training the methods and sciences of the "West" and to achieve a synthesis between the tradition and the "modern world" as they understood it. These came to dominate modern Jewish scholarship in the United States, the Jewish community of Palestine (later the state of Israel), and Central Europe before World War II. The absence of traditional training, combined with the presence of spiritual initiation provided by a crisis of faith and conscience in abandoning the *yeshiva,* therefore, were regarded as insuperable obstacles in the path of a Jewish scholar.

We have so far concentrated on broad social structures, movements, and ideal types. We may now consider how a significant individual exemplified the process of modernization and suffered from it. He was Louis Ginzberg, professor of Talmud at the Jewish Theological Seminary of America for the first half of the twentieth century, a highly regarded *yeshiva* student in his youth and later a doctor of philosophy in Semitic philology in a German university. Ginzberg's magnum opus, his commentary on the Palestinian Talmud, was both modern and traditional— that is, modern in its choice of text, for the traditional academies neglected the Palestinian Talmud in favor of the Babylonian one, but modern in little else.

To be sure, Ginzberg's extensive philological training led to a new range of questions and interests, but his commentary remained just that—a *commentary*—mostly exegetical but always compendious. Texts were contrasted with one another not to make the traditional *hiddush* (new point) but to make something much like it in a modern mode. Stress was laid on finding the right "readings," but traditional doctors of the law were not indifferent to invariant readings. The texts were read, by and large, in a fundamentalist spirit. That is, if the text stated that a certain rabbi had issued a decree, it was assumed not only that such a decree was issued but that it was therefore carried out; stories were not sub-jected to the kind of higher criticism commonplace in biblical studies, classics, and history.

As in traditional literature, no serious effort was made to organize the data or to spell out in a clear and abstract language the consequences of the author's research. The only framework of organization was the text itself, just as it was in the traditional schools. No index was provided; nor was any very substantial introduction prepared to explain what the au-thor had contributed, although an elaborate statement about the Palestin-ian Talmud—in English, unlike the commentary itself—was included. The text was paradigmatic, exemplifying the divisions between the tradi-tional and modern modes in Ginzberg's mind.

Nor should it be thought that the man himself exhibited a more soundly integrated personality. As reported by his son, Ginzberg never fully achieved a separation from the attitudes and affirmations of the *yeshivot* of Eastern Europe, by the best of whose products he was trained —and fathered. He is quoted as believing that a Jew should eat *kosher* and think *tref* (that is, not *kosher*); he should conform to the traditional laws but preserve the freedom to think in new ways. Orthopraxy is not new in Judaism. What is new is the suspension of intellectual endeavor to unite traditional practice with a new way of understanding the tradition—that is, the effort to integrate faith and practice.

Ginzberg's failure to find some sort of an integrated perception of the faith is most dramatically illustrated by a simple fact. Toward the end of his life he grew increasingly concerned about the breach his approach and method had caused among his father and his father's father and him-self. His son, Eli Ginzberg, reports: "He told me regretfully that he could never have published his *Commentary* during his father's lifetime." The despair he felt at the death of his father four decades earlier seems an ap-propriate foil: "My father was the embodiment of all the noble and great Rabbinical Judaism has produced and his death takes away from me the concreteness of my 'Weltanschauung,'" he wrote. He later said: "I know my poor father did not die peacefully on account of my becoming a scholar instead of a gaon [talmudic sage] and on account of my bachelor-ship." Shortly afterward he married, but he was never able to retrace the path that had led him from the East.

Louis Ginzberg wrote:

> The vitality of an organism is shown in its power of adaptation. Judaism in modern time . . . was confronted with the almost insurmountable dif-ficulty of adapting itself to modern thought . . . Judaism passed from the fifteenth century into the nineteenth, and this could not take place with-out a formidable shock. That it withstood this shock is the best proof of the power and energy inherent in Judaism.

Ginzberg himself—making the transition from the scholarly modes of one world to those of another, required by the facts of psychology and the affirmations of theology not to give up the one in the acquisition of the other—more nearly absorbed that shock in his person than did others of his day. He seemed more aware of it, suffered more deeply from its effects, and in the end proved unable to preserve health within the tensions it imposed. Those who preceded him, like those who followed, accepted the given as normal. It was he who had to make his way across the abyss between traditional and modern scholarship.

This brings us to another figure who illustrates the shift in a field of learning from one institutional setting to another. He is Saul Lieberman. Born in Motol, near Pinsk in Byelorussia, Lieberman studied traditional Jewish sciences—the exegesis of the Babylonian Talmud and related documents, for instance—in the *yeshivas* of Malch and Slobodka. Leaving that subject, Lieberman went on to study medicine at the University of Kiev in the 1920s, went to what was then Palestine, and promptly left for France, where he continued his studies. He again settled in Jerusalem in 1928 and reverted to his original subject, particularly talmudic philology. But he added to his curriculum Greek language and literature, and this represented what was new. For it was not common for Talmud scholars to introduce classical philology into talmudic exegesis, although from the time of S. Krauss's *Griechische und Lateinische Lehnwörter im Talmud, Midrasch, und Targum* (1898–99), it was generally recognized that talmudic philology required knowledge of Greek. Accordingly, what Lieberman did was new for someone of his origins and interests but was commonplace for learning.

In the *yeshivas* only one of the two Talmuds, the Babylonian, was subjected to study. In defining the new approach to the received literature, Lieberman chose to concentrate on the other, the Talmud of the Land of Israel, also known as the Yerushalmi (for "Jerusalem Talmud"). This he did at the Hebrew University, where he was appointed lecturer in Talmud in 1931. In 1934 he became dean at the Harry Fischel Institute for Talmudic Research in Jerusalem. After his appointment at the Hebrew University terminated,* in 1940 he emigrated to the United States, where he became professor of Palestinian literature and institutions (meaning the Talmud of the Land of Israel, or the Yerushalmi) at the Jewish Theological Seminary of America, a rabbinical school for the education of rabbis for Conservative Jewish congregations. In 1949 he was appointed dean and in 1958 rector.

Lieberman's first book was called simply *On the Palestinian Talmud*, and in it he emended texts and conducted a set of lower critical studies. Although unconventional for the *yeshivas*, the intellectual enterprise—bits and pieces of novellae on isolated texts—was hardly new. A further set of mostly literary and philological studies followed. His greatest work was a systematic study of the Tosefta (1937–39), a compilation of sayings in the name of authorities who also appear in the Mishnah. His analytical and exegetical work, covering the entire Tosefta, a sizable document, proposed textual revisions based on a diversity of manuscript representa-

---

*The decisive impact of that termination on Lieberman's life and career—he left the country and went to America, he had to learn a new language and find a place for himself in a rabbinical seminary that was not Orthodox—cannot be overestimated.

tions and citations of the work in medieval commentaries and also supplied explanations for numerous difficult passages.

When Lieberman came to America, he decided to write in English and also to write on subjects of broad interest to his new scholarly environment—for example, historical and cultural topics. *Greek in Jewish Palestine* (1942) and *Hellenism in Jewish Palestine* (1950) dealt with a number of concrete cultural matters, and his one important historical effort, on the history of the Jews in Palestine, will presently occupy our attention. However, he abandoned the effort to address the larger academic world of America, as I shall argue, because he could not accomplish that task of reframing not only his mode of address but also his mode of thought. In the 1950s and for the remainder of his life, Lieberman reverted to Tosefta-exegesis, done in Hebrew, vastly expanding it in many volumes.

The work of the 1940s therefore captures Lieberman's effort at moving from one world to another, one country to another, and one paradigm of learning to another. Lieberman represents the transition from one institution to two others: from the old-world *yeshiva*, which pursued the exegetical study of commentaries to and codes of the law of Judaism, beginning with the Talmud of Babylonia, to an Israeli university and an American, non-Orthodox rabbinical seminary. In making that move, he sought a fresh program of inquiry into the received literature. He found it in the use of classical philology for the exegesis of words and phrases of the Talmud and related writings and in the compilation of a compendious commentary to a critical text of some of those same writings. At the Hebrew University, he continued the philological work he was trained to do in the *yeshivas*, but he did it on a broader basis and drew upon a wider range of information. That is to say, in the move from East European *yeshiva* to the Hebrew University, founded as it was on the German model, he studied the old books in new ways. The American move then challenged him to study new subjects, topics of history and culture, in ways new to him. That he could not do. Lieberman's move from *yeshiva* to university in the German tradition and onward to an American rabbinical seminary carried him over considerable territory.

The academy thinks in propositions: the *yeshiva* reads words and phrases like atoms, one by one. It is hardly surprising, therefore, that Lieberman just did not know how to compose coherent arguments made up of sentences joined together in the service of a common syllogism. In fact, he showed himself capable of exegesis of words and phrases but unable to write histories and treatises on culture. Thus Lieberman shows us how, at the end of the received paradigm of learning, in the movement from one institutional setting to another, the *forms* of the old system persist but are not understood and so enter a stage of decadence. Misunderstanding the received discipline of thought, he simply took it for granted that sustained, continuous argument, with one thought joined by proposition and logical sense to the next, was not part of cogent discourse. But then he found no alternative principle of cogent discourse to take the place of the fixed association that made sense in the *yeshiva* and provided self-evident connections between thought and thought. The result was that, when he had to address a Western reader and produce a set of coherent historical generalizations, he blundered. After a few efforts, he gave up trying entirely. What he was left to do after the 1940s was to redo work he had already done in the 1930s, only bigger and better.

A complete paragraph shows us how Lieberman's propensity to write through free association leads hither and yon but never to a cogently stated proposition, at best only to an implicit and somewhat confused one:

> [1] We conclude our short survey with the position of the Patriarch and the Jewish scholars in the Roman system of taxation. [2] The role of the former in the distribution of the tax-burden and his responsibility to-wards the government are [sic!] not clear. [3] However, it is certain that the Patriarch had to pay vast sums to the government and offer gifts to the officials. [4] The Midrash relates that the Patriarch asked R. Simeon b. Laqish to pray for him, because "the government is very wicked," and this is demonstrated by the following episode: "A woman brought the Patriarch a small salver (*diskarion*) with a knife on it. He took the knife and returned the salver to her. Then a courier (*beredarios, veredarius*) of the government came and he saw it, coveted it, and took it."[1]

I have numbered the sentences so that the simple point may be clear. Sentences 1 through 3 form a cogent statement. The break at sentence 4 is stunning. In fact, this is no paragraph at all, only a set of generalizations followed by a case that in no way proves commensurate, or even congruent, with the generalizations and, in my judgment, is not even relevant to the issue.

In his move from *yeshiva* to an American setting, Lieberman faced the task of shifting from one intellectual paradigm to another. The first was a somewhat modernized continuation of the exegetical-philological modality of the inherited system of thought. Just as in traditional study of the Talmud people read words and phrases and said things about them, so the so-called scientific (that is, *wissenschaftliche*) students of the Talmud did the same. They added attention to variant readings, and they learned languages not ordinarily learned in *yeshivas*. But what they did with what they knew was not different in morphology, in fundamental mode of logical discourse, from what people in *yeshivas* did. When he moved from Slobodka to Jerusalem, Lieberman moved to a world that was different from but intellectually continuous with the world in which he originated. When he left Jerusalem and came to New York, he encountered a different world altogether. He tried to meet its challenges but did not have the intellectual equipment to do so, and so he turned back to his earlier success with the Tosefta and recapitulated it. And as to the prior hope of presenting the Talmud of the Land of Israel with a critical text and an ample commentary, so opening it for contemporary study—beyond his earliest efforts and excepting only some bits and pieces on this and that—Lieberman never even tried. Nor did he encourage anyone else to.

To state the matter simply, what we find in Lieberman is simply the incapacity either to generalize or to compose a cogent propositional statement in which connections between two facts are made to yield a conclusion. Fixed association has in Lieberman's mind, as shown in his writing, given way to free association. He presents us with an exemplary figure who excelled at the hunting and gathering, the collecting and arranging of information, which is always best presented in the form of a commentary. But Lieberman in English presents us with an accurate portrait of the workings of the modern Judaic mind in transition. He shows us how difficult it was to make the move from the *yeshiva* to the academy; he never succeeded. In fact, Ginzberg was a far more successful figure, transferring the values of the academy to the *yeshiva*.

CHAPTER 31

The Unbroken Myth

We have traced much change, but also many points of continuity, in the four cases of modernization we have reviewed. From description and analysis we now move to interpretation. How are we to interpret the situation of modern Jews? I have suggested that archaic Judaism constituted a rich, mythic structure, realized in important elements in every sort of experience. The issue of modern Judaism is not whether Jews still believe in the old myths. It is rather how the old myths have been transformed. Which of them have vanished, ceased to shape the consciousness, the view of reality, of ordinary Jews? And which ones persist and continue to shape the Jewish interpretation of ordinary events? What we referred to as "the Jewish tradition" has become, in the felicitous phrase of Professor Ben Halpern "the Jewish consensus." Halpern says:

> If certain laws, rituals, linguistic and literary traditions, together with the myth of Exile and Redemption, were the universal values that bound Jews together, then with their loss the Jewish people should have disintegrated. But these values *were* lost and the Jews did *not* fall apart. In the nineteenth century, values which have been universal among traditional Jewry still continued to be shared—but only by part of the Jews. There were some who no longer shared them, yet these dissenters continued to be regarded as Jews by the remainder who preserved the old values. . . . Apparently there must have been a different "consensus" binding them together—that is, a set of values that were *universally* shared among the Jews.[1]

What were these values? Halpern denies that it is necessary to define them. He points out:

> What was the most striking thing . . . about the cohesion and the survival . . . of traditional Jewry? It was the fact that they were united and sur-

vived without many of the shared values that are generally believed to
hold a normal people together and constitute essential parts of the consensus of comparable groups.

Judaism had few dogmas, and the Jewish law and courts were backed by
little power or hierarchical authority.

We turn to Halpern to ask what constituted this inchoate consensus.
Halpern sees it in a "community of fate" rather than of "faith." He writes:
"Only because they are constantly involved in the consequences of each
other's acts need each care what the other wants." It was a consensus, too,
of shared sensitivity. The Jews remained what they had been in earlier
times: a singular people, not quite like any other. And Judaism, instead
of positing a providence receptive to the prayers and responsive to the
deeds of Jewry, became instead the repository of those experiences Jews
could share in common, however much they differed.

It seems to me, however, that the fundamental mythic structure in important ways is unbroken. Highly secular Jews continue not only to recognize the sociological facts of their group life but to interpret them as
important—that is, worth maintaining and transmitting to their children.
Difference is still destiny, still normative and meaningful. And the vast
majority of Jews, secular and religious, still continue to respond to this-
worldly events through the pattern of the classical Judaic myth.

By way of illustration, let me cite a guidebook—published by the
American Jewish Congress, a secular organization—to the monuments
and memorials in Europe and Israel in memory of the victims of the Holocaust. The booklet states:

> Why should the vacationer go out of his way to visit the places where
> European Jewry suffered its catastrophe? Not a vow of hate toward the
> murderers. Not a feeling of shame that a crime of such enormity should
> have taken place in our time. Not even the renewed pledge to be a "good
> Jew" in the future. We want only that the visitor standing at the gate of
> Dachau or the grave of Bergen Belsen recognize that he too was behind
> barbed wire; that his own children were led into the gas chamber.[2]

Here we have not merely an explicit reference to, not merely an echo of,
the Passover liturgy but rather an authentic example of participation in
its existence, in the mythic being that sees people as themselves redeemed
from Egyptian bondage, although they live in a free land many centuries
later.

Another telling example is the view, held almost universally by Jews,
that the events of Europe from 1933 to 1945 and of the Middle East from
1948 to 1969 (and beyond) are interrelated and meaningful in a more than
commonplace way. It was not just the killing of millions of people that
happened in Europe, not merely the creation of another state in the
Middle East; it was a holocaust and a rebirth, the fulfillment of prophecy,
interpreted by prophetic teachings about dry bones, the suffering servant,
and the return to Zion. These supposedly secular people see *themselves* as
having been asphyxiated at Auschwitz and reborn in the state of Israel.

They understand their group life in the most recent times as conforming to the paradigm of ancient prophecy. The state is not merely another nation, but the state of *Israel*. Events of the day remain highly charged and full of meaning.

Israelis and European and American Jews alike respond to ordinary happenings in an extraordinary way, and this response, it seems to me, is the very essence of mythic being. Whether we call the myth "religious" or not depends on our definition of religion; but the phenomenon of contemporary Jewish responses to, and Jewish shaping of, reality constitutes a striking continuation of archaic mythical structure, an exemplification of what it means to live in and by myth.

Let me confess that I have never read the vision of the valley of the dry bones without tears. We Jews were the dry bones in 1945, without hope. We Jews were given sinew, flesh, and the breath of life in 1948 and afterward—until in 1967 we returned to the old Temple wall. All these events bore immense meaning not only for the religious sector within Jewry but also for millions of secular, assimilated individuals who long had supposed they were part of no particular group, least of all the Jewish one into which they were born.

The myths of old live because no one thinks they are other than accurate and ordinary descriptions of what happens. What people claim they *know* to be true, not what they profess to *believe*, constitutes the testimony that myth continues to shape their view of reality. That events have meaning, that the only kid yet lives, that the dry bones have risen—these affirmations profoundly shape the contemporary Jewish imagination. As to creation, revelation, and redemption—the complex symbolism that embodies them and the action-symbols that express them—these too remain, if in subtle ways, central categories by which the world is understood and interpreted. Much has changed, but the people who began at Sinai to interpret reality *as a people*—that people endures. In the study of the history of religions in postarchaic times, Judaism must occupy a special place, for without the perspective of the history of religions, no one would imagine that today such a phenomenon as Judaism continues at all.

Still, perhaps Judaism does not endure. One might argue that what seems to be a continuity of myth—an abiding effort to interpret events in the light of ancient archetypes of suffering and atonement, disaster and salvation—is really sentimentality. How are we to know whether seeing oneself as saved from Auschwitz is merely practical wisdom or whether it is continuing participation in archaic mythical structures? Where does mythic being end and bourgeois nostalgia begin? Perhaps we have dignified the secular and profane artifacts of American Jewish middle-class life by our effort to understand them as something more profound than they really are. We have established no sound, theoretical criterion by which we may separate spurious and cheap emotionalism from exacting and penetrating spirituality.

If archaic piety is the only true piety, then the classical tradition of Judaism endures only within the circles of the archaic Orthodoxy in the state of Israel, Great Britain, the United States, and elsewhere. The larger part of world Jewry, then, cannot be said to constitute a religious group at all, and its cultural and imaginative life supplies no data for the study of religion in modern times. But if that is so, then one must admit modernity excludes the possibility of true religiosity. And such an admission denies the self-understanding of modern people, aware of the abyss between themselves and the classic formulation of their ancient religious traditions yet nonetheless certain of the authenticity and reality of their religious experience. Are we to take the modern people at their word? Then religiosity endures and, with it, the modern modes of Judaic religiosity described here. Perhaps it is too soon to tell, for modernity has been a brief experience, and its full meaning has yet to be deeply and completely apprehended. Meanwhile, we are left with ambiguity and perplexity. God alone knows that truth from fraud.

CHAPTER 32

Into the Twenty-First Century: The Age of New Beginnings

The last third of the twentieth century has witnessed a vast movement of "return to tradition," or reversion, affecting all of the Judaic systems of the past two hundred years, from Orthodoxy to Reform, inclusive of American, European, and Israeli Jewry. The Judaic system of reversion encompasses large numbers of Jews who have moved from an essentially secular and naturalist view to a profoundly religious and supernatural view of Israel as God's people and of themselves as well. They have adopted the way of life of the received Judaism of the dual Torah or of one of its continuators, whether Reform, Orthodox, or Conservative systems of Judaism. The single most striking trait of the contemporary Judaic religious world, in all its diversity, is the return to Judaism on the part of formerly secular Jews or the movement from less rigorous to more complete observance of the holy way of life. All together, these diverse phenomena fall under the category of reversion, "return to tradition" in theological language or renewed religiosity in more descriptive terms. Reversion both marks a movement and defines a particular Judaic system.

Let me make this picture of the return to Judaism more concrete. When, as happens not uncommonly, American Jews decide to observe the dietary laws and the Sabbath, to say prayers every day and to identify with a Torah-study circle in a *yeshiva*, they adopt a way of life and a world view new to them. The generality of American Jews have defined their lives in other terms. Reversion marks the entry of Jews not born and brought up within the Judaic system of the dual Torah into the way of life defined by the dual Torah and the adoption of the viewpoint and values of that same Torah. Reversioners enter into the Israel to whom the dual Torah speaks, entering an intense social life lived in a round of daily and Sabbath prayers, study sessions, celebrations. Leaving Judaic systems that favor or accommodate integration, they choose a Judaic system that, in effect if not in articulated policy, creates a life of segregation. The shift from world to world marks entry into a stunningly powerful Judaic system.

Yet in interpreting the Judaic mode and system of reversion, we may not take for granted that we witness a mere "return to tradition." Some maintain that the "return" is exactly that. Quite to the contrary, whatever is meant by "tradition," reversioners in their context represent new, not traditional choices. The reversioners do undertake to redefine—for themselves, but they are exemplary—that way of life and world view that they received as traditional from their parents. But that was *not* the received system of the dual Torah, its world view, its way of life. So to the reversioners the new is what (they say) is old, even as what was old is new to them. Accordingly, our analysis requires us to treat as fresh not the received system but the way the reversioners receive it: A system of reversion is fresh, even though that to which people return draws them (in its own terms) upward to Sinai.

Extant Judaisms of the last third of the twentieth century all bear the marks of reversion. When people wish to find their way home, they generally move over one chair. That could mean from total estrangement from the synagogue to involvement with a Reform temple, or it could mean from one Orthodox *yeshiva* of a less segregated character to another one that totally rejects secular learning. All the Judaic systems of the last third of the twentieth century have witnessed a renewal of observance and a return to more classical formulations of the faith. But a particular reversionary system has also taken shape. It has led utterly secular but searching young Jews into one or another of the Orthodox Judaic systems both in America and in the state of Israel. Let us speak first of the movement that imparted a style of its own to existing Judaisms, all of which at the end of the twentieth century saw themselves as "more traditional" than they had earlier been.

Reversion to Judaism in America began with the third generation, the grandchildren of the immigrants of 1880–1920, when millions of Eastern European Jews came to this country. But it reached its height with the fourth generation and beyond, and it now is obvious that reversion will mark the formation of Judaic systems into the twenty-first century. That movement that I have called "reversion" uses the language of "return," which in Hebrew, as *teshuvah*, bears the further sense of repentance. The Judaic systems of return or repentance invoke profoundly moral and theological dimensions that are not characteristic of the four movements reviewed in previous chapters. All of the Judaic systems of the late nineteenth and twentieth centuries explained a process of distance, a movement away from "the tradition." The Judaic style and system of the present propose to account for the opposite: a return, a closing of the gap between the Jew and the Torah.

That is the explanation for using the word *return* to describe the movement to the Judaic way of life and a religious rather than secular world view. Reversionary Judaisms see Israel as God's people, who *by nature and by definition* should keep the Torah. All Jews who do not keep the Torah ought to return to their true calling and character. So the title of the movement expresses its world view and its theory of who is Israel and what it is natural for Israel to become. Jews are perceived as alienated from "the Tradition" to which they must "return." The way of life, on the surface, is simply that mode of behavior prescribed by "the Tradition" for whatever chair the reversioner chooses to occupy.

We may wonder why Jews growing up in secular circumstances opt for a religious Judaism. More important, we want to know how that tendency on the part of individuals became a movement and generated the one fresh Judaism that we see as we turn toward the twenty-first century. To answer these questions we have to take note of the highly secular character of American Judaism, which stresses institutions and organizations rather than the inner life of faith, learning, and observance. That system has provided a mode of "being Jewish" in the context of an open and free society, when one wanted to be both Jewish and also part of an undifferentiated society. It involved essentially secular activity—fund raising, political organizing—and left untouched the inner life and values of the participants. But the success of American Judaism has had an unexpected effect. People took seriously the powerful emotions elicited by the appeals characteristic of fund-raising and organizational propaganda, such as rehearsals of the Holocaust and engagement with the ongoing crises of the state of Israel. American Jews were sold a version of Judaism that they find partial and incomplete.

As the 1970s unfolded, the stress on a high level of emotion, joined to only occasional activity and then essentially neutral activity, affected younger people in a curious way. People sold on the centrality of "being Jewish" in their lives required modes of expression that affected their lives more deeply and in more ways, rather than the limited way of life offered by American Judaism. In search once more for values, rejecting what they deemed the superficial, merely public Jewish activities of their parents, they resolved that tension between being Jewish and not being too Jewish. They looked not for activity but for community, not for an occasional emotional binge but for an enduring place and partnership: a covenant. In America, reversioners have come from Reform and secular backgrounds, Conservative and Orthodox ones. It hardly matters. In all cases we find a conversion process, a taking up of a totally new way of life and a rejection of the one inherited from parents. In the state of Israel, reversioners derive from three different sources: Jews from America, Israelis of European background, and Israelis of Asian or African origin.[1] The movement dates from the mid-1960s and begins in a rejection of Western culture. So much for reversion as a generalized characteristic of diverse Judaic systems.

Reversion has formed not only a mode and a style for Judaic systems of all sorts but also a Judaic system of its own. The definitive chronicle of the matter, by Janet Aviad, provides a systematic picture of the ideology and way of life as well as a synoptic portrait of the movement as a whole. The movement's American component derived, she says, from the youth rebellion of the 1960s:

> Protesting a war they regarded as immoral, a situation that permitted terrible injustices to ethnic minorities, what appeared as a wasteful direc-

tionless use of technology, youth struck out in various directions. One direction was toward new forms of a religious life.[2]

Involved was a rejection of the "tradition of skeptical, secular intellectuality which has served as the prime vehicle for three hundred years of scientific and technical work in the West." These reversioners had earlier in the 1960s experimented with diverse matters, including drugs, poetry, and religion. Among the religions, some Jews tried Judaism. The quest involved travel, and Judaism "was often only the end station of a long search."[3] They came to Judaism through chance meetings with rabbis or religious Jews but stayed there because of the *yeshivas* that received them. Yet another group of reversioners derived from Reform and Conservative synagogues; they wanted to improve their knowledge and raise their level of practical observance of piety. A further group, Israelis of Western background, compared overall with this second group. They had seen themselves as secular but sought to become, in Israeli terms, religious. Their search for meaning brought them to the *yeshivas* ready to receive them. The final group Aviad surveys were Israelis of poorer and Asian or African origin. To them, too, reversion represented a religious conversion from life "experienced as empty or meaningless to one experienced as fully, whole, and holy."[4]

In all, we deal with a Jewish expression of a common, international youth culture of the 1970s and 1980s, just as we found in American Judaism a version, in a Judaic idiom, of a larger cultural development in American life of the 1960s and early 1970s. When the massive rise in the birth rate following World War II took place, it pointed the way to, among other things, the youth culture that would emerge twenty years later. When we find that Jews rejected the values they deemed secular and shallow and opted for a new way of life they found authentic and Godly, we do well to wonder whether, in other groups, young people were reaching the same conclusions. A generation in search, a shared quest for something to transcend the ("merely") material achievements—that generation grew up in the prosperity that followed the end of World War II.

These were children of successful parents, with leisure and resources to go in quest. Some turned to drugs, others to social concerns, still others to a search for a faith that would demand more than the (to them shallow, compromising) religiosity of their parents. Whether the search led to Roman Catholic Pentecostalism, Protestant Biblical affirmation (called "fundamentalism"), Judaic reversion, Islamic renewal from Malaya to Morocco (also called "fundamentalism" or "extremism"), the international youth movement exhibits strikingly uniform traits: young people in rebellion against the parents' ways, in search of something more exacting and rigorous.

If the Judaism of the dual Torah insisted that Jews are not only Jews all the time but never anything else, then we may characterize as a return to that theory of Israel the movement of reversion. But it is only in that sense. For as an acutely contemporary movement, part of a large-scale rejection of secular, humanistic, and liberal values of a generation concerned with living an affable life, the reversion to Judaism presented much that was fresh, unprecedented, but above all selective.

The reversioners in fact formed part of a larger world movement, a youth movement of resentment of the parents' generation and affirmation of the children's: a Jewish equivalent of the Cultural Revolution of far-away China. They expressed in the Judaic idiom an international message and viewpoint, no less than did Jewish socialism, Yiddishism, Zionism, and in their way, Reform, Orthodox, and Conservative Judaisms. Let us review the simple facts. Jewish socialism was part of international socialism; Yiddishism, idiomatic expression of romantic linguistic nationalism; Zionism, the Jewish statement of ethnic nationalism. Reform, Orthodox, and Conservative Judaisms presented in their arguments and modes of thought little more than Judaic versions of Protestant historicistic theology in the aftermath of Kant and Hegel. All these Judaic systems were composed within categories available, so to speak, in the larger world of humanity. And so were the reversionary Judaisms of the later decades of the twentieth century.

The system of reversion drew its categories, its values, its goals from a larger setting as well. These it then adapted to the Judaic circumstance: a totally fresh, totally new, totally autonomous Judaic system. Was the system invented or discovered? Both, but to begin with, it was invented. In her description of reversion in the state of Israel, Aviad (whom I shall cite at length) uses such language as this: ". . . who turned outward . . . who noticed a change in the spiritual climate." That is a mark of invention, I think. But, then, assuredly it was also a Judaism discovered and recovered: "The traditional world of Judaism contains all truth." So the idiom may have proved new, as Aviad says, but the content was more than welcome: It was what they had brought with them. The world view of reversionism in the present form is part of a larger international style, a Judaic statement of what a great many people were saying, all of them in the language and categories of their own.

The movement of reversion flourishes throughout the Jewish world. It attains realization as a system, however, in the *yeshivas*, the centers for full-time study of Torah, comparable to monasteries in the holy way of life they provide for all their participants. The *yeshivas* in the state of Israel lead the movement and give full expression to its world view and way of life. But, interestingly, the *yeshivas* that succeed in embodying the ideals of reversion derive not from Israeli Orthodox rabbis but from American ones living in Jerusalem. It was American Orthodox rabbis trained in *yeshivas* who saw the opportunity and the issue. They understood as self-evident that all Jews should live by the Torah and study it, but they had the wit to recognize a generation of young Jews who were prepared to revert to that way of life and world view. And they further undertook to give form and full expression to the system of reversion. The *yeshivas* that received the newcomers came into being because of American rabbis settled in Jerusalem:

They discerned a new openness to religion. . . . They felt strongly that Orthodox Judaism would appeal to the young Jews being drawn to non-

Jewish religious groups . . . the problem seemed merely technical: how to make young people aware of orthodox values and beliefs as a way of life.[5]

191
*Into the
Twenty-First
Century*

What these rabbis found points to the freshness of the movement at hand, for in fact the established *yeshivas* took no interest in the possibilities at all. They did not think they could absorb the types of students coming their way. So the American rabbis founded autonomous schools.

That fact alerts us to the presence of an innovative system that, to begin with, finds itself rejected and ignored by another system of the same family. The new system will have difficulty claiming to form an incremental outcome of the old system, the institutions of which prove by their own word utterly incompatible. In the movement of reversion, as well as in the systemic formulations of "return," there is a transvaluation of that critical value: Gifts of the spirit take priority and endow the gifted with status out of all relationship to his (or her) intellectual attainment. The addition of the "or her" of course provides another signal of a system aborning, for the familiar *yeshiva*-world makes slight provision for women's participation in its Judaism. But the system of reversion worked out within the Judaic system of the dual Torah flourishing in the state of Israel founded *yeshivas* for women and understood the importance of equality for them within the received system, an astounding and important mark of innovation and renewal.

That is only one indicator that we deal with something fresh and novel. The initiative involved in identifying the opportunity further provides solid evidence that a new system is under way. The total negation of Western culture that forms the centerpiece of the world view at hand finds no ample precedents in the received dual Torah, which found itself entirely at home in diverse circumstances and drew both deliberately and unselfconsciously on the world in which it flourished. We need hardly point to obvious precedents for a policy of selecting what was appropriate. But the policy of rejecting the entire world beyond finds few precedents and, in the balance, presents an egregious exception to a long history of, not integration, but mediation. However, if we look toward another wellspring of reversion, we readily discern the precedent. The world view of reversion, resting on the principle of total rejection of "Western culture," in fact corresponded point by point with the world view of comparable movements of its time and circumstance. It was the youth revolution of the 1960s. Rejecting parents and their values, the authority of their youth, and the conventions of society, the juvenile revolutionaries sought radical change in politics, music, clothing, food, drugs— and, for some, religion—of their choice rather than their parents'.

The view that the reversion was a homecoming, that the values of reversionism simply replicated for the occasion the theology of the Judaic system of the dual Torah, contradicts the movement's particular structure, points of value, and emphasis. The questions at hand come from the circumstance; the answers then derive from a process of selecting and arranging proof-texts provided by the canonical writings and, if truth be told, the everyday way of life of the Judaic system of the dual Torah. The whole then compares to other wholes, other Judaic systems: a work of selection along lines already determined, a system dictated by its own inventive framers to answer questions urgent to themselves in particular, a Judaism.

To conclude this introduction to the twenty-first century, let me spell out why I single out the movement of reversion as the key to what is coming in the century ahead. It is because I find in the contemporary mode evidence of renewal and regeneration, whether within Reform Judaism or far-out Orthodoxy. The source of the rebirth is the world as it is; the motive and the power are provided by the teachings of the Torah. The reversionary Judaisms mix resentment of a social present with a right and natural reflection on an awful, near-at-hand past. The reversion to the dual Torah marks the generations beyond the murder of the Jews of Europe, facing the demographic loss. It affects the generations that made the state of Israel, addressing the perpetual insecurity of the bastion become beleaguered fortress. It touches deeply the great-grandchildren of the immigrants who formed American Jewry, the children of the framers of American Judaism, looking backward at integration fully realized and forward toward what they fear will be no future at all. With no family untouched by out-marriage (whether demographically advantageous), and with many families living outside all relationship with distinctively Judaic or even culturally Jewish activity (however defined), the future has come under doubt. For their part, the reversionary Judaic systems say no to two hundred years of Judaic system building. They reject the premises and the programs of the essentially economic and political Judaic systems, socialism and Zionism, for example, as well as the ones that affirm religious viewpoints and ways of life. Since these systems by definition come into being as the creation of children—great, great-grandchildren, really—of the nineteenth-century reformers, they mark the conclusion of the age of modernization.

The pressing problem they address seems to me clear. The Jews en route to the dual Torah once more ask very profound, very pressing human questions such as "Why do I live?" "What do I do to serve God?" "What should I do with my life?" No wonder Orthodoxy cannot cope with them. The reversioners come to study Torah as God's word, not as a source of historical facts. They take up a way of life quite alien to that they knew from their parents as an act of conversion to God, not as a means of expressing or preserving their Jewishness. They repudiate, yes, but only to affirm. If I had to explain, in a single sentence, the remarkable power of reversionary Judaisms, I would invoke a single consideration. The one question ignored by the former Judaic systems, the human question, found its answer here, and after two hundred years of change, the final turning of the wheel brought up the original issue afresh.

What questions had the Judaic system of the dual Torah set at the center of discourse, if not the ones of living a holy and a good life? For those long centuries in which Christianity defined the frame of reference for all Western society, Jews understood that the question pressed, that its answers demanded attention. The Judaism of the dual Torah addressed that

Jew who was always a Jew and who was only a Jew, delivering the uncompromising lesson that God demanded the human heart, that Israel was meant to be a kingdom of priests and of a holy people, and that the critical issues of life concerned conduct with God, the other, and the self. That piety explained from day to day what it meant to be a *Mensch*, a decent human being; it answered the question that through the Christian centuries the West understood as critical: How shall I live so as decently to die?

The issues of modern times shifted from the human questions framed by humanity in God's image and in God's likeness to an altogether different set of urgent concerns. These had to do with matters of politics and economics. The received Torah echoed with the question "Adam, where are you?" The Torahs of the nineteenth century answered the question "Jew, what *else* can you become?" For millennia, Jews had not wanted to be more than they were, and now the Jewish question, asked by Gentiles and Jews alike, rested on the premise that to be Jewish did not suffice. Now Jews wished not totally to integrate, but also not entirely to segregate themselves. They no longer had in mind a place in which a people dwells alone. The Judaic systems of the twentieth century, with their stress on politics for professionals, ephemeral enthusiasm for everybody else, reconstituted the people that dwells alone—for fifteen minutes at a time. No wonder then that, at the end of two hundred years, the heirs of a set of partial systems would go in search of a whole and complete one, one that provided what all the established ones did not, that same sense of center and of the whole that, for so long, was precisely what Jews did not want for themselves. The protracted love affair over, some Jews reengaged the received Torah, the one in two parts, in a long-term union. Not many, not experienced, sometimes awkward, often forced and unnatural, they in time would find their path—and in ways they could not imagine or approve, they would lead the Jewish world.

The capacity of Judaic systems, drawing upon the Judaism of the dual Torah, to come to grips with the acutely contemporary issues of Jews' lives forms the source of their remarkable power to change lives, to bring about what in secular terms one would call conversion and in Judaic terms return. The reversionary Judaisms—and they include Reform, Orthodoxy, and Conservatism, each one in its many formulations—take up today's concerns and draw them into the framework of an enduring program of lively reflection. That capacity to form a relationship between the individual, here and now, and the social entity—holy, supernatural Israel—in the far reaches of time and unto eternity, takes the measure of Judaic systems. By that criterion, the systems of reversion, however limited their actual effect in numbers, exercise moral authority and therefore enjoy remarkable success. I discern only one source of that success: the Judaic system of the dual Torah, its enduring power to address the human condition of Israel, the Jewish people everywhere, in God's name: *"And he believed the Lord, and he reckoned it to him as righteousness."*

Notes

CHAPTER 4

1. Yehezkel Kaufmann, "The Biblical Age," in *Great Ages and Ideas of the Jewish People*, ed. by Leo W. Schwarz (New York: Random House, 1956), pp. 77*ff*.
2. Wilfrid Cantwell Smith, "Traditional Religions and Modern Culture," address at the Eleventh Congress of the International Association for the History of Religions, Claremont, Calif., 9 September 1965. Published in *Proceedings of the Eleventh International Congress of the International Association for the History of Religions* (Leiden: E. J. Brill, 1968), vol. 1, *The Impact of Modern Culture on Traditional Religions*, pp. 55*ff*. This entire analysis follows Smith's paper, and all quotations are drawn from it.

CHAPTER 5

1. *Midrash on Psalms* to Psalm 90:3, Louis Ginzberg, *The Legends of the Jews*, Vol. 1, trans. by Henrietta Szold (Philadelphia: Jewish Publication Society, 1947), p. 3.
2. The best brief account of biblical religion is Yehezkel Kaufmann, "The Biblical Age," in *Great Ages and Ideas of the Jewish People*, ed. by Leo W. Schwarz (New York: Random House, 1956), pp. 3–93.
3. Ibid., p. 15.

CHAPTER 9

1. Gary G. Porton, "Midrash: The Palestinian Jews and the Hebrew Bible in the Greco-Roman Period," in Hildegard Temporini and Wolfgang Haase (eds.), *Aufstieg und Niedergang der romischen Welt* (Berlin and New York, 1979), II. 19.2, p. 104. See also Gary G. Porton, "Defining Midrash," in *The Study of Ancient Judaism I: Mishnah, Midrash, Siddur*, ed. by Jacob Neusner (New York: Ktav, 1981), pp. 55–92; Gary G. Porton, *Understanding Rabbinic Midrash: Text and Commentary* (New York: Ktav, 1985); and Gary G. Porton's forthcoming entry on Midrash in the *Anchor Bible Dictionary*.

2. For examples of the same rabbinic comments appearing as midrashic statements and nonmidrashic statements, see Porton, *Understanding Rabbinic Midrash*, pp. 6–8.

CHAPTER 11

1. Frederick J. Streng, *Understanding Religious Man* (Belmont, Calif.: Dickenson, 1968), p. 56.
2. Ibid., p. 57.
3. E. P. Sanders, *Paul and Palestinian Judaism* (Philadelphia: Fortress, 1977).

CHAPTER 12

1. *Weekday Prayer Book,* ed. by the Rabbinical Assembly of America Prayerbook Committee, Jules Harlow, Secretary (New York: Rabbinical Assembly, 1962), p. 42.
2. Ibid., p. 141.
3. Ibid., pp. 45–56.
4. Ibid., pp. 50*ff*.
5. Frederick J. Streng, *Understanding Religious Man* (Belmont, Calif.: Dickenson, 1968), p. 57.

CHAPTER 13

1. Jules Harlow (ed.), *A Rabbi's Manual* (New York: Rabbinical Assembly, 1965), p. 45. The "seven blessings" said at a wedding are printed in traditional Jewish prayerbooks.

CHAPTER 14

1. Maurice Samuel (trans.), *Haggadah of Passover* (New York: Hebrew Publishing, 1942), p. 9.
2. Ibid., p. 26.
3. Ibid., p. 13.
4. Ibid., p. 27.
5. *Weekday Prayer Book,* ed. by the Rabbinical Assembly of America Prayerbook Committee, Jules Harlow, Secretary (New York: Rabbinical Assembly, 1962), pp. 97–98.

CHAPTER 15

1. Judah Goldin (trans.), *The Grace After Meals* (New York: Jewish Theological Seminary of America, 1955), pp. 9, 15*ff*.

CHAPTER 17

1. *Weekly Prayer Book,* ed. by the Prayer Book Commission of the Rabbinical Assembly of America, Gershon Hadas, Chairman, and Jules Harlow, Secretary (New York: Rabbinical Assembly, 1961), pp. 56–67.

CHAPTER 18

1. Traditional prayer; author's translation from the Hebrew.

2. Abraham J. Heschel, *The Sabbath: Its Meaning for Modern Man* (New York: Farrar, Straus & Young, 1951), p. 8.

3. Ibid., p. 10.
4. Hayyim Schauss, *The Jewish Festivals from Their Beginnings to Our Own Day* (New York: Union of American Hebrew Congregations, 1938), pp. 40*ff.*
5. Ibid., pp. 86*ff.*
6. Traditional prayer; author's translation from the Hebrew.

Chapter 19

1. Abraham Z. Idelsohn, *The Ceremonies of Judaism* (New York: National Federation of Temple Brotherhoods, 1930), p. 120.
2. Jules Harlow (ed.), *A Rabbi's Manual* (New York: Rabbinical Assembly, 1965), p. 96.
3. Idelsohn, *Ceremonies of Judaism*, p. 133.

Chapter 21

1. Abraham S. Halkin, "The Judeo-Islamic Age," in *Great Ages and Ideas of the Jewish People*, ed. by Leo W. Schwarz (New York: Random House, 1956), p. 235.
2. Ibid., pp. 238–39.
3. Ibid., p. 245.
4. Julius Guttmann, *Philosophies of Judaism: The History of Jewish Philosophy from Biblical Times to Franz Rosenzweig*, trans. by David Silverman (New York: Holt, Rinehart & Winston, 1964), p. 158.
5. Ibid., p. 158.
6. Halkin, "Judeo-Islamic Age," p. 251.
7. Ibid., p. 251.
8. Ibid., pp. 251–52.
9. Alice Lucas (trans.), quoted in Bernard Martin, *Prayer in Judaism* (New York and London: Basic Books, 1968), pp. 84–85.
10. Halkin, "Judeo-Islamic Age," p. 253.
11. Ibid., p. 253.
12. Cited from Isaak Heinemann, "Judah Halevi, Kuzari," in *Three Jewish Philosophers*, ed. by Isaak Heinemann, Alexander Altmann, and Hans Lewy (Philadelphia: Jewish Publication Society, 1960), p. 33.
13. Ibid., p. 72.
14. Ibid., p. 75.
15. Ibid., p. 75.
16. Ibid., pp. 126–29.
17. Guttmann, *Philosophies of Judaism*, p. 125.
18. Ibid., p. 125.
19. Ibid., p. 126.
20. Frederick J. Streng, *Understanding Religious Man* (Belmont, Calif.: Dickenson, 1968), p. 92.
21. Ibid.

Chapter 22

1. Scholom Alchanan Singer (trans.), *Medieval Jewish Mysticism: The Book of the Pious* (Northbrook, Ill.: Whitehall, 1971), pp. 37–38.

2. Abraham J. Heschel, "The Mystical Elements of Judaism," in *The Jews: Their History, Culture, and Religion,* ed. by Louis Finkelstein (New York: Harper & Row, 1971).
3. Ibid., pp. 284–85.
4. Ibid., pp. 292–93.
5. Gershom G. Scholem, "Major Trends in Jewish Mysticism," in *Understanding Rabbinic Judaism,* ed. by Jacob Neusner (New York: Ktav, 1977), pp. 253–54.

CHAPTER 23

1. Israel Abrahams, *Hebrew Ethical Wills,* Vol. 2 (Philadelphia: Jewish Publication Society of America, 1948), pp. 207–18.
2. For an excellent account of medieval Jewish life, see Cecil Roth, "The European Age," in *Great Ages and Ideas of the Jewish People,* ed. by Leo W. Schwarz (New York: Random House, 1956), pp. 267–314.

CHAPTER 24

1. Cited from Franz Kobler, *A Treasury of Jewish Letters,* Vol. 2 (Philadelphia: Jewish Publication Society of America, 1954), pp. 565–67.
2. Cited from "The Jewish Woman: An Anthology," *Response: A Contemporary Jewish Review,* no. 18 (Summer 1973): 76.

CHAPTER 25

1. G. G. Scholem, *Major Trends in Jewish Mysticism* (New York: Shocken, 1961), p. 288.
2. Salo W. Baron, "The Modern Age," in *Great Ages and Ideas of the Jewish People,* ed. by Leo W. Schwarz (New York: Random House, 1956), pp. 313–484.
3. Ibid., p. 317.
4. Raul Hilberg, *The Destruction of the European Jews* (Chicago: Quadrangle, 1961), p. 3.
5. Ibid., p. 17.
6. Ibid., p. 765.
7. The works of Emil Fackenheim, Leo Baeck, A. J. Heschel, and Richard Rubenstein exemplify theological responses to the Holocaust.

CHAPTER 26

1. Jacob Katz, *Tradition and Crisis* (New York: The Free Press, 1961).
2. Ibid., pp. 214–15.
3. Marcus Lee Hansen, "The Problem of the Third Generation Immigrant," *Commentary* 14 (1952): 492–500.

CHAPTER 27

1. Solomon Freehof in his preface to W. Gunther Plaut, *The Rise of Reform Judaism* (New York: World Union for Progressive Judaism, 1963), p. viii.
2. Quoted in Samuel Raphael Hirsch, *Nineteen Letters* (New York: P. O. Feldheim, 1960).

3. Ibid.
4. Ibid.

CHAPTER 28

1. Joseph L. Blau, *Modern Varieties of Judaism* (New York: Columbia University Press, 1966), p. 121.
2. Ibid., p. 124.
3. Ibid., p. 140.
4. Arthur Hertzberg, *The Zionist Idea* (New York: Doubleday, 1959), pp. 14*ff.*
5. Ibid., p. 20.

CHAPTER 29

1. Charles S. Liebman, "Orthodoxy in American Jewish Life," *American Jewish Yearbook 1966* (Philadelphia: Jewish Publication Society, 1966), pp. 27*ff.*
2. Quoted in Melech Epstein, *Profiles of Eleven* (Detroit: Wayne State University Press, 1965), p. 17.
3. Joseph C. Landis, "Who Needs Yiddish? A Study in Language and Ethics," *Judaism* 13, no. 4 (1964): 1–16.

CHAPTER 30

1. Saul Lieberman, "Palestine in the Third and Fourth Centuries," *Jewish Quarterly Review* 36 (1946): 359–62.

CHAPTER 31

1. Ben Halpern, "The Jewish Consensus," *Jewish Frontier*, September 1962.
2. *In Everlasting Remembrance: A Guide to Memorials and Monuments Honoring the Six Million* (New York: American Jewish Congress, 1969), p. 2.

CHAPTER 32

1. Janet Aviad, *Return to Judaism: Religious Renewal in Israel* (Chicago: University of Chicago Press, 1983), p. ix.
2. Ibid., p. 2.
3. Ibid., p. 4.
4. Ibid., p. 10.
5. Ibid., p. 16.

Glossary

Adon Olam: "Lord of the World," hymn containing dogmas of divine unity, timelessness, providence.

aggadah: lit.: telling, narration; generally: lore, theology, fable, biblical exegesis, ethics.

ahavah: love; *Ahavah rabbah*: great love; first words of prayer preceding *Shema*.

Alenu: "It is incumbent on us": first word of prayer.

aliyah: going up; migration to the Land of Israel.

Am haarez: lit.: people of the land; rabbinic usage: boor, unlearned, not a disciple of the sages.

Amidah: lit.: standing. The main section of obligatory prayers morning, afternoon, and evening called "the eighteen benedictions" but containing nineteen sections: (1) God of the fathers; (2) praise of God's power; (3) holiness; (4) prayer for knowledge; (5) prayer for repentance; (6) prayer for forgiveness; (7) prayer for redemption; (8) prayer for healing the sick; (9) blessing of agricultural produce; (10) prayer for ingathering of dispersed Israel; (11) prayer for righteous judgment; (12) prayer for punishment of wicked and heretics; (13) prayer for reward of pious; (14) prayer for rebuilding Jerusalem; (15) prayer for restoration of house of David; (16) prayer for acceptance of prayers; (17) prayer of thanks; (18) prayer for restoration of Temple service; (19) prayer for peace.

amora: rabbinical teacher in Palestine and Babylonia in talmudic times (ca. C.E. 200–500).

Apikoros: Hebrew for Epicurus; generally: belief in hedonism.

Ashkenaz(im): European Jews who follow the customs originating in medieval German Judaism.

Ashré: "Happy are they," Psalm 145; read in morning and afternoon worship.

Av, Ninth of: Day of Mourning for destruction of Jerusalem Temple in 586 B.C.E. and C.E. 70.

Baal Shem Tov: (ca. 1700–1760): Master of the Good Name, Founder of Hasidism.

bar mitzvah: ceremony at which thirteen-year-old boy becomes adult member of Jewish community; an adult male Jew who is obligated to carry out the commandments (*mitzvah/mitzvot*).

bat mitzvah: adult female Jew who is obligated to carry out commandments; marked by ceremony, as for *bar mitzvah*.

B.C.E.: before the common era; used in place of B.C.

Berakhah: benediction, blessing, praise.

Bet Am: house of people; early word for synagogue.

Bet Din: court of law judging civil, criminal, and religious cases according to *halakhah*.

Bet Midrash: house of study.

Bimah: place from which worship is led in synagogue.

Birkat HaMazon: blessing for food; Grace After Meals.

brit milah: covenant of circumcision; removal of foreskin of penis on eighth day after birth.

C.E.: common era; used instead of A.D.

Central Conference of American Rabbis: association of Reform rabbis.

cohen/kohen: priest.

Conservative Judaism: religious movement reacting against early Reform movement; attempts to adapt Jewish law to modern life on the basis of principles of change inherent in traditional laws.

dayyan: judge in Jewish court.

Decalogue: Ten Words; the Ten Commandments (Hebrew: *'Aseret HaDibrot*).

Derekh Eretz: lit.: the way of the land; normal custom, correct conduct; good manners, etiquette.

diaspora: dispersion, exile of Jews from the Land of Israel.

dietary laws: laws pertaining to animal food. Pious Jews may eat only fish that have fins and scales, animals that part the hoof and chew the cud (for example, sheep and cows but not camels or pigs). Animals must be ritually slaughtered (Hebrew: *shehitah*) in a humane method accompanied by a blessing of thanks. Jews may not eat shellfish, worms, snails, flesh torn from a living animal, and so on. Any mixture of meat and milk is forbidden; after eating meat, one may not eat dairy products for a period of one to six hours, depending on custom. Fish are neutral (*pareve*). See *kosher*.

El, Elohim: God, divinity.

erev: evening, sunset, beginning of a holy day.

Etrog: citron, one of four species carried in synagogue on *Sukkot*, from Leviticus 23:40, *fruit of a goodly tree.*

exilarch: head of the exile; Aramaic: *Resh Galuta;* head of the Jewish community in Babylonia in talmudic and medieval times.

galut: exile; belief that Jews not living in the state of Israel are political exiles. See *diaspora*.

gaon: eminence, excellency; title of head of Babylonian academies; later on, distinguished talmudic scholar.

Gedaliah, Fast of: third day of autumn month of *Tishri*, commemorating assassination of Gedaliah (II Kings 25, Jeremiah 40:1).

Geiger, Abraham (1810–1874): early reformer in Germany; produced modern prayerbook; wanted Judaism to become a world religion.

Gemara: completion; comments and discussions of Mishnah. Mishnah + *Gemara* = Talmud.

get: bill of divorce, required to dissolve Jewish marriage.

golus: Ashkenazic pronunciation of *galut:* exile; life in diaspora; discrimination, humiliation.

Hadassah: U.S. women's Zionist organization.

halakhah: "the way things are done," from *halakh:* go; more broadly, the prescriptive, legal tradition.

Haskalah: Jewish Enlightenment, eighteenth-century movement of rationalists.

Hebrew Union College—Jewish Institute of Religion: founded in Cincinnati in 1875; center for training Reform rabbis and teachers; campuses in Los Angeles, Cincinnati, New York City, Jerusalem.

heder: room; elementary school for early education.

hiddush: novella; new point, insight, given as a comment on classical text. Often ingenious, sometimes hair-splitting.

Hillel: first-century Pharisaic leader who taught, "Do not unto others what you would not have them do unto you."

Hillul HaShem: profanation of God's name; doing something to bring disrepute on Jews or Judaism, particularly among non-Jews.

Hillul Shabbat: profanation of the Sabbath.

Hol HaMoed: intermediate days of festivals of Passover and *Sukkot.*

huppah: marriage canopy under which ceremony takes place.

Jehovah: transliteration of Divine name, based on misunderstanding of Hebrew letters *YHWH.* Jews did not pronounce name of God but referred to him as *Adonai,* Lord. Translators took vowels of *Adonai* and added them to consonants *JHVH;* hence JeHoVaH.

Jewish Theological Seminary: founded 1888; center for training conservative rabbis and teachers; campuses in New York City, Los Angeles, Jerusalem.

Judah the Prince: head of Palestinian Jewish community, C.E. 200; promulgated Mishnah.

kabbalah: lit.: tradition; later, the mystical Jewish tradition.

kaddish: doxology said at end of principal sections of Jewish service; praise of God with congregational response, "May his great name be praised eternally." Has eschatological emphasis and conveys hope for speedy advent of Messiah. Also recited by mourners.

Karaites: eighth- to twelfth-century Middle Eastern Jewish sect that rejected oral Torah and lived by written one alone.

kehillah: Jewish community.

Keneset Israel: assembly of Israel; Jewish people as a whole.

Keriat Shema: recital of *Shema.*

ketuvah: marriage contract specifying obligations of husband to wife.

Ketuvim: writings; biblical books of Psalms, Proverbs, and so on.

kibbutz: collective settlement in state of Israel where property is held in common.

kibbutz galuyyot: gathering together of the exiles; eschatological hope that all Israel will be restored to the land; now applied to migration of Jewish communities to the state of Israel.

Kiddush: sanctification, generally of wine, in proclamation of Sabbath or festival.

Kiddush HaShem: sanctification of the name of God; applies to conduct of Jews among non-Jews that brings esteem on Jews and Judaism; in medieval times, martyrdom.

Kol Nidré: all vows; prayer opening Yom Kippur eve service, declaring that all vows made rashly during the year and not carried out are null and void.

kosher: lit.: fit, proper; applies to anything suitable for use according to Jewish law.

Lag BeOmer: thirty-third day in seven-week period of counting the *Omer,* from second day of Passover to Pentecost (Leviticus 23:15); day of celebration for scholars.

Lamed Vav: thirty-six unrecognized men of humble vocation by whose merit the world exists; they bring salvation in crisis.

lulav: palm branch used on *Sukkot*.

Maariv: evening service.

Magen David: shield of David; six-pointed star; distinctive Jewish symbol after the seventeenth century.

Mah Nishtannah: "Wherein is this night different from all others," opening words of four questions asked by child at Passover *seder*.

Mahzor: prayerbook for New Year and Day of Atonement.

Malkhuyyot: sovereignties, section of New Year Additional Service devoted to theme of God's sovereignty.

Maoz Tsur: "Fortress, Rock of My Salvation"; Hanukkah hymn.

maror: bitter herbs consumed at Passover *seder* in remembrance of bitter life of slaves.

mashgiah: supervisor of rituals, particularly ritual slaughter; must be expert in laws, pious and God-fearing. Ignorant man, motivated by financial gain, cannot supervise religious rites.

maskil: enlightened man, follower of *Haskalah* (Enlightenment).

masorah: tradition.

matzah: unleavened bread, used for Passover.

mazzal: lit.: constellation, star.

mazzal tov: good luck.

Megillah: scroll; usually scroll of Esther, read at Purim.

Melavveh Malkah: "accompanying the queen"; Sabbath meal held at end of holy day to prolong Sabbath celebration.

menorah: candelabrum; nine-branched menorah used at Hanukkah; seven-branched menorah used in ancient Temple.

Messiah: eschatological king to rule in end of time.

Mezuzah: parchment containing first two paragraphs of *Shema*, rolled tightly and placed in case that is attached to doorposts of home.

Midrash: exegesis of Scripture; also applied to collection of such exegeses.

mikveh: ritual bath or immersion to wash away impurity; baptism.

minhah: afternoon prayers.

minyan: number needed for quorum for worship; ten.

Mishnah: code of law promulgated by Judah the Prince (ca. C.E. 200); in six parts, concerning agricultural laws, festival and Sabbath law, family and personal status, torts, damages, civil law, and laws pertaining to the sanctuary and to rules of ritual cleanness.

mitnaged: opponent; opposition to Hasidism on the part of rationalists and talmudists.

mitzvah: commandments; technical sense: scriptural or rabbinic injunctions; later on, also used in sense of good deed; every human activity may represent an act of obedience to divine will.

moed: festival.

mohel: ritual circumciser.

Musaf: additional service on Sabbath and festivals, commemorating additional offering in Temple times.

musar: lit.: chastisement; instruction in right behavior; movement in modern Judaism emphasizing study and practice of ethical traditions, founded by Israel Salanter (1810–1883).

nasi: prince.

navi: prophet.

neder: vow.

Neilah: closing service at end of Yom Kippur, at nightfall when fast ends.

niggun: melody, traditional tune for prayer.

Olam Hazeh, Olam Haba: "this world," "the world to come."

omer: sheaf cut in barley harvest.

Oneg Shabbat: Sabbath delight.

Orthodoxy: traditional Judaism; belief in historical event of revelation at Sinai of oral and written Torah, in binding character of Torah, and in authority of Torah sages to interpret Torah.

Passover: (Hebrew: *Pesah*) festival commemorating Exodus from Egypt, in spring month of *Nisan* (April).

peot: corners; Leviticus 19:27 forbids removing hair at corners of head, meaning not to cut earlocks.

peshat: literal meaning of Scripture; distinct from *derash*, or homily.

Pharisee: (Hebrew: *Parush*) separatist; member of party in ancient Judaism teaching that oral Torah was revealed at Sinai along with written one, both preserved among prophets and sages down to the Pharisaic party; espoused prophetic ideals and translated them to everyday life of Jewry through legislation. Distinctive beliefs, according to Josephus: (1) immortality of the soul, (2) existence of angels, (3) divine providence, (4) freedom of will, (5) resurrection of the dead, (6) oral Torah.

pilpul: dialectical reasoning in study of oral law.

piyyut: synagogue poetry.

Purim: festival commemorating deliverance of Persian Jews from extermination in fifth century B.C.E., as related in Scroll of Esther; on fourteenth of *Adar*, generally in March.

rabbi: "my master"; title for teacher of oral Torah.

Rabbinical Assembly: association of Conservative rabbis.

Rabbinical Council: association of Orthodox rabbis in United States.

Rashi: a name for R. Solomon Isaac (1040–1105), composed of *Rabbi SHlomo Yizhak: RSHY*, hence *Rashi*. He was the writer of the most widely consulted of all commentaries on the Bible and the Talmud.

Rava: fourth-century talmudic master, head of Babylonian school at Mahoza.

Reconstructionism: movement to develop modern, naturalist theology for Judaism; founded by Mordecai M. Kaplan (1881–1982); emphasizes Jewish peoplehood, sees Judaism as natural outgrowth of Jewish people's efforts to ensure survival and answer basic human questions.

Reform: religious movement advocating change of tradition to conform to conditions of modern life. Holds *halakhah* to be human creation, subject to human judgment; sees Judaism as historical religious experience of Jewish people.

Rosh Hashanah: New Year, first day of *Tishri* (September).

Rosh Yeshivah: head of talmudic academy.

Sabbatai Zevi (1626–1676): messiah, kabbalist; made mystical revelations; announced himself as Messiah in Smyrna (Turkey) synagogue, 1665; went to Constantinople to claim his kingdom from sultan; was imprisoned and converted to Islam.

Sabbatianism: movement of followers of Sabbatai Zevi (1626–1676), messianic leader who became an apostate. Followers believed this apostasy was part of divine plan.

Sadducees: sect of Temple priests and sympathizers; stressed written Torah and the right of the priesthood to interpret it against Pharisaic claim that oral tradition held by Pharisees was means of interpretation; rejected belief in resurrection of dead, immortality of soul, angels, and divine providence.

Sanhedrin: Jewish legislative-administrative agency in Temple times.

seder: order; Passover home service.

sefer Torah: scroll of Torah.

Selihot: penitential prayers recited before New Year.

semikhah: laying on of hands; ordination.

Sephardi(m): descendants of Spanish Jewry, generally in Mediterranean countries.

shaharit: morning service; dawn.

shalom: peace.

Shammai: colleague of Hillel, first-century Pharisaic sage.

Shavuot: Feast of Weeks; Pentecost; commemorates giving of Torah at Mt. Sinai.

shehitah: ritual slaughter; consists of cutting through both windpipe and gullet with sharp knife and examining to see that both have been cut through.

Shekhinah: presence of God in the world.

Shema: proclamation of unity of God: Deuteronomy 6:4–9 and 11:13–21, Numbers 15:37–41.

Shemini Atzeret: "eighth day of solemn assembly" (Numbers 30:35); last day of *Sukkot*, a holy day in itself.

Sheva Berakhot: "seven blessings" recited at wedding ceremony.

Shiva: seven days of mourning following burial of close relative.

shohet: ritual slaughterer.

shofar: ram's horn sounded during high-holy-day period, from a month before New Year until end of Yom Kippur.

Shoferot: *shofar*-verses concerning revelation that are read in New Year Additional Service.

Shulhan Arukh: prepared table; code of Jewish law by Joseph Karo, published in 1565, which is authoritative for Orthodox Jewry.

Siddur: Jewish prayerbook for all days except holy days.

simhah: celebration.

Simhat Torah: "rejoicing of law"; second day of *Shemini Atzeret*, on which the Torah-reading cycle is completed; celebrated with song and dance.

sukkah: booth, tabernacle.

Sukkot: autumn harvest festival, ending high-holy-day season.

synagogue: Greek translation of Hebrew *bet hakeneset* (house of assembly). Place of Jewish prayer, study, assembly.

takkanah: decree, ordinance issued by rabbinic authority.

tallit: prayer shawl; four-cornered cloth with fringes (Numbers 15:38) worn by adult males in morning service.

Talmid Hakham: "disciple of the wise."

Talmud: Mishnah plus commentary on the Mishnah produced in rabbinical academies from about ca. C.E. 200 to 500 (called *Gemara*) form the Talmud. Two Talmuds were produced—one in Palestine, the other in Babylonia. From C.E. 500 onward, the Babylonian Talmud was the primary source for Judaic law and theology.

Talmud Torah: study of Torah; education.

Tanakh: Hebrew Bible; formed of Torah, Nevi'im, Ketuvin, Pentateuch, Prophets, and Writings; hence *TaNaKh*.

tanna: one who studies and teaches; a rabbinical master mentioned in Mishnah is called a *tanna*.

tefillin: phylacteries worn by adult males in morning service, based on Exodus 13:1 and 11 and Deuteronomy 6:4–9 and 11:13–21. These passages are written on parchment, placed in leather cases, and worn on the left arm and forehead.

Tehillim: psalms.

tekiah: sounding of *shofar* on New Year.

Teref, terefa: lit.: torn; generally: unkosher food.

Torah: lit.: revelation; at first the Five Books of Moses, then Scriptures as a whole, then whole corpus of revelation, both written and oral, taught by Pharisaic Judaism. Talmud Torah: study of Torah. Standing by itself, *Torah* can mean "study," the act of learning and discussion of the tradition.

Tosafot: novellae on the Talmud, additions generally to the commentary of *Rashi*. The *Tosafists*, authorities who produced *Tosafot*, flourished during the twelfth and thirteenth centuries in northern France.

Tosefta: supplements to the Mishnah.

tzaddik: righteous man; in Hasidism, intermediary or master of Hasidic circle.

tzedakah: righteousness; used for charity, philanthropy.

Tzidduk HaDin: justification of the judgment; prayer of dying man.

tzitzit: fringes of *tallit*.

Wissenschaft des Judentums: "science of Judaism"; scientific study using scholarly methods of philology, history, and philosophy of Jewish religion, literature, and history; founded in nineteenth-century Germany.

yahrzeit: anniversary of death of relative.

Yahveh: Jehovah.

Yamim Noraim: Days of Awe; Rosh Hashanah, intervening days, and Yom Kippur; ten days in all.

yeshiva: session; talmudic academy.

Yetzer HaRa, Yetzer Tov: evil inclination, good inclination.

Yiddish: Jewish language of Eastern Europe, now used in addition to vernacular in United States, Israel, Argentina, and Mexico; originally a Judeo-German dialect with a large number of Hebrew and Slavic words.

Yom Kippur: Day of Atonement; fast day for penitence.

Zikhronot: remembrances and prayers in New Year Additional Service on theme of God's remembering his mercy and covenant.

Zionism: movement to secure Jewish state in Palestine, founded in 1897 by Theodor Herzl.

Zohar: medieval kabbalistic (mystical) book, completed by fourteenth century in Spain; mystical commentary on biblical passages; stories of mystical life of the *tanna*, Simeon b. Yohai.

R. J. Zwi Werblowski and Geoffrey Wigoder, eds., *The Encyclopedia of the Jewish Religion* (New York: Holt, Rinehart & Winston, 1966) has been consulted throughout.

Suggestions for Further Reading

If you have time to read only one more book and want to know what it means to be a Jew in the classical tradition, read Abraham J. Heschel, *God in Search of Man: A Philosophy of Judaism* (Philadelphia: Jewish Publication Society, 1956); it is the single best introduction to the intellectual heritage of Judaism.

My students greatly enjoy James Michener, *The Source* (New York: Random House, 1965), a practically painless way to learn about the whole history of the Jews; and Herman Wouk, *This Is My God* (New York: Doubleday, 1959), a warm-hearted and enthusiastic account of Judaism by a faithful Orthodox Jew. Both are classics in their own way. A good history of Jewish thought is Robert Seltzer, *Jewish People, Jewish Thought: The Jewish Experience in History* (New York: MacMillan and Collier, 1980). Three books of mine expand on the approach to Judaic history presented here: *First Century Judaism in Crisis: Yohanan ben Zakkai and the Renaissance of Torah* (New York: Ktav, 1981); *From Politics to Piety: The Emergence of Pharasaic Judaism* (New York: Ktav, 1978); and *There We Sat Down: Talmudic Judaism in the Making* (New York: Ktav, 1978).

For the history of the Jews in modern times, Howard M. Sachar, *The Course of Modern Jewish History* (New York: World, 1958), is an engaging narrative.

On the Judaic way of life, a wonderful account of the Sabbath ("life under the law") is Abraham J. Heschel, *The Sabbath: Its Meaning for Modern Man* (New York: Farrar, Straus, and Young, 1951). An imaginative and thoughtful "how to" book on being Jewish is Richard Siegel, Michael Strassfeld, and Sharon Strassfeld, *The Jewish Catalog*, 2 vols. (Philadelphia: Jewish Publication Society, 1975). A most engaging account of how Judaism reads Scripture is in Maurice Samuel, *Certain People of the Book* (New York: Knopf, 1955).

For relationships between Judaism and Christianity, see Malcolm Hay, *Europe and the Jews* (also published as *The Foot of Pride*) (Boston: Beacon, 1960), and Edward Flannery, *The Anguish of the Jews* (New York: Macmillan, 1965).

On the destruction of the Jews of Europe, I recommend Raul Hilberg, *The Destruction of the European Jews* (Chicago: Quadrangle, 1961), and Lucy S. Dawidowicz (ed.), *A Holocaust Reader* (New York: Behrman House, 1975).

On Zionism and the state of Israel, Amos Elon does not have the capacity to write a bad or boring book, and both of his pertinent works— *Herzl* (New York: Holt, Rinehart & Winston, 1975) and *The Israelis: Founders and Sons* (New York: Holt, Rinehart & Winston, 1971)—deserve rereading. Walter Laquer, *A History of Zionism* (New York: Holt, Rinehart & Winston, 1972), is a more formal history.

Two works of mine deal with subjects not treated here but pertinent to the appreciation of Judaism: *Death and Birth of Judaism: The Impact of Christianity, Secularism, and the Holocaust on Jewish Faith* (New York: Basic Books, 1987), and *The Enchantments of Judaism: Rites of Transformation from Birth Through Death* (New York: Basic Books, 1987; second printing, Atlanta: Scholars Press for University of South Florida Studies in the History of Judaism, 1991).

Index